AF531170

CAPE COD

AND THE NATIONAL SEASHORE

A PHOTOGRAPHIC ESSAY BY

CHARLES FIELDS

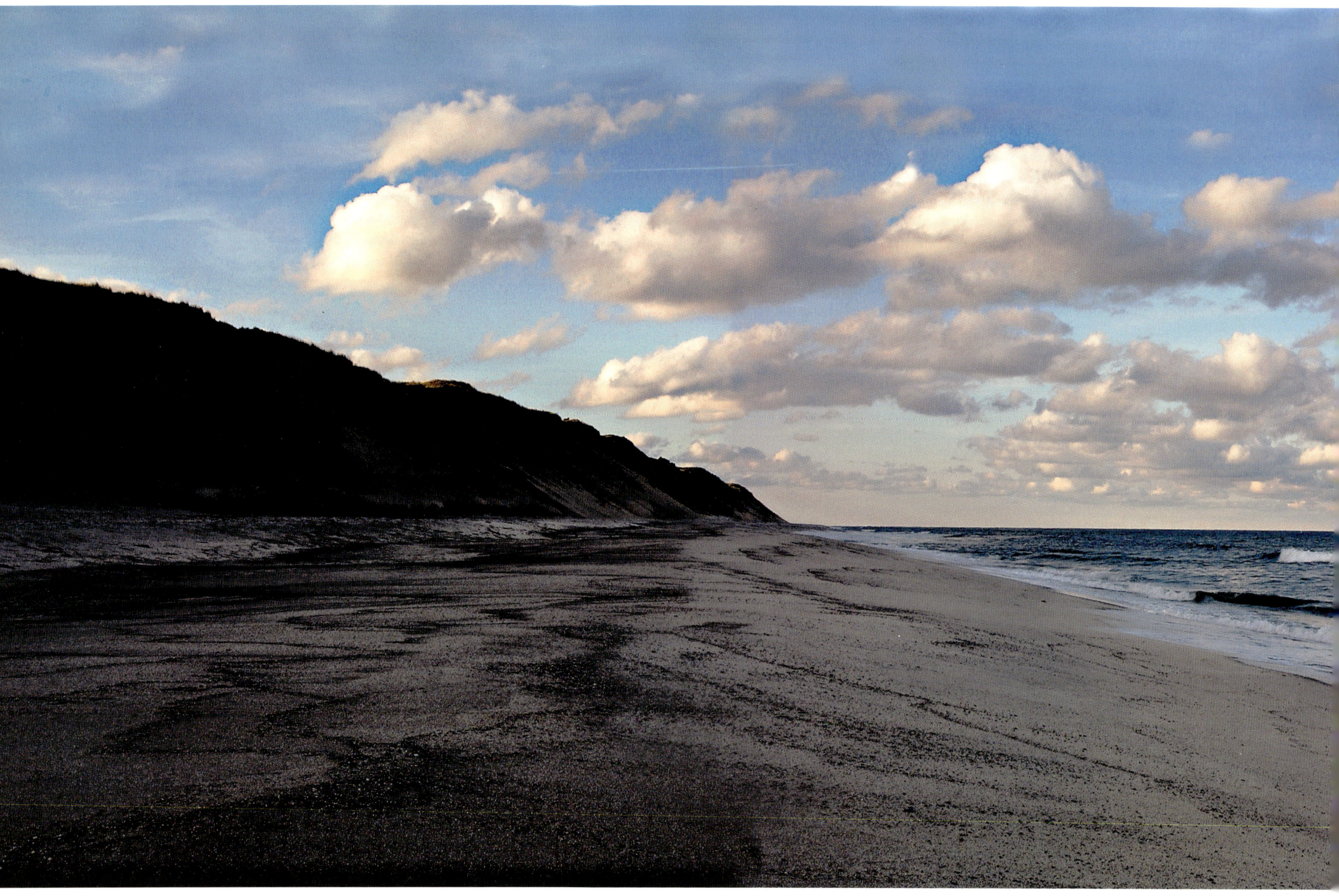

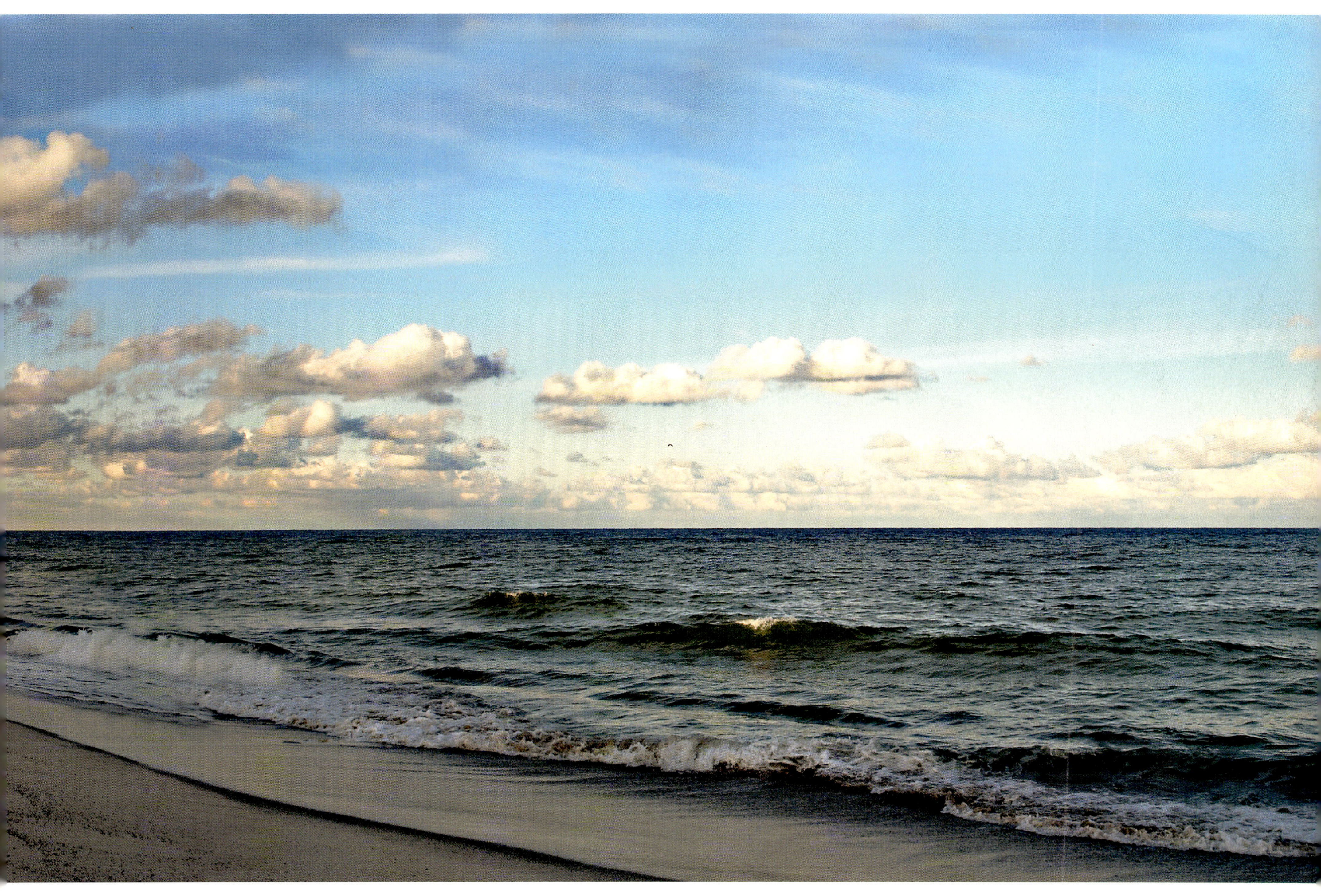

Coast Guard Beach, Truro

INTRODUCTION

It's often the case that we fail to fully explore our own backyards. As a Provincetown resident I, too, was guilty of not fully exploring the remainder of the Cape—an arm of land I largely ignored for years in between my route from my home in Connecticut and my new haven at the extreme tip of the Cape. This project changed all that. With one successful essay book on Provincetown and the National Seashore already under my belt, I was spurred on with the desire to uncover the beauty and people that populate "the rest of Cape Cod" or—as Henry David Thoreau eloquently described it—the land where "a man may stand...and put all America behind him."

Indeed, Cape Cod has always lent a reflective perspective to its visitors and new and longtime residents alike. It seems that artists and writers in particular have been attracted to the pace and aura out here on "the bended arm"—an analogy made famous by Thoreau in his eponymous treatise "Cape Cod." And since Thoreau's adventures from Boston to Cape Cod 150 years ago, more contemporary authors have carried on the Cape's artistic and literary tradition with the works of painters Edward Hopper and Anne Packard, the Sandwich Glass Factory, and writers Norman Mailer, Stanley Kunitz, Robert Finch, and Henry Beston, whose quintessential 1928 "The Outermost House: A Year of Life on the Great Beach of Cape Cod" remains a classic today. I draw on such topical work to inspire and motivate my own artistry today.

Thoreau was the first to capture the essence of the Cape when his posthumously published book chronicled three pilgrimages here in 1849, 1850, and 1855. He wrote of his walks from Provincetown to Eastham, recounting the land's geologic and natural history and remarking on the solitary life of its people. He described his stays in the home of a Wellfleet Oysterman, his walks along the bluffs at Truro's Cape Cod Light, and his conversations with locals during Provincetown's Golden Age when ship captains and merchants were making massive fortunes from the sea.

It's all a bit humbling, but in many ways, I feel that this book—this visual history—retraces some of Thoreau's steps and haunts that have stood the test of time. Have a look inside and you'll see: oysters are still being harvested in Wellfleet Bay, Cape Cod Light continues to keep watch, albeit slightly inland from its original perch, while Provincetown, Thoreau's described "flourishing town," experiences a new gilded age of artistry, new commerce and gentrification unfolding year-in, year-out.

And so this book began as the New England seasons unfurled themselves to me in their subtle majesty; a changing natural grandeur which is pervasive, deliberate and mysteriously slow but always dramatic, especially along the Cape's volatile Atlantic shore. Thoreau had a stagecoach and sturdy walking shoes; I a camera, a pickup truck, and well-worn hiking boots, ready to go and explore the nooks and crannies of the Cape coastline unfamiliar and ever-changing, patiently awaiting my visit.

A guest of many Cape innkeepers, I traversed the region—first explored 9,000 years ago by Native Americans—from the shoulder of Buzzard's Bay, the elbow at Chatham, up to the wrist at Truro, and up on home to the sandy fist at Provincetown. Wherever I roamed, I was invariably met with enthusiasm and Yankee hospitality, affording me some of the area's quaintest and most historic lodgings. In experiencing this comfort first-hand, I logged thousands of miles, foraging as a modern-day photographer to capture the varied region here in a collective, close-up portrait of my adopted home.

At times, the task was daunting and dizzying as I visited almost every Cape historical society. In the process, I left thousand of images on my cyber cutting floor, always managing to bask in the luminosity of Cape light as it bounced off the water and sand and back again to my lens. I was in my glory. After all, where else on earth can you capture both a sunrise and sunset over water as I so often do here on the Outer Cape?

This photographic essay is my Cape Cod—my personal and unique connection to the land and people I've met along the way. It is my experience and my back yard, slightly more familiar and cherished than a year ago. It is my newcomer's perspective, hopefully both fresh and timeless to you the reader and me the resident photographer. It's my wish that this photographic journey offers a glimpse into the past. It does for me, and it may too, for you.

Certain experiences and images captured in the process will forever be indelible in my mind: Gail dreaming in the early morning light of a National Seashore dune shack inhabited by the great Provincetown poet Henry Kemp; the aerial abstract of a fall-hued Cape cranberry harvest; Edward Hopper's Truro home still standing tall; and Brewster's Paine's Creek, where every spring, millions of herring alewives enter the fresh waterway to spawn before returning to salt water. Like these herring, artists too, have long been attracted to this quiet stream. I especially loved its unexpected beauty.

Like a graceful and patient nude model, the Cape sits still. Time and weather sculpts its aging visage but its heart and spirit remain much the same—fierce, wild, and independent. The Cape, formed by glaciers millions of years ago, continues to cast its spell. It challenges me to discover and remain engaged as a professional artist. In spite of my mania for technology, I happily temper this trait with a continued connection to nature—one that keeps me centered but ready to discover.

"When Thoreau wrote 'Cape Cod' and Beston 'The Outermost House,' neither had a digital camera, only their five senses. Today, my visual acuity and other senses are enhanced by an ever-changing photographic technology." But some things remain equal in the ability to experience and chronicle our times and Cape Cod. Beston spent a solitary year secluded in a two-room cottage in the dunes of Eastham's Nauset Beach where he related nature's seasonal sights, sounds, and smells in a place of "outermost" exposure.

Beston wisely wrote, "Listen to the surf, really lend it your ears, and you will hear in it a world of sounds: hollow boomings and heavy roarings, great watery tumblings and tramplings, long hissing seethes, sharp rifle-shot reports, splashes, whispers, the grinding undertone of stones, and sometimes vocal sounds that might be the half-heard talk of people in the sea."

Though Beston's cottage was swallowed up by the Blizzard of 1978, his unforgiving friend—the Atlantic—remains still talking, still whispering, still there playing at its whim and chatting away the hours with whomever takes the time to stop and listen." I took the time and, today, Thoreau and Beston's Cape Cod is my Cape Cod. Won't you come inside?

——Charles Fields

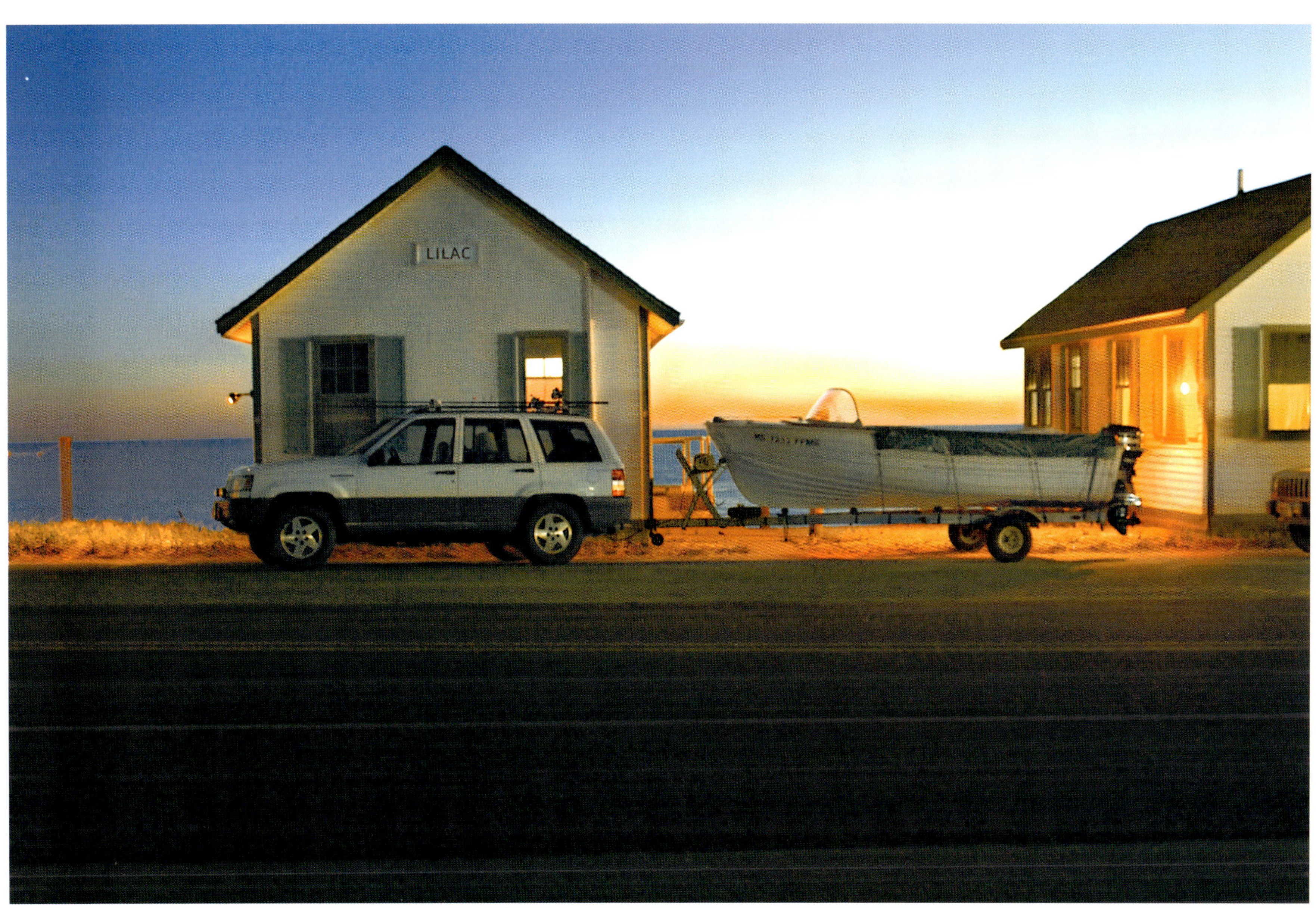

Days' Cottages, Cape Cod Bay, North Truro

To Gail,

Without whose patience and perseverance this book would not be possible. For your tireless work and your dedication and support—this book is for you.

—Charles

First Edition

Library of Congress Catalogung-in-Publication Data

Fields, Charles.

Fields, Cape Cod and the National Seashore: photography and commentary / by Charles Fields. —1st ed.

144 pages, 27.94 x 30.48 cm.

ISBN 0-9715458-2-0

Library of Congress Control number 2003092918

1. Cape Cod—United States-—Photographs I. Title. II. Title: National Seashore-—Cape Cod -—Massachusetts -—Photography

Photo pages 2-3: Coast Guard Beach, Truro, MA

Book Design by Charles Fields and Gail Fields
Introduction edited by Gerry Desautels
Picture Captions edited by Bill DeSousa
Color Consultant Glenn Bassett

Printed in Korea

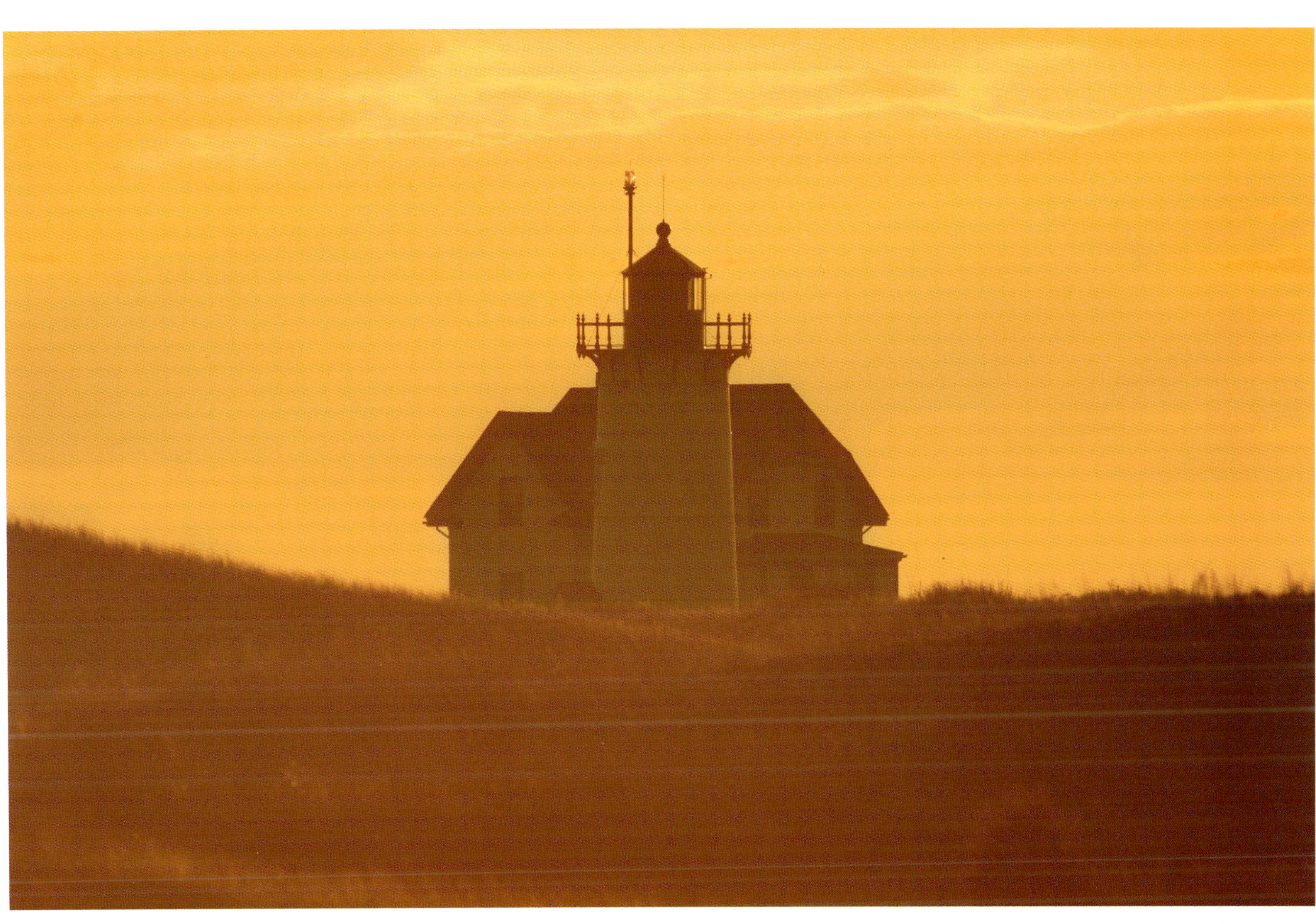

11 **Race Point Light, Provincetown**

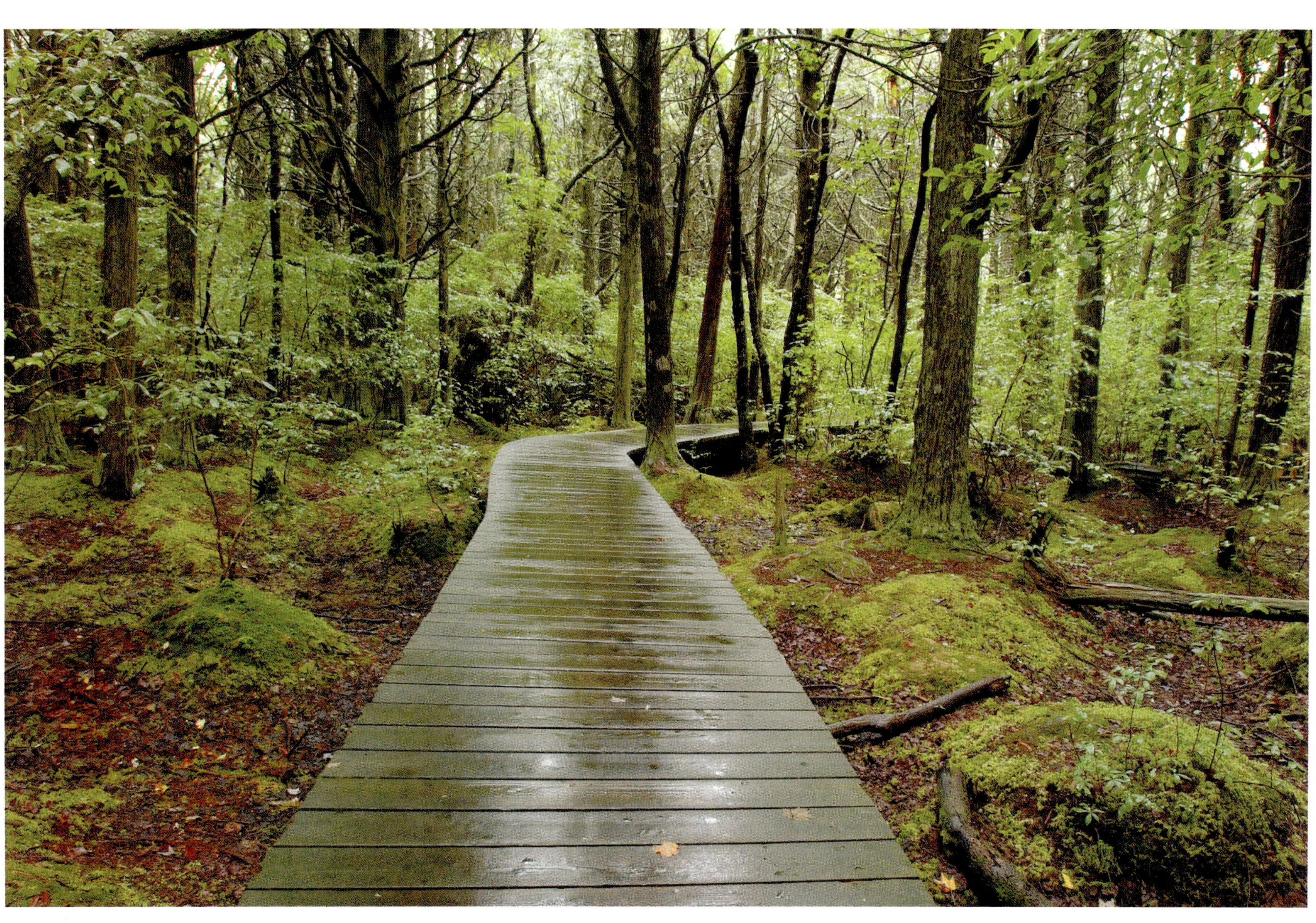

Great Atlantic Cedar Swamp, Eastham

FOREWORD

Cape Cod—a place of eternal warring between land and the sea—is a dynamic place. Shifting sands, wind and the ocean work their sometimes nefarious magic to continually change its face. But that face is, in some ways, enduring and unchangeable. Millions know and recall with delight familiar feelings of personal freedom and exhilaration crossing one of the behemoth bridges onto the peninsula. The lure is unmistakable.

Four hundred years ago, Bartholomew Gosnold left Falmouth, England, to explore the New World. After journeying across the Atlantic, he and his crew sailed into an unknown bay. There, they encountered land they first christened Shoal Hope. Later that day, a fellow voyager related: "Neere this Cape we came to Anchor in fifteene fadome, where wee tooke great store of Cod-fish, for which we altered the name and called it Cape Cod."

On November 9, 1620, the Mayflower with 102 passengers sailed into Provincetown Harbor in Cape Cod Bay. The Pilgrims decided to settle on Cape Cod but, before doing so, executed the Mayflower Compact, the first written constitution in the New World. In the four centuries since, whaling and trading, agriculture, fishing and commerce have altered the economy and landscape of Cape Cod. But not its abiding persona. It remains today, preserved as much as any place can be in the 21st century, pristine, proud and welcoming.

The Cape Cod peninsula is host to more than 13 million visitors annually. Small wonder— once one has meandered its beaches, dunes, byways and villages—that it ranks as one of America's most recognizable and popular resort destinations. Internationally renowned for its shoreline, pristine waters, dunes, marsh and wetlands, cranberry bogs, waterways, story book villages, architecture and culture, Cape Cod enchants all who visit, instilling in them lifelong memories. Cape Codders are the stewards of this magical land. Within its rolling hills, moors and heath, bays, ponds and forests, Cape Cod's magic lives on. From first landfall this side of the bridges to the reverie which inevitably accompanies leaving Cape Cod, visitors will relish a range of emotions and experiences. All of these are wonderfully supplemented by warm, wonderful welcomes and sad partings. But no one enters or leaves Cape Cod unmoved.

The photographic essay upon which you are about to embark will delight, inspire and move you. Each photograph was painstakingly taken exactly at the moment when light and subject were optimal. Charles Fields has captured Cape Cod unaware of itself—candid and true. Each image is evocative and provocative. The Cape's fleeting shadows and ethereal light have been captured precisely to embody the Cape's very essence. And Nature is not always conciliatory. Occasional inconvenient fogs or sudden downpours have dampened Fields' planned endeavors, but provided other, unwished for, photographic opportunities whose composition and effect far exceeded the original. And Fields' photographic essay features abundant serendipitous achievements.

Cape Cod cannot be taken home, except in one's heart and mind. But, within the pages of this Cape Cod photographic essay, with its palette of photographic experiences, featuring locales visited and yet unseen, exploring the uniqueness of Cape lifestyles and its people, architecture, majestic shoreline and unequalled diversity of terrain, one is transported here merely opening the cover. Just as the fussy eater wisely savours each morsel, thus did Charles Fields savour his picture-taking forays. Rejoicing in the light and passage of the seasons, this endeavor is, more than anything, a celebration of a timeless land whose stark beauty and natural gifts are the equal of any of America's greats.

——*Bill DeSousa*

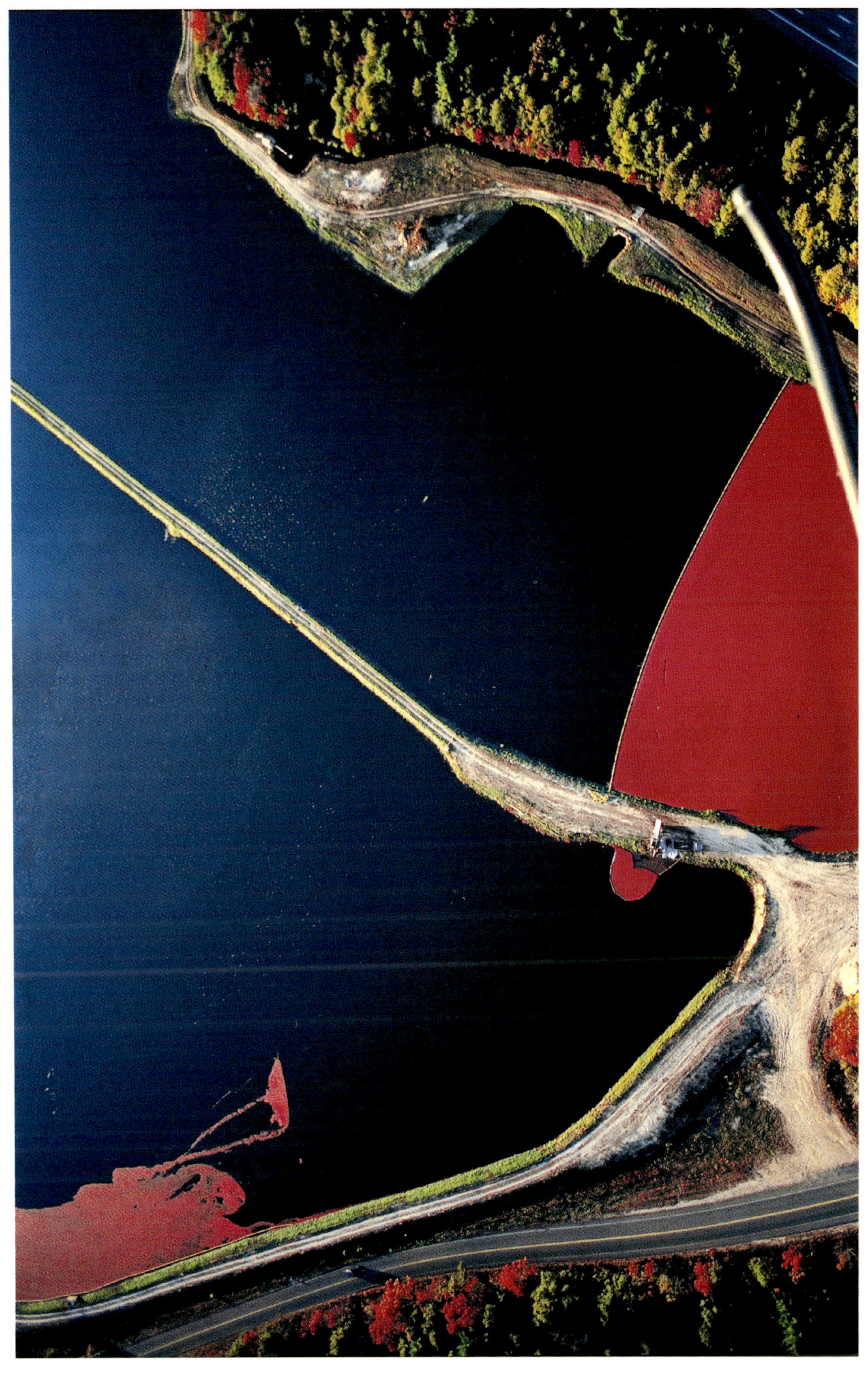

 Cranberry Harvest, Abstract

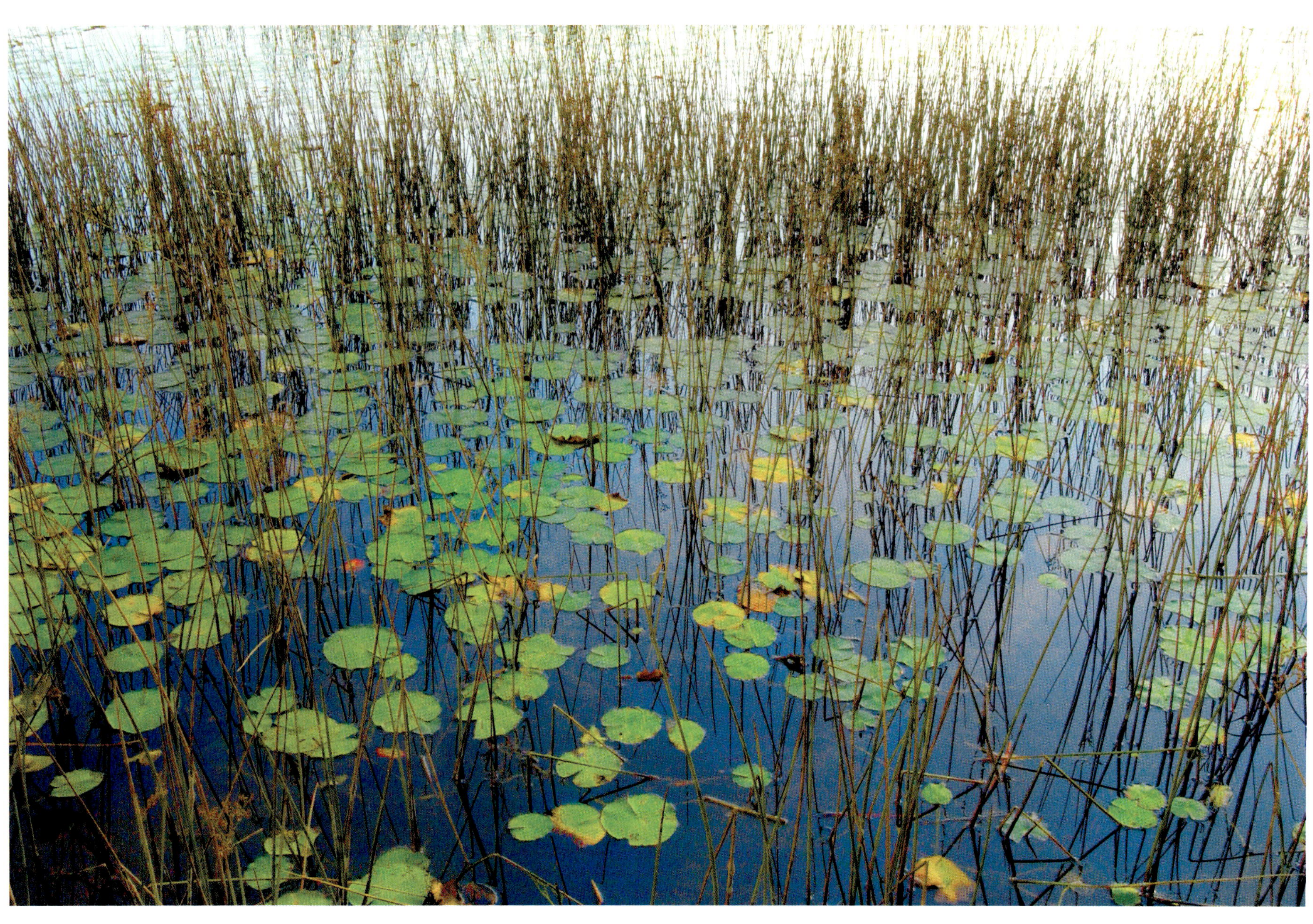

Water Lilies, Kettle Pond, Truro

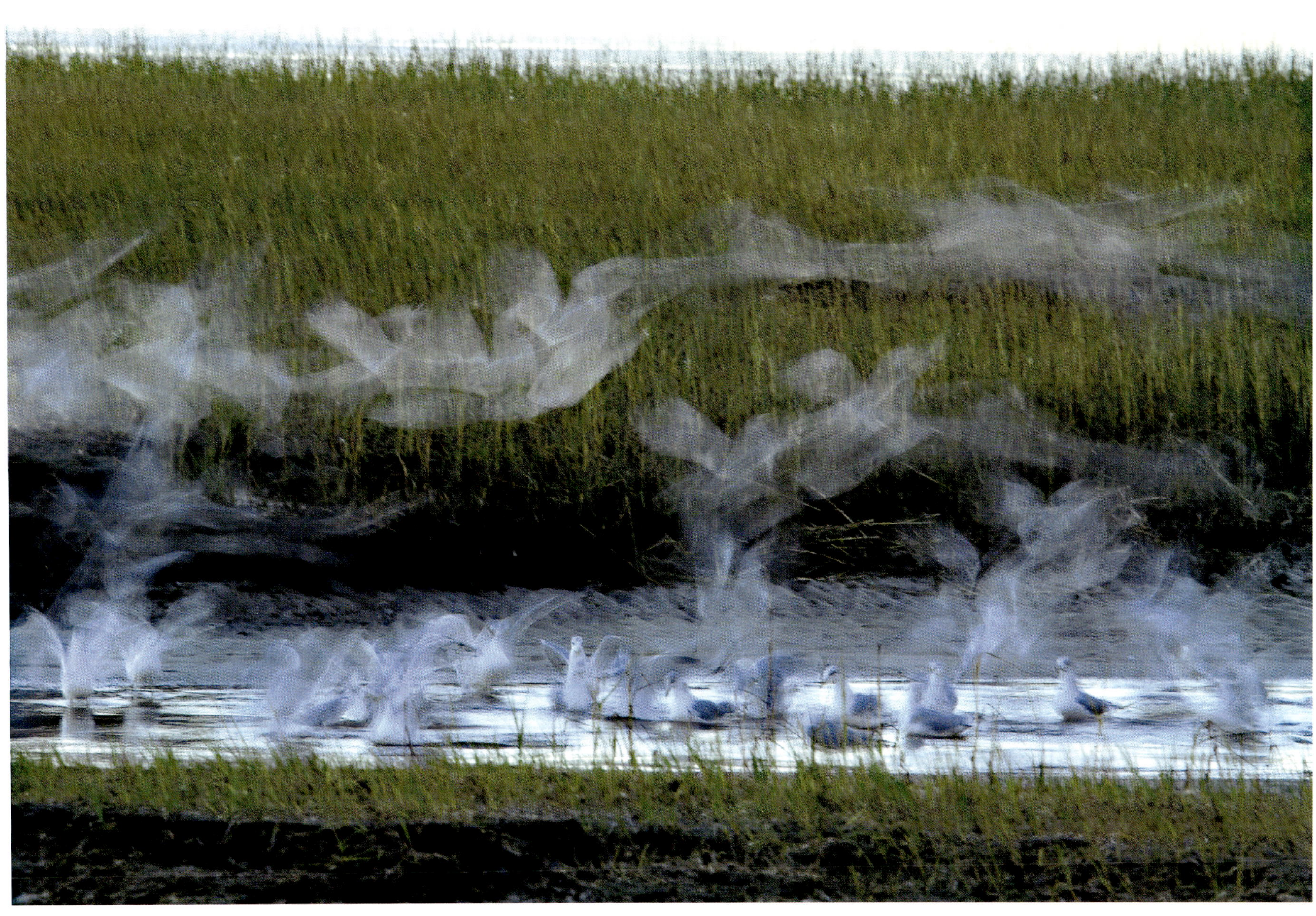

17 **Gulls in Flight, Paine's Creek, Brewster**

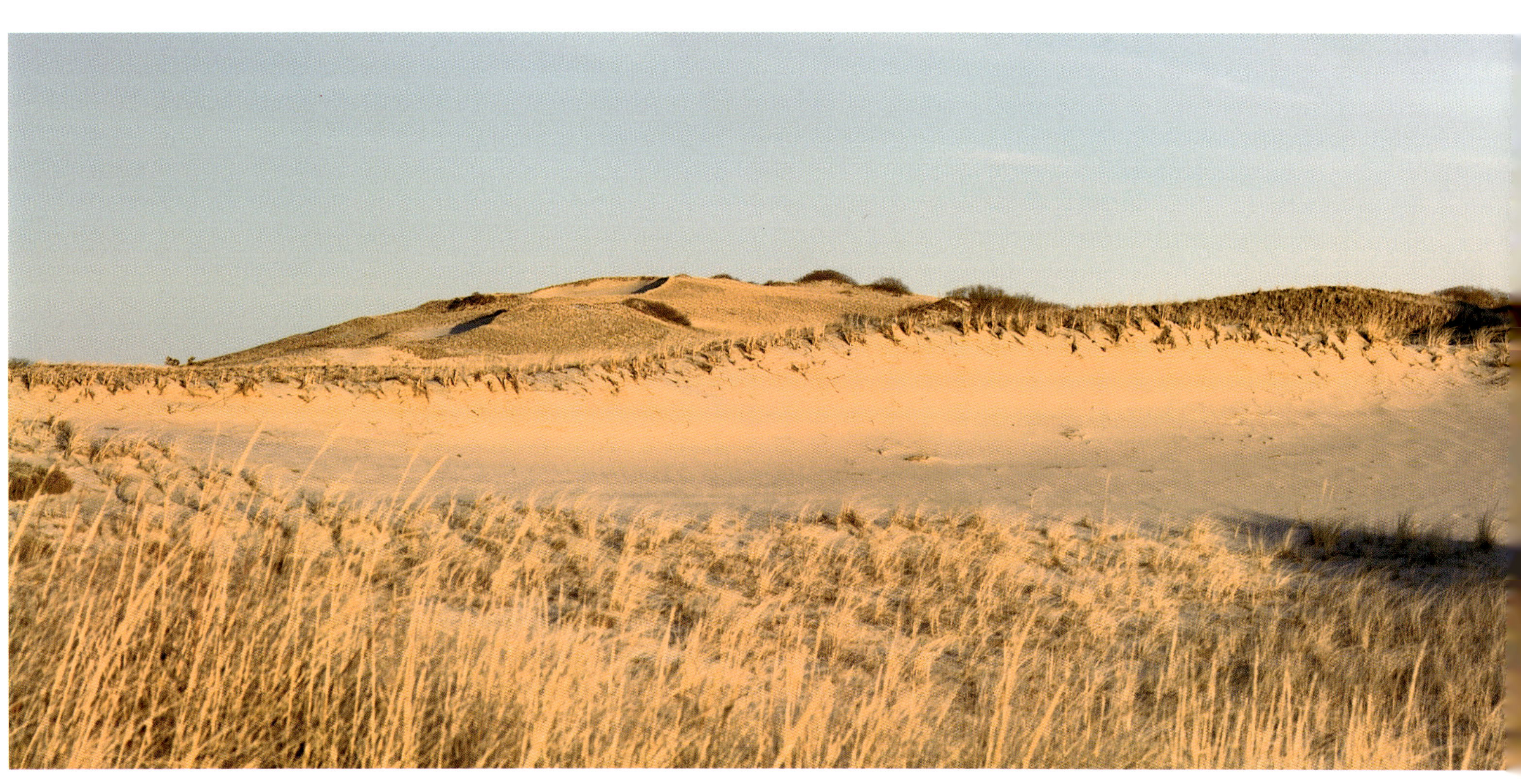

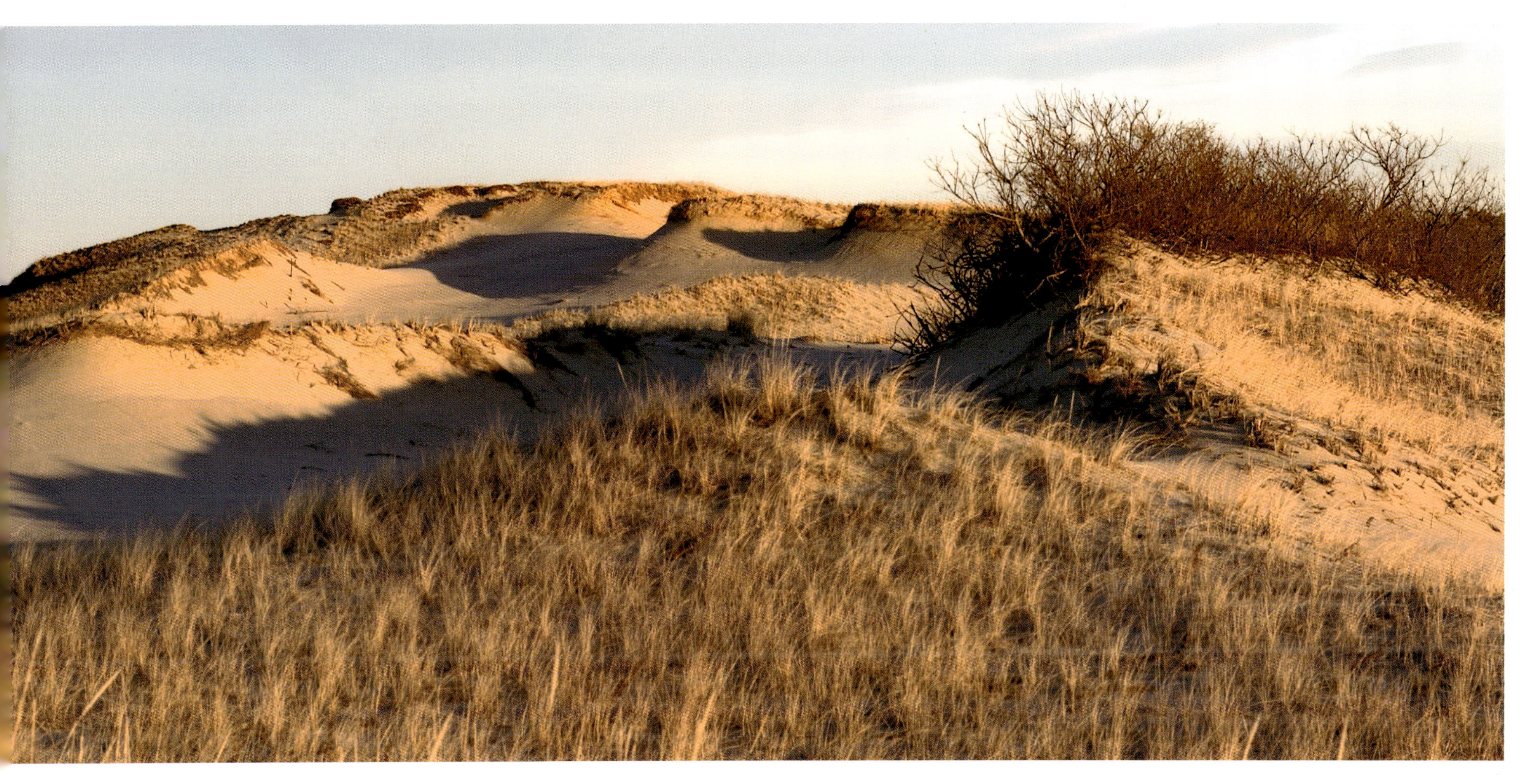

Dunes, Province Lands, Provincetown

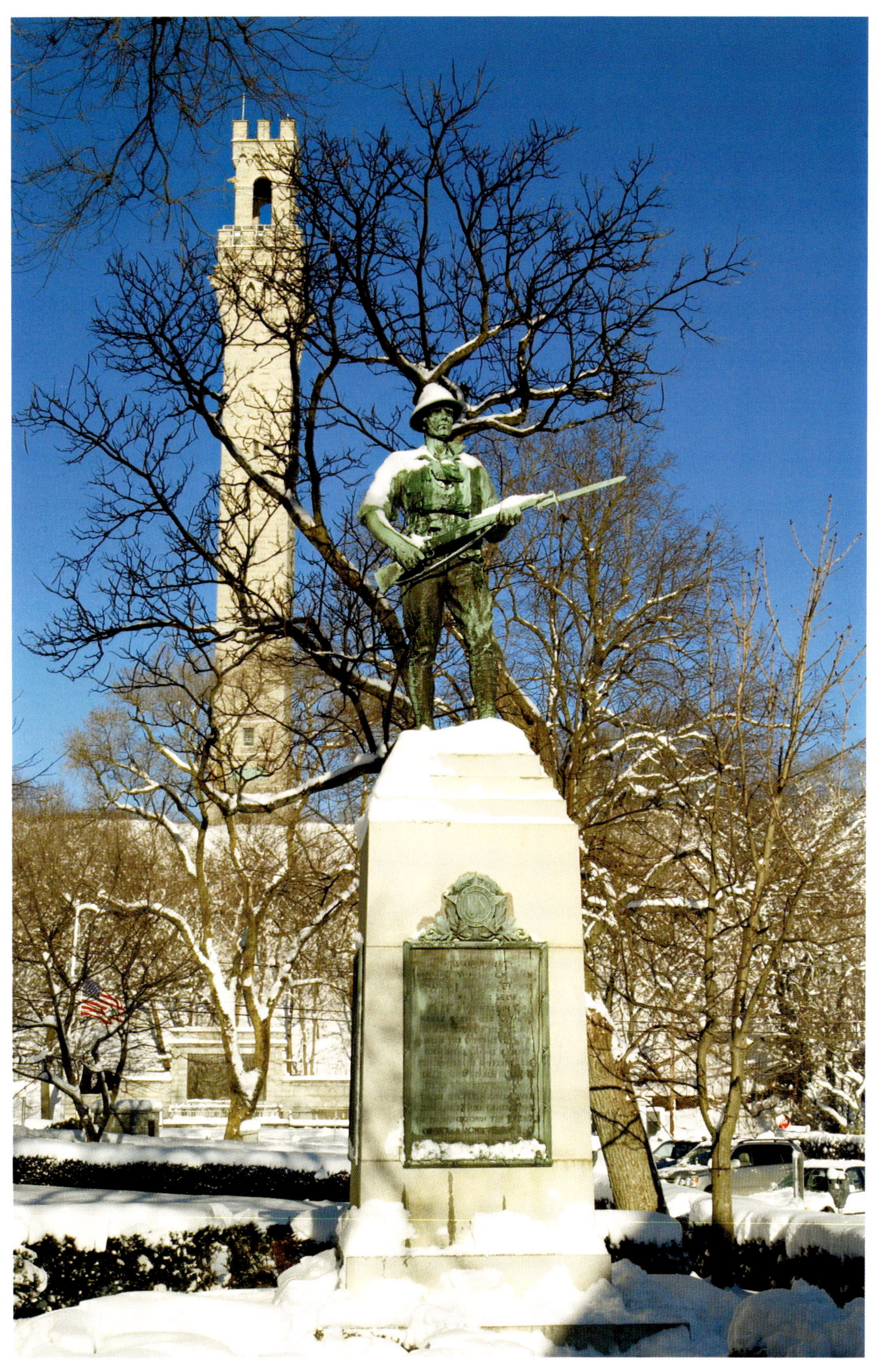

WWI Statue, Provincetown

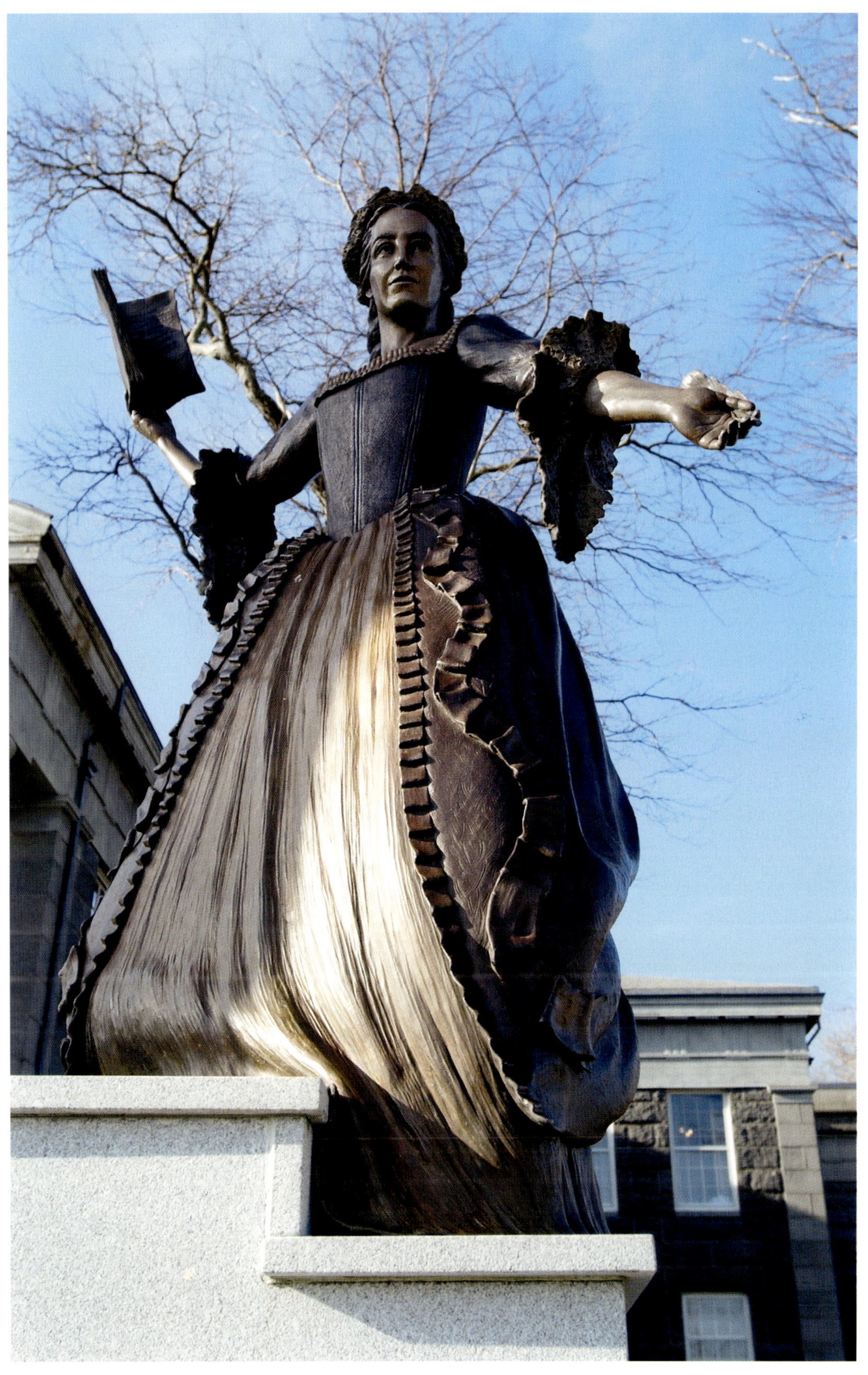

21 **Patriot, Mercy Otis Warren (1728-1814), Barnstable Superior Courthouse, Barnstable**

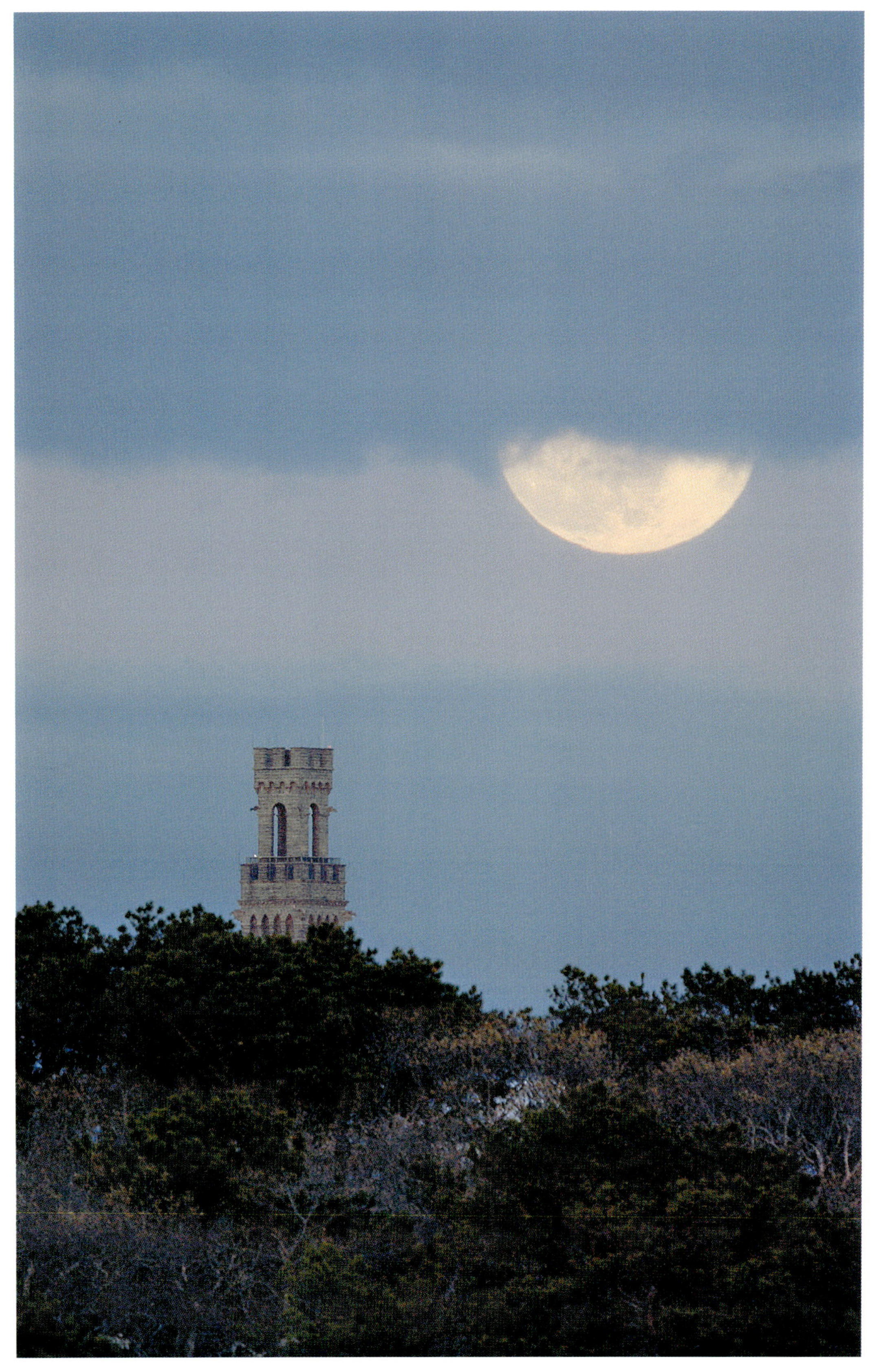

Moon Rising Over Pilgrim Monument, Provincetown

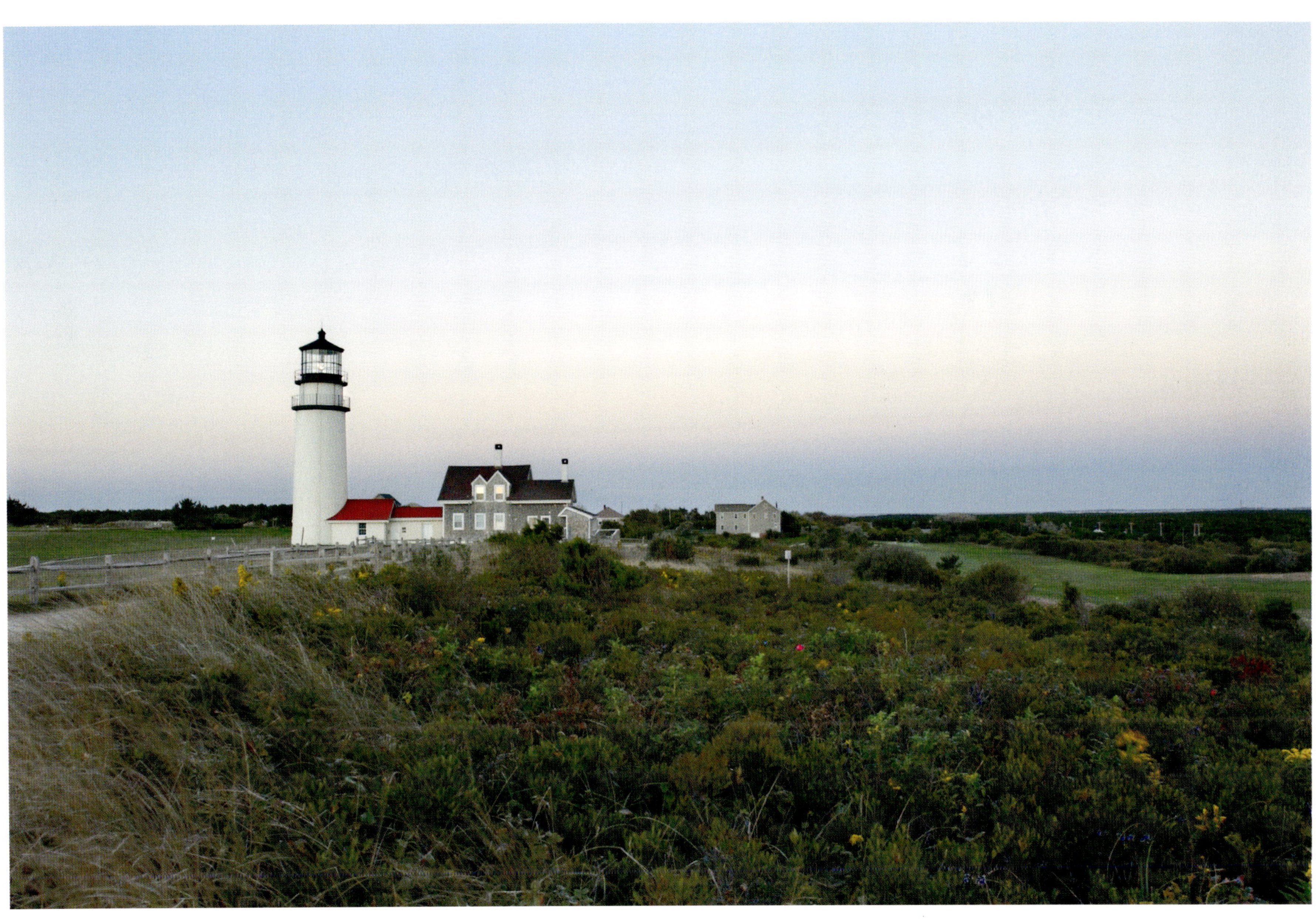

 Highland Light, North Truro

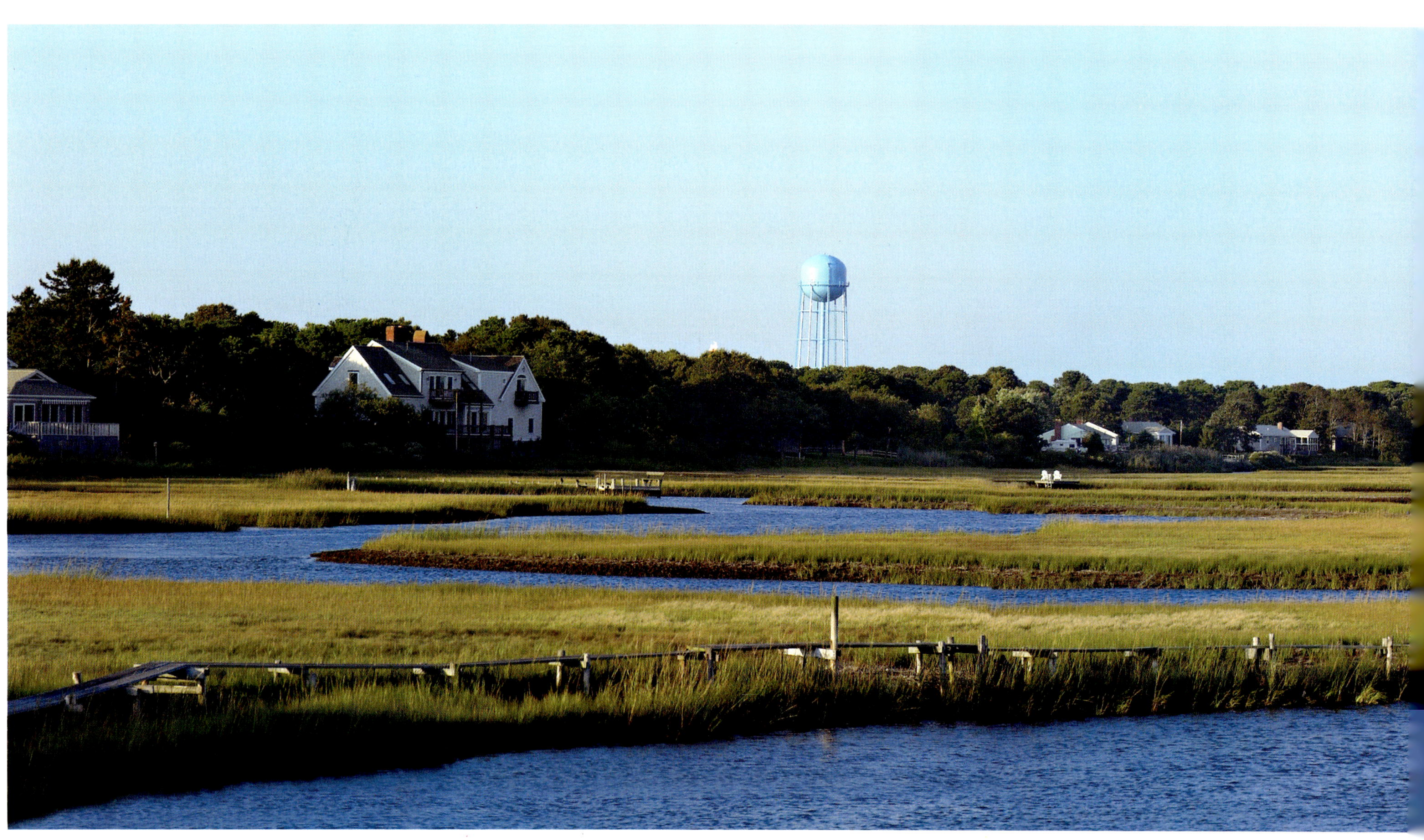

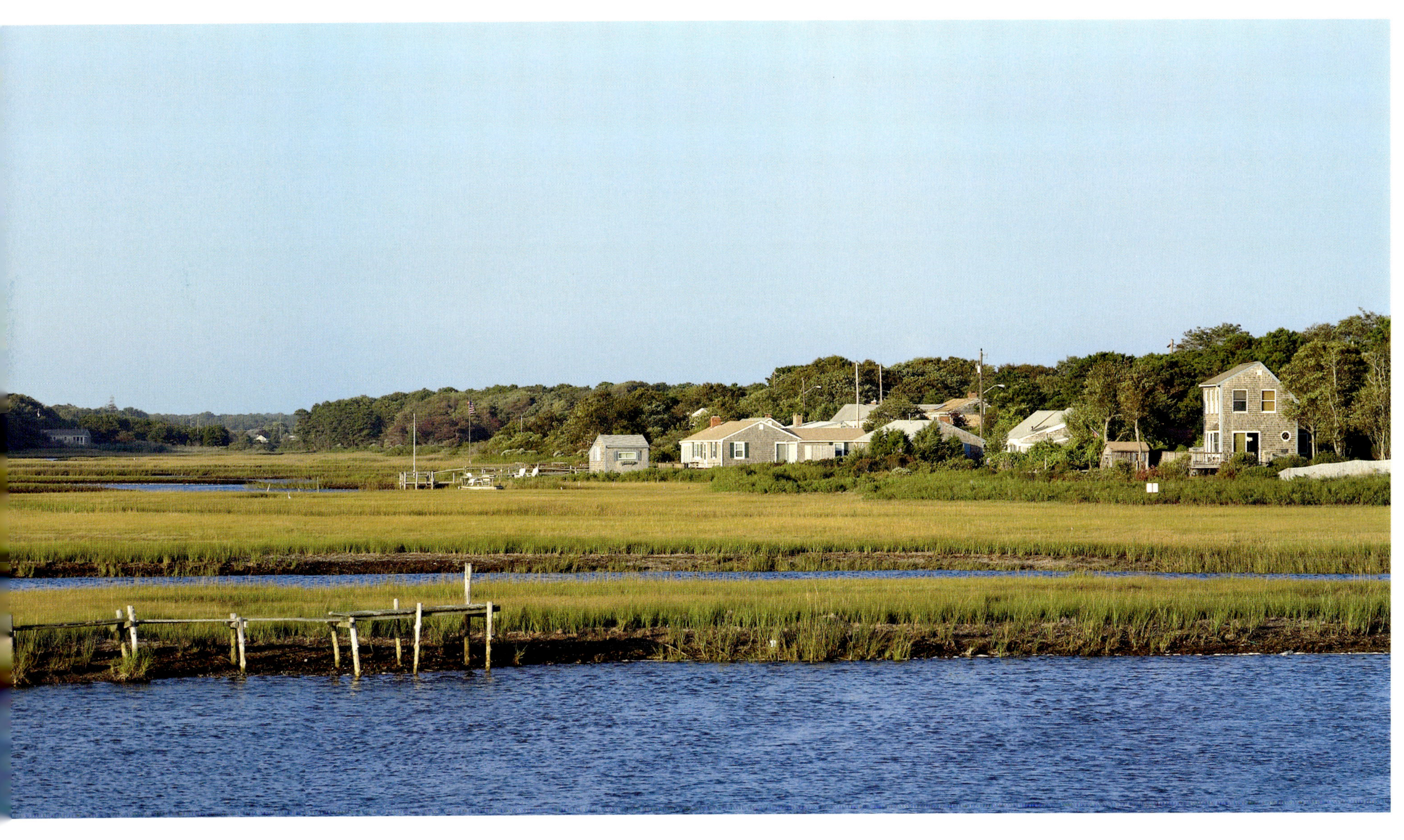

Bass River, Dennis

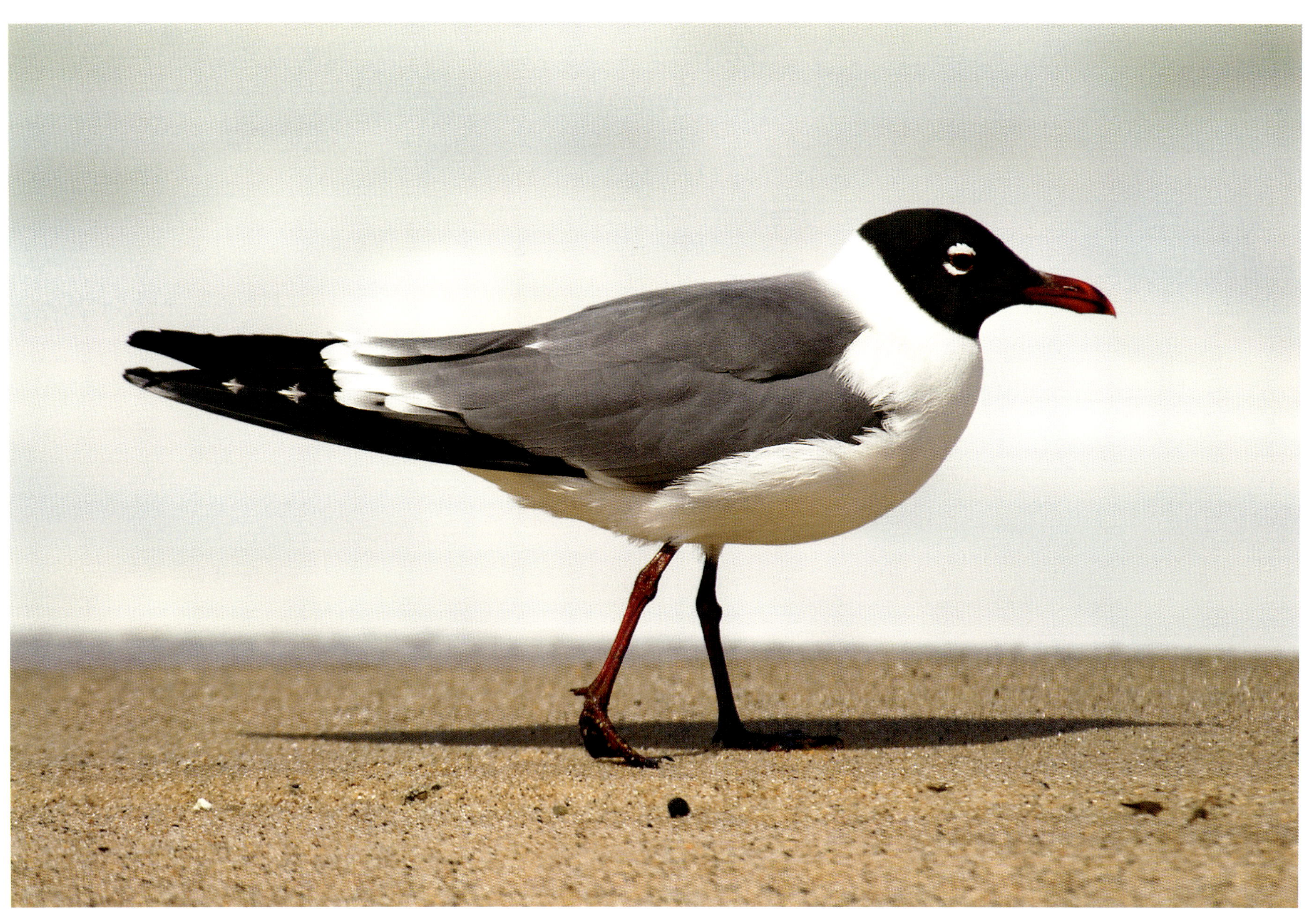

Laughing Gull

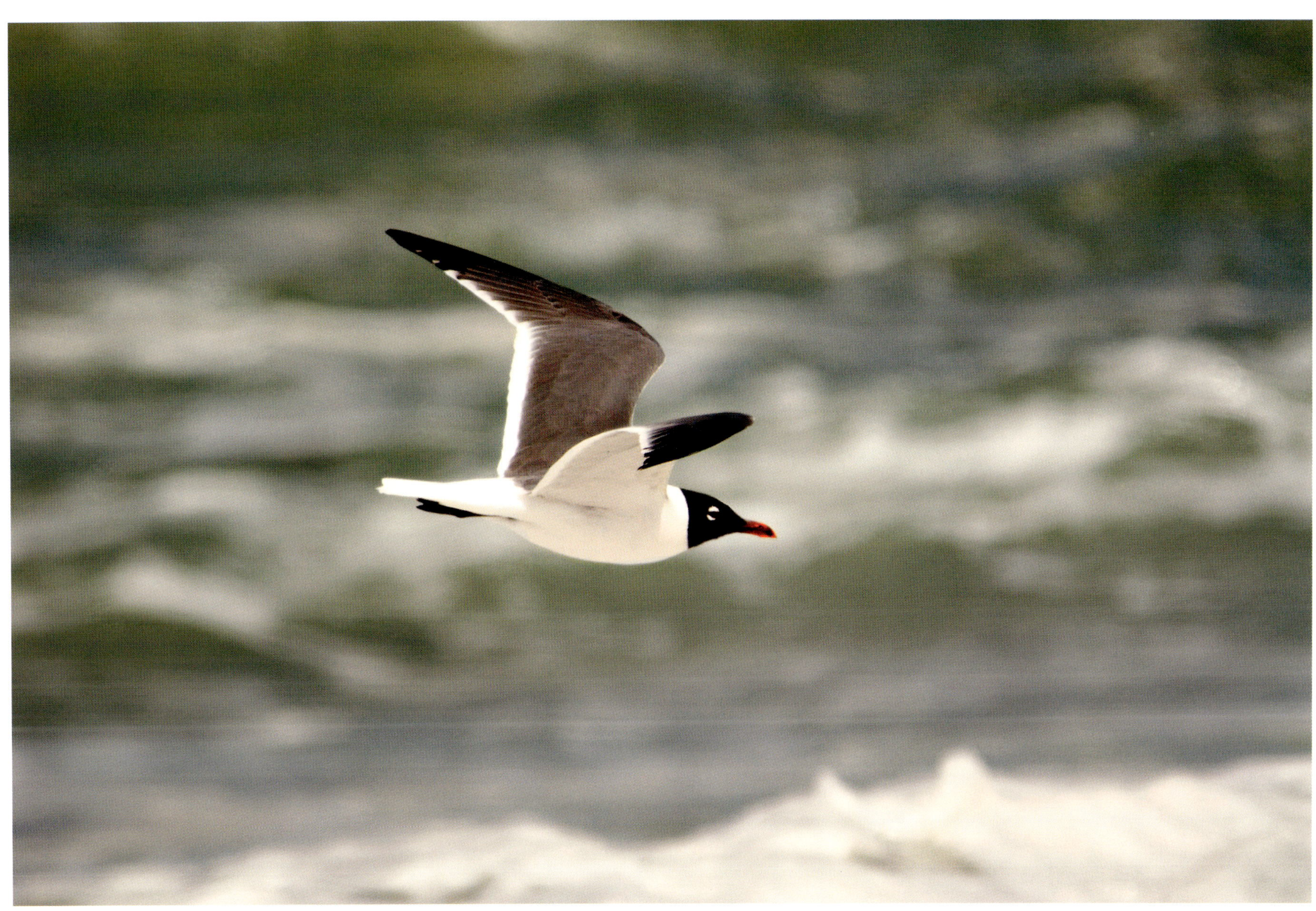

27 **Laughing Gull in flight**

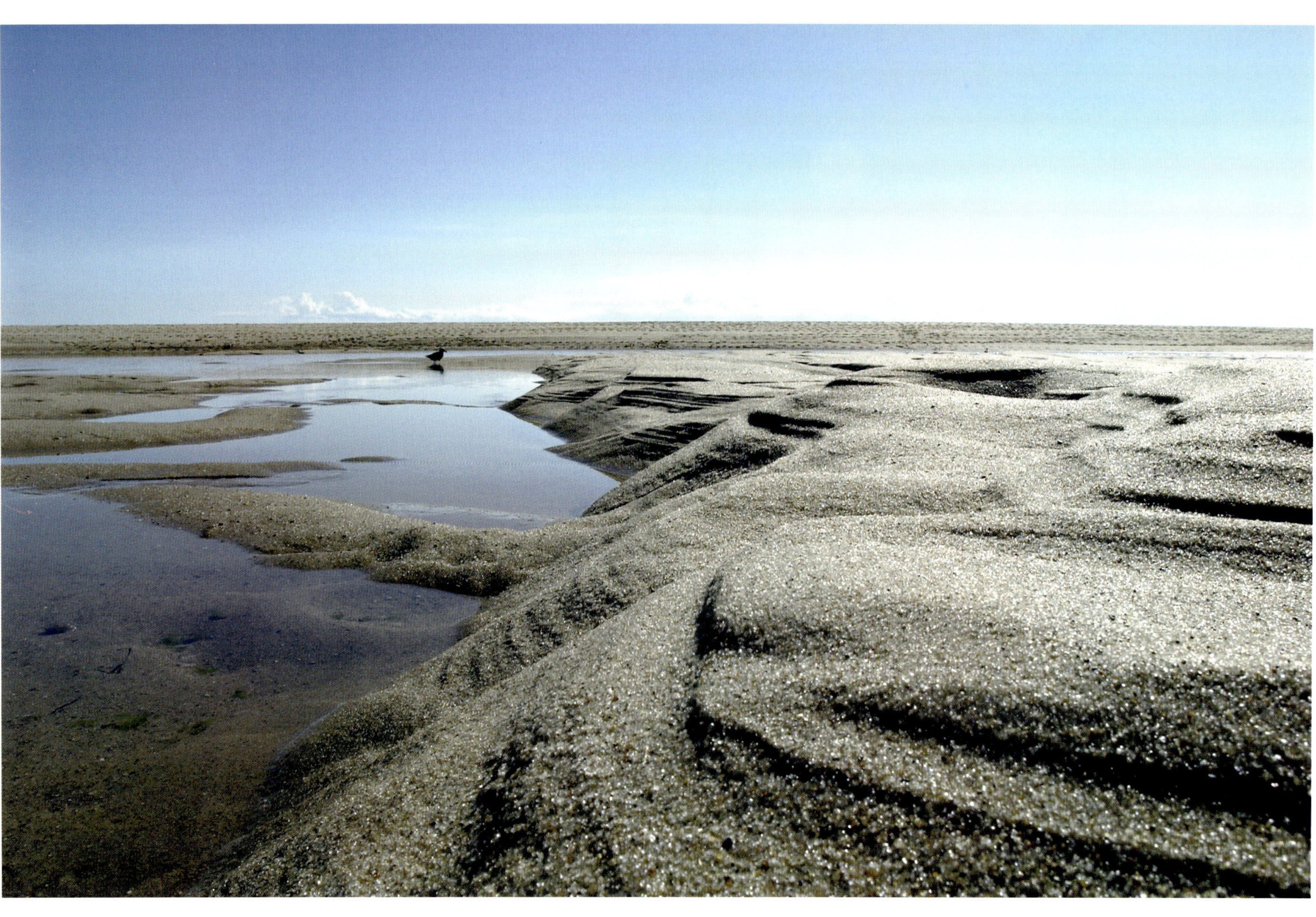

Hatches Harbor, Provincetown

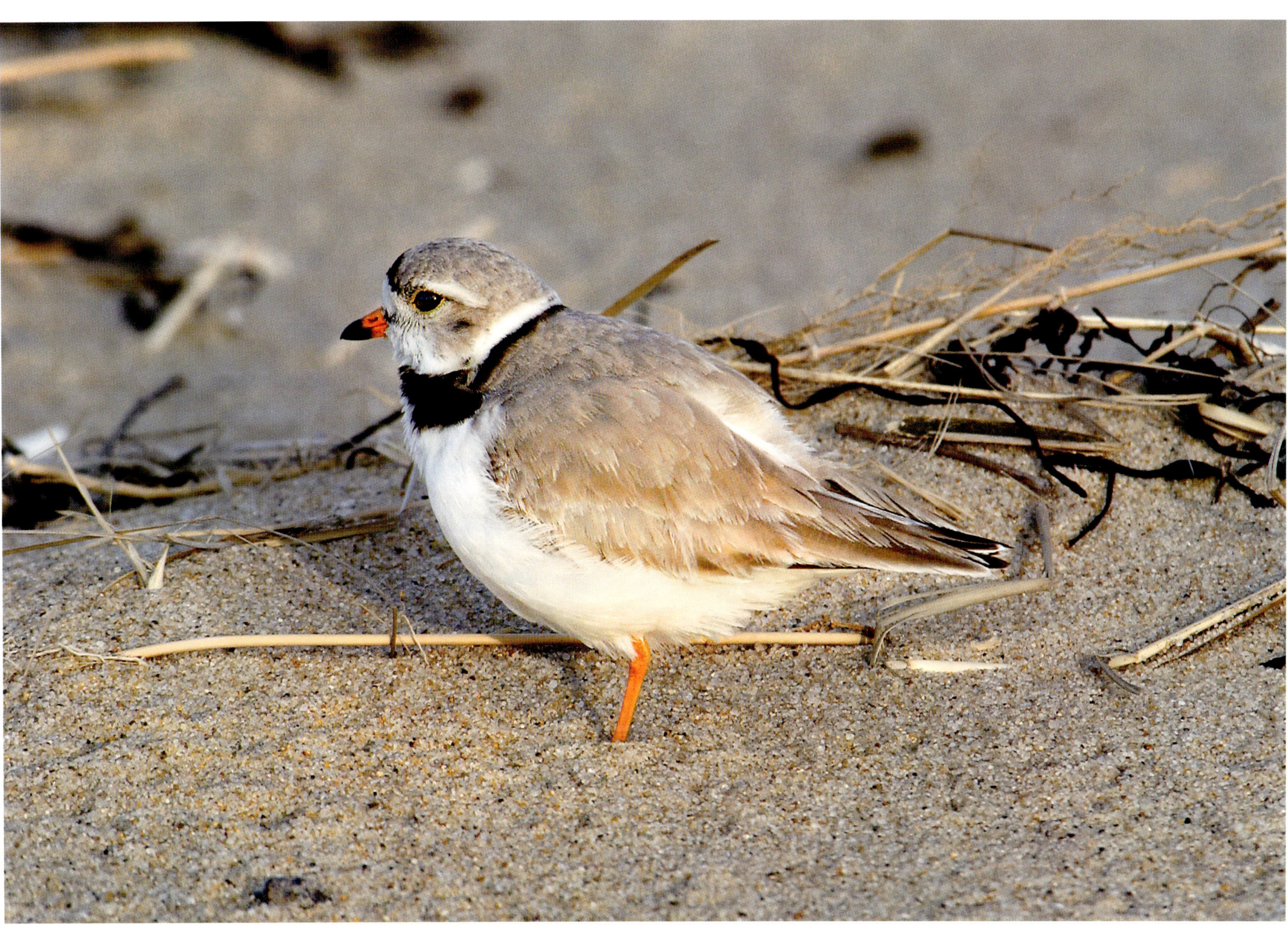

29 **Piping Plover, Provincetown**

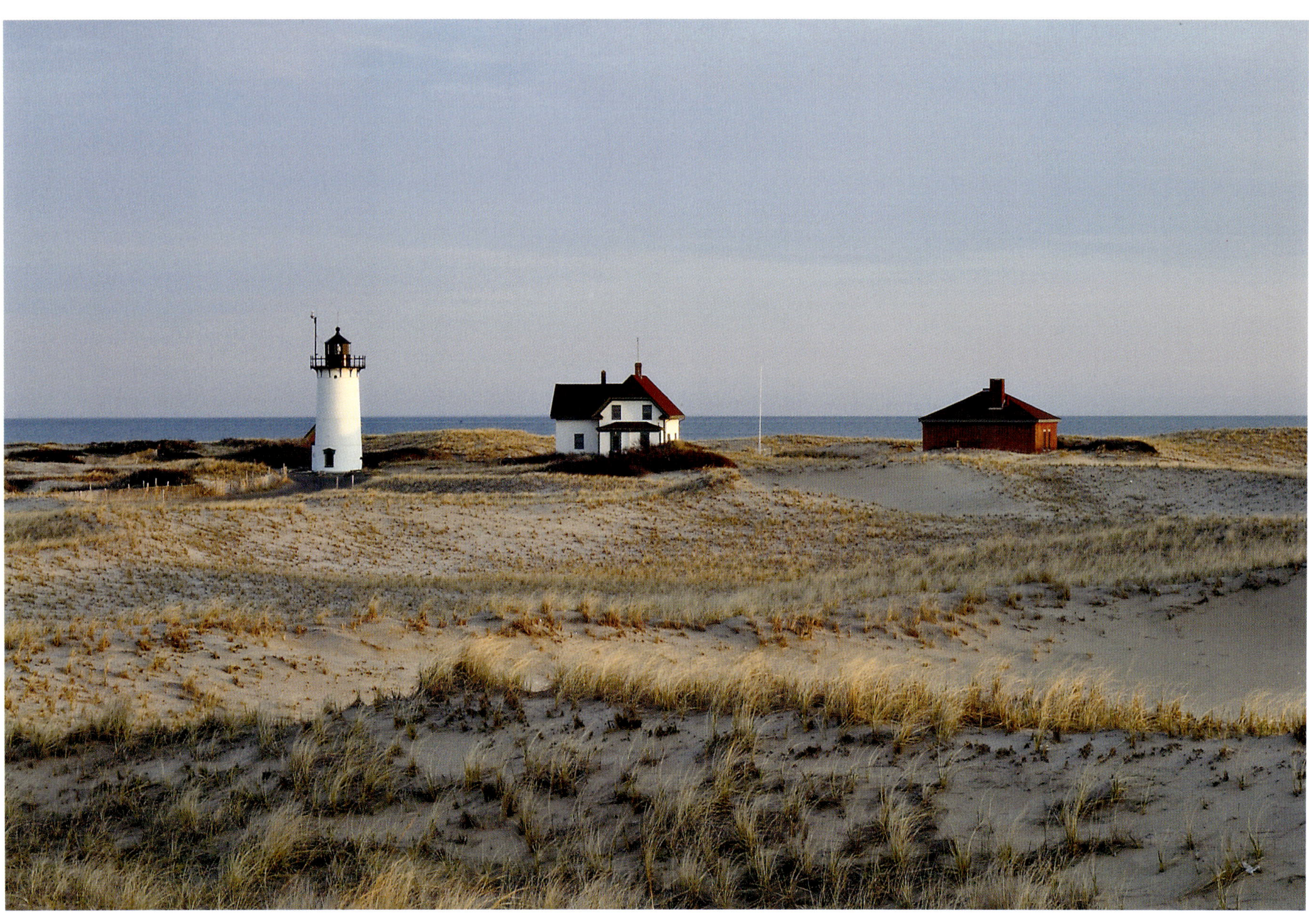

Race Point Light, Provincetown

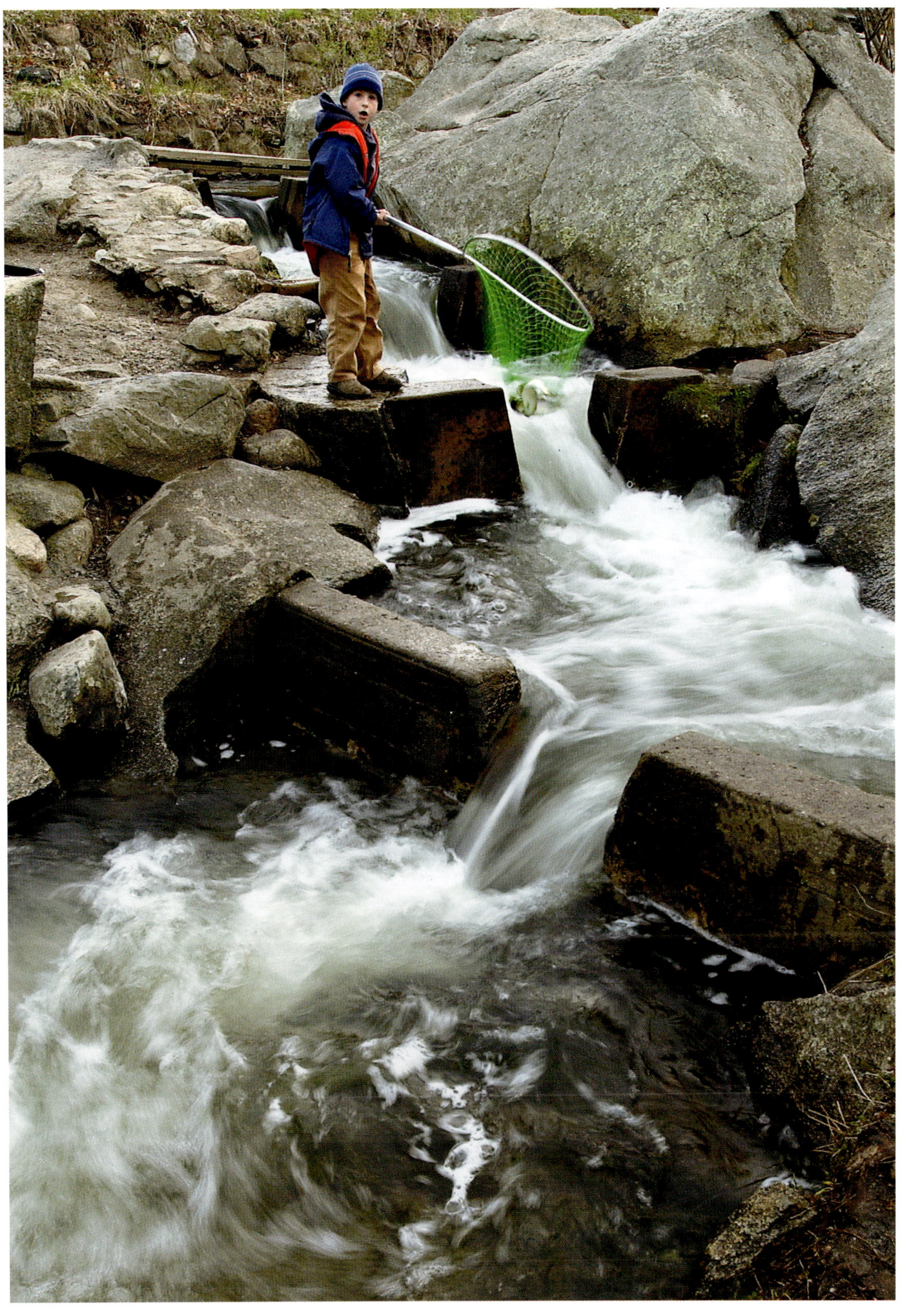

 Stony Brook Herring Run, Brewster

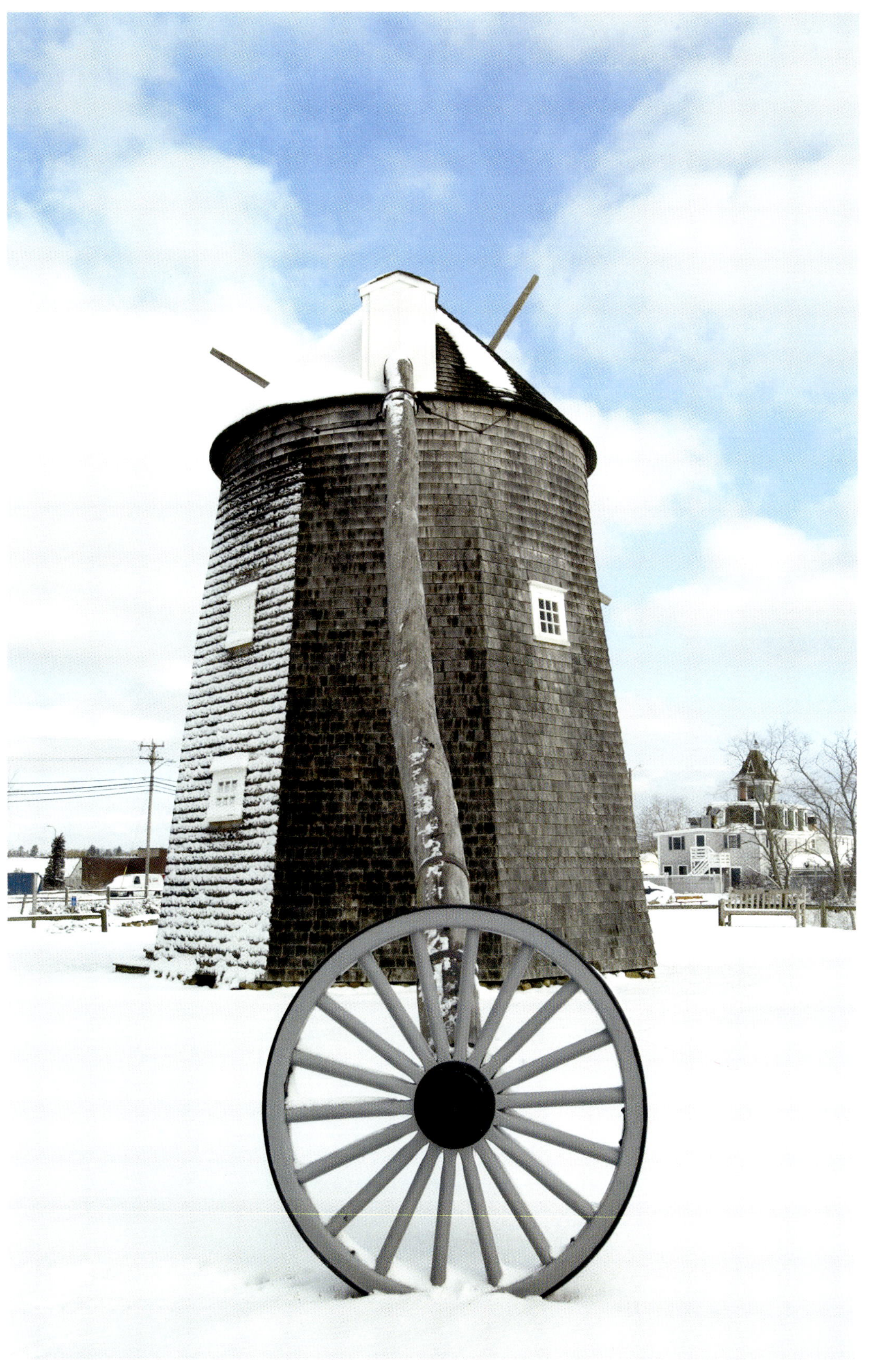

Windmill, Orleans

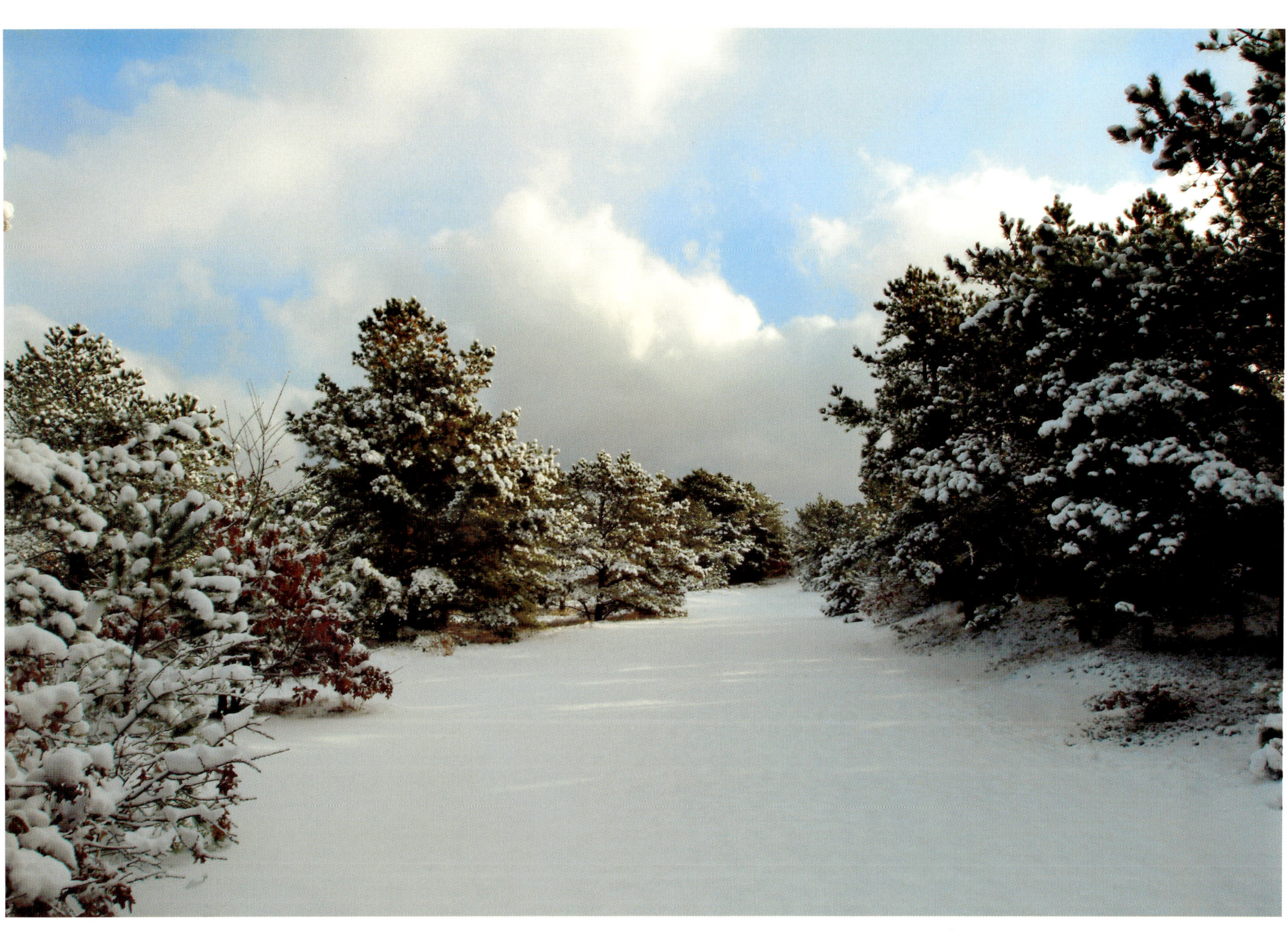

 Old Wireless Road, Marconi Station, Wellfleet

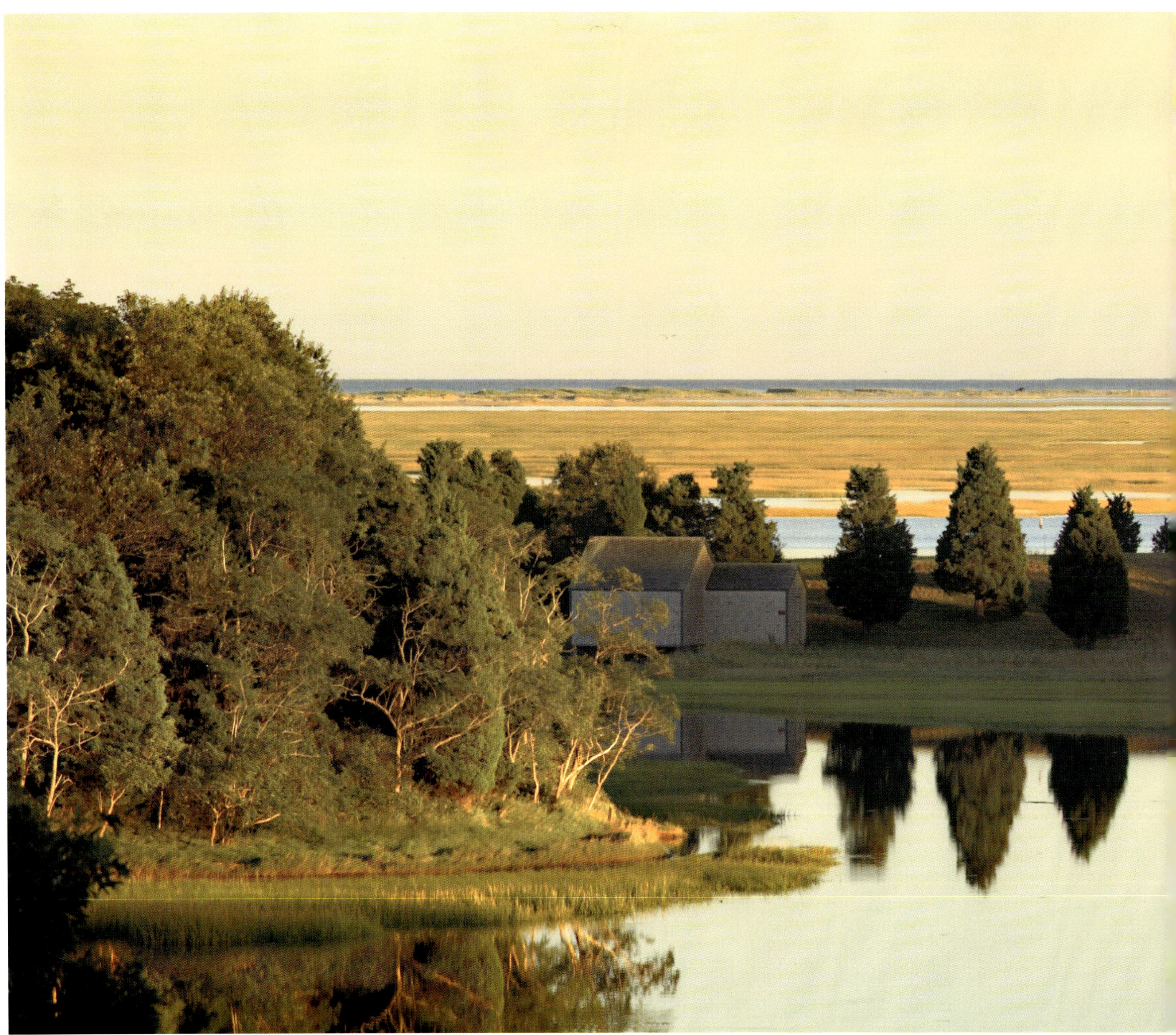

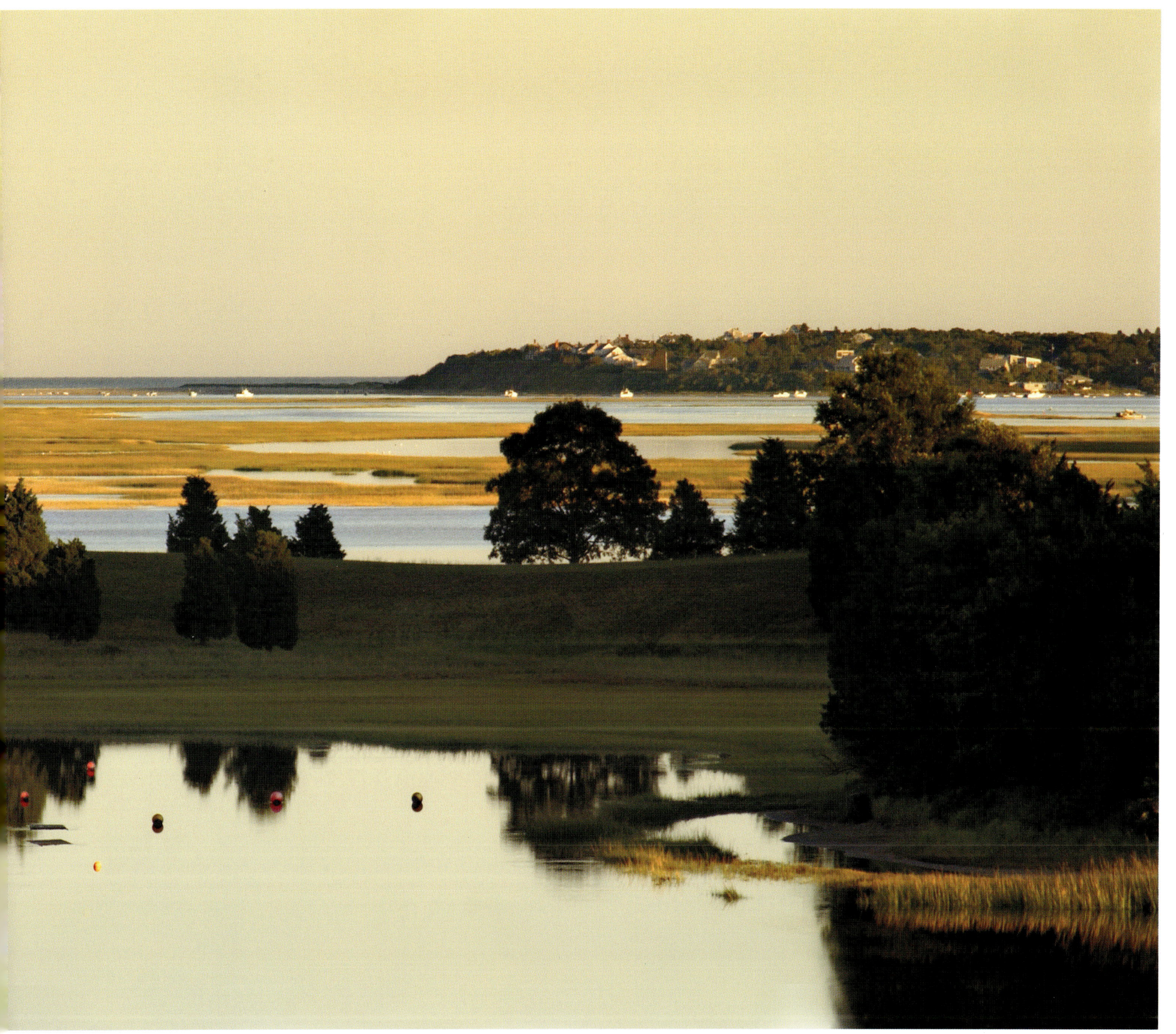

Salt Marsh View from National Seashore Visitors Center, Eastham

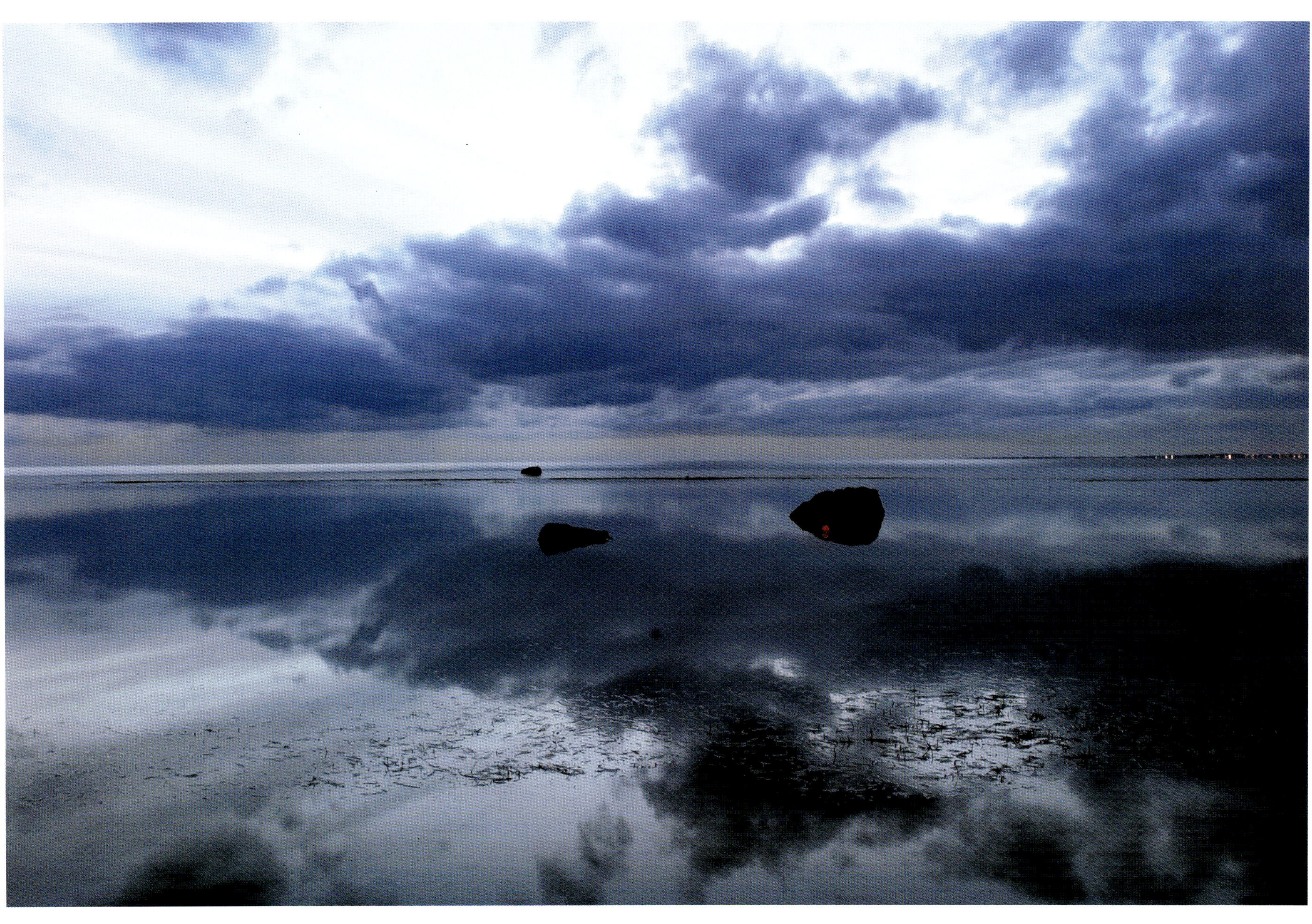

Corn Hill Beach, Truro

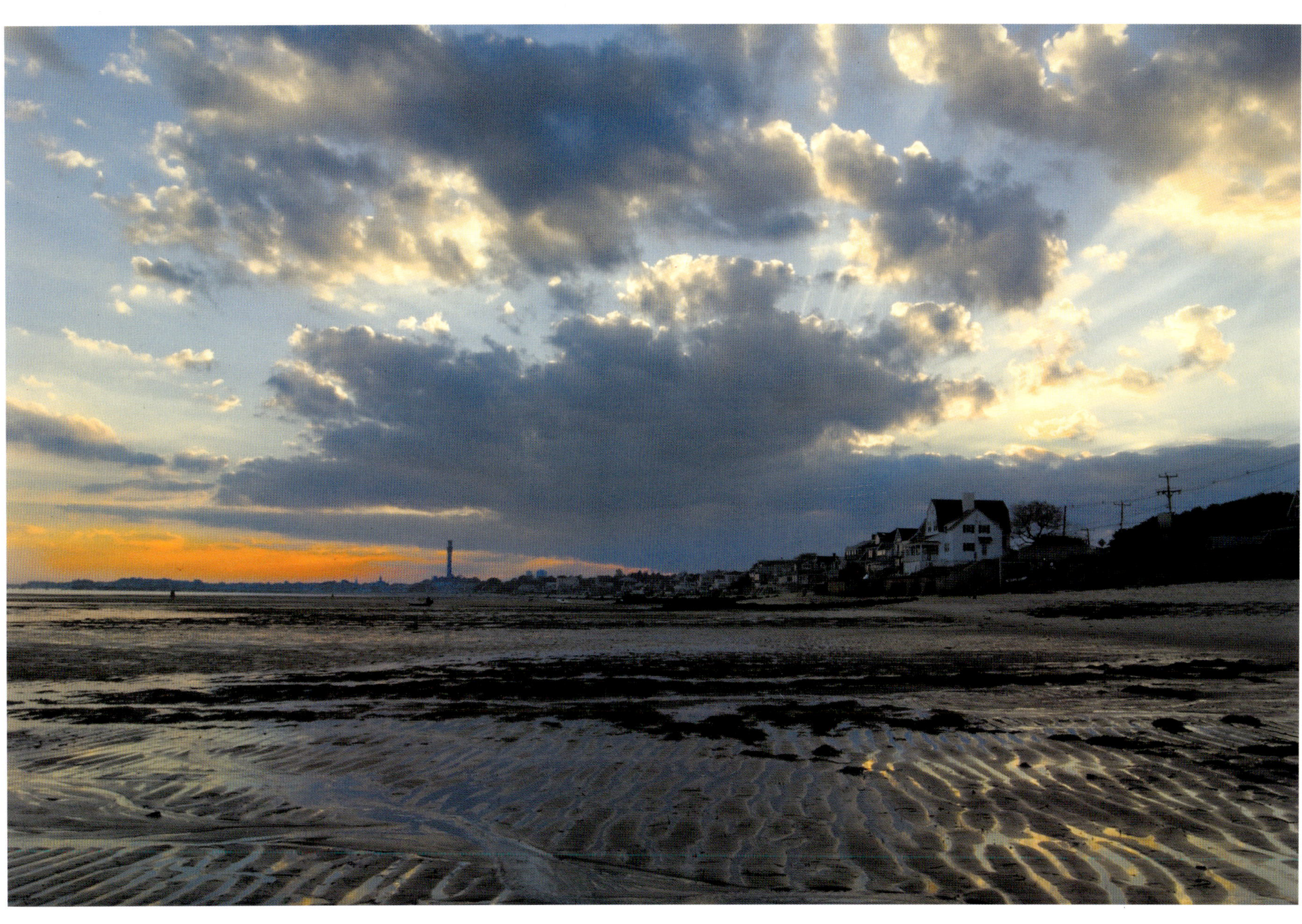

37 **View from East End, Provincetown**

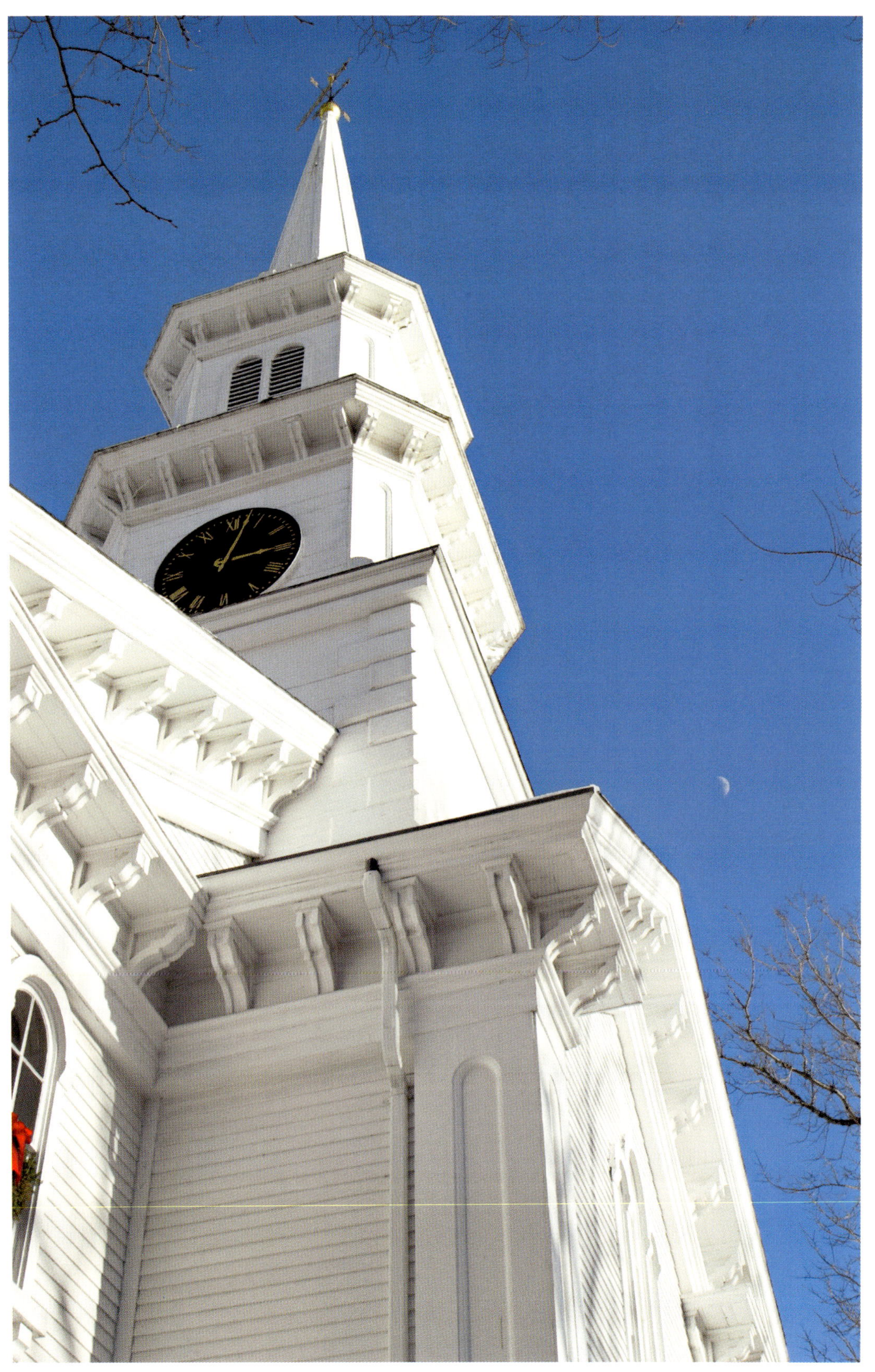

First Congregational Church, Falmouth

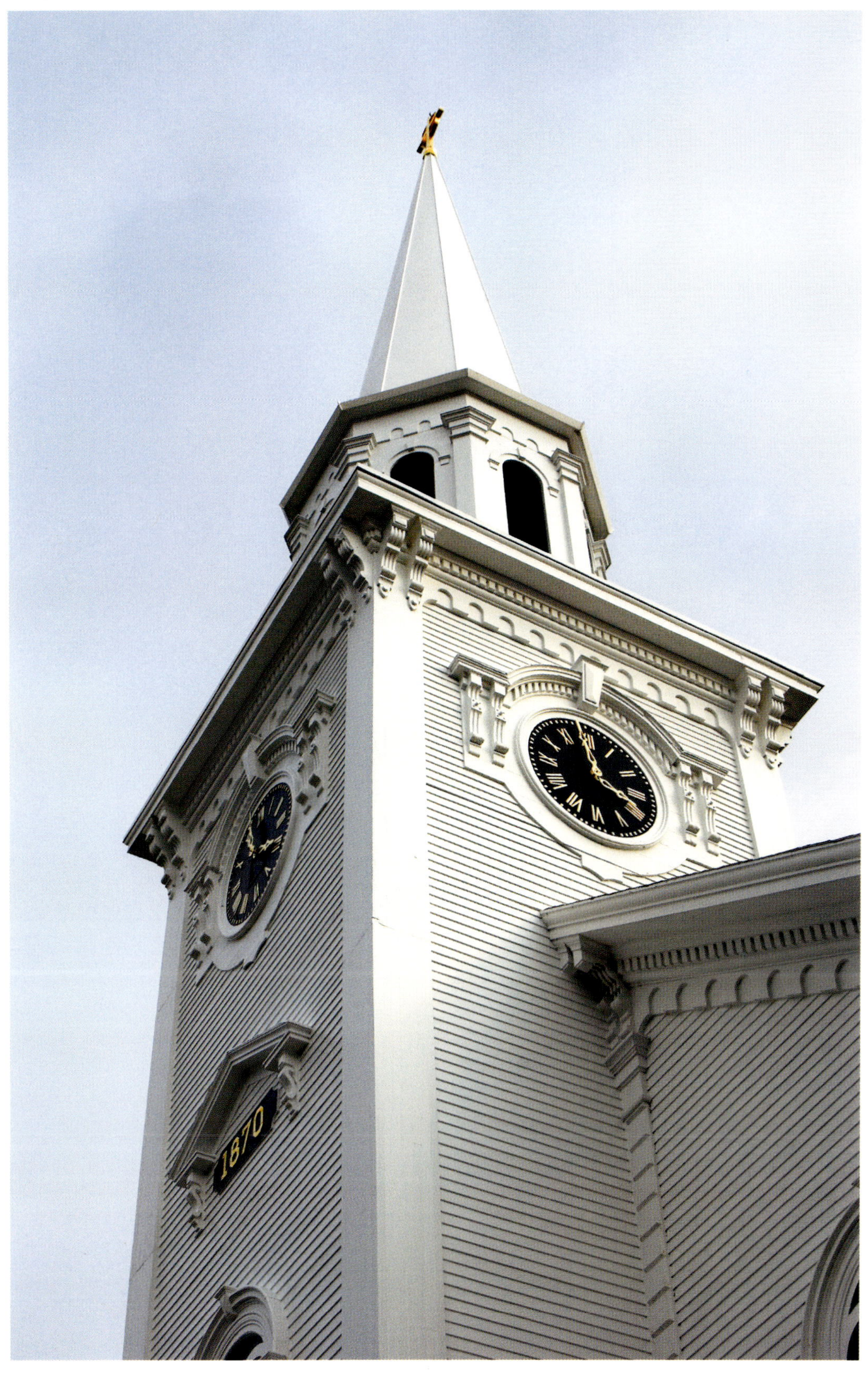

 First Congregational Church, Yarmouth

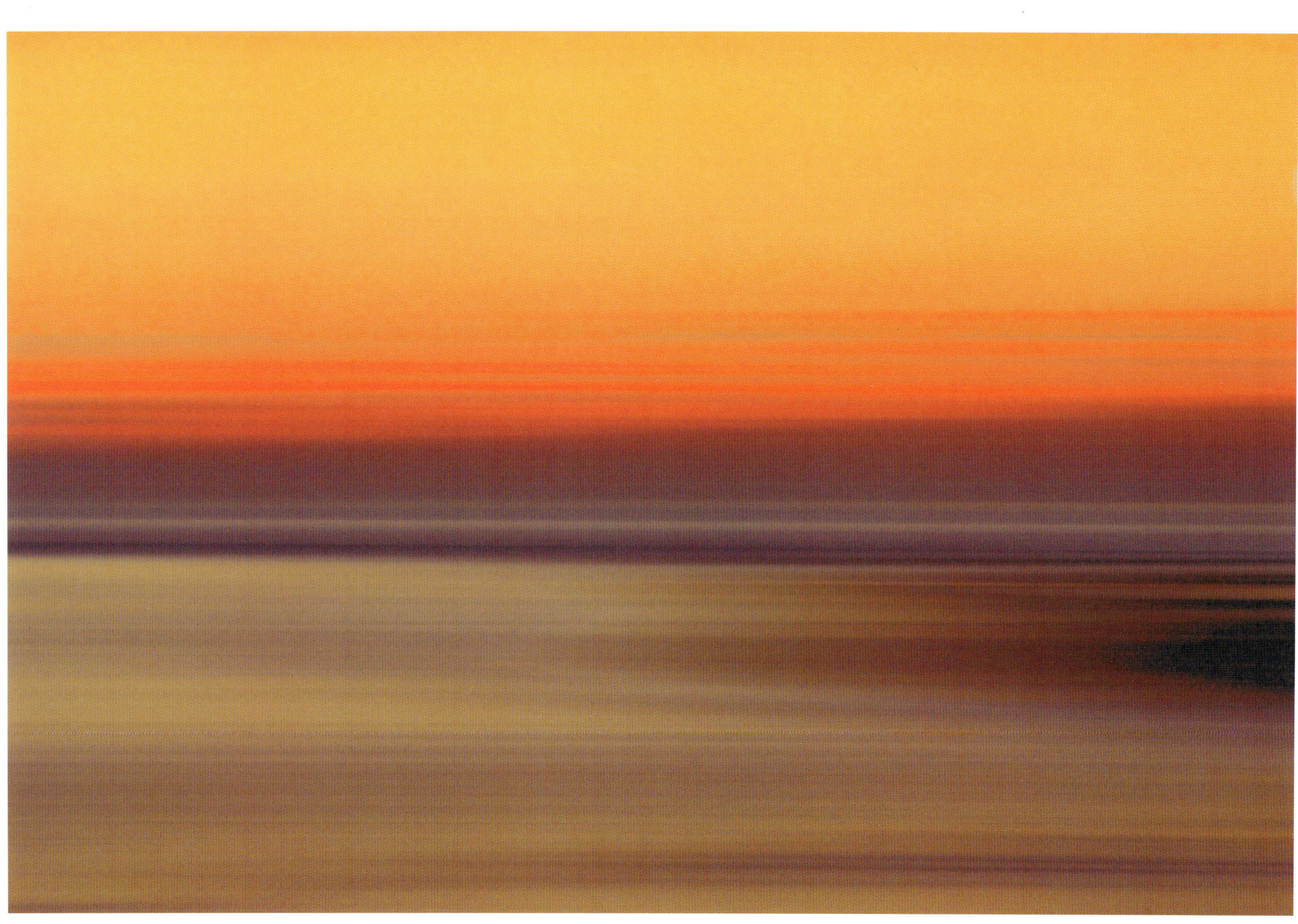

Sunrise, Chatham

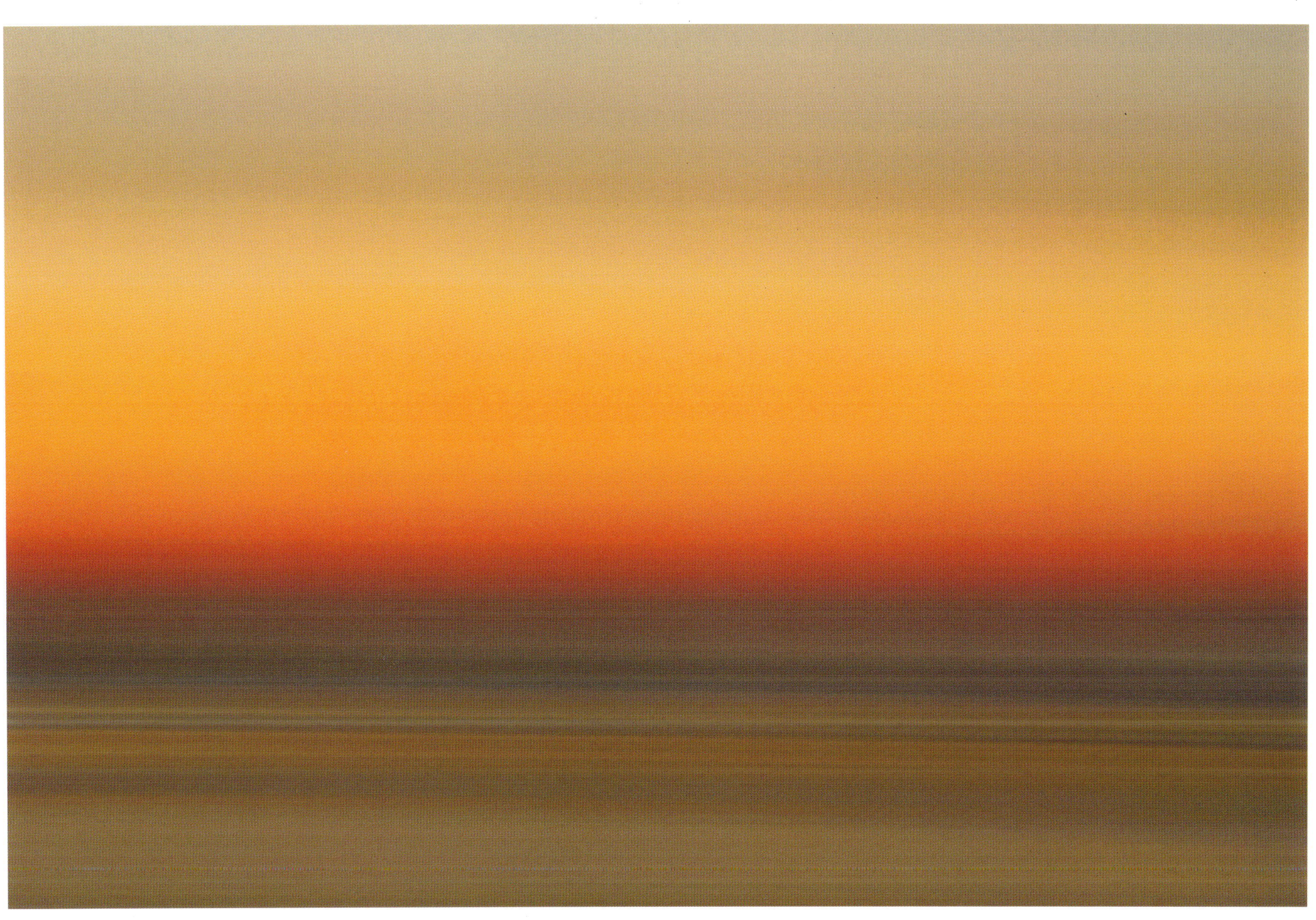

41 **Sunrise, Chatham**

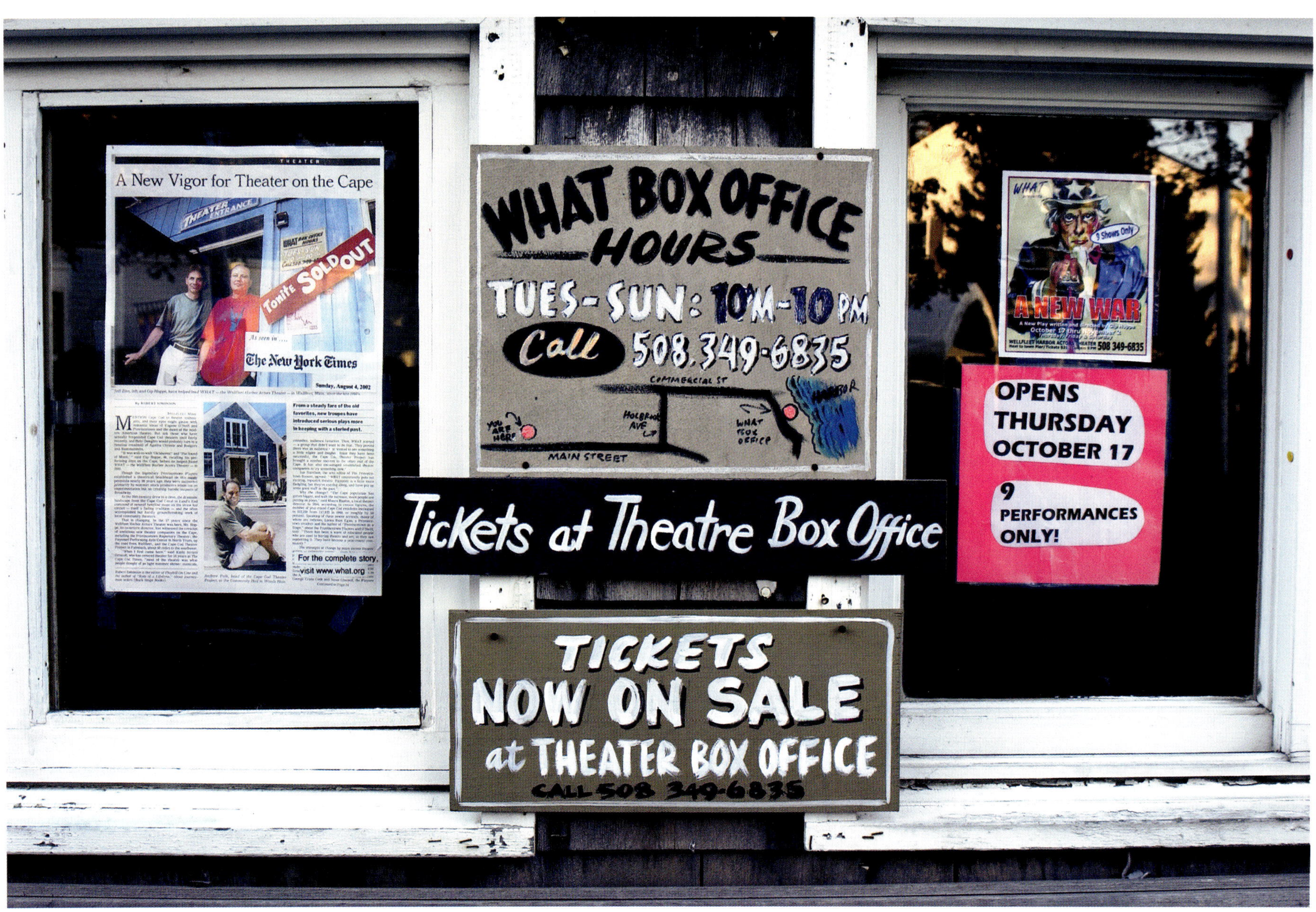

Wellfleet Harbor Actors Theater Box Office (WHAT), Wellfleet

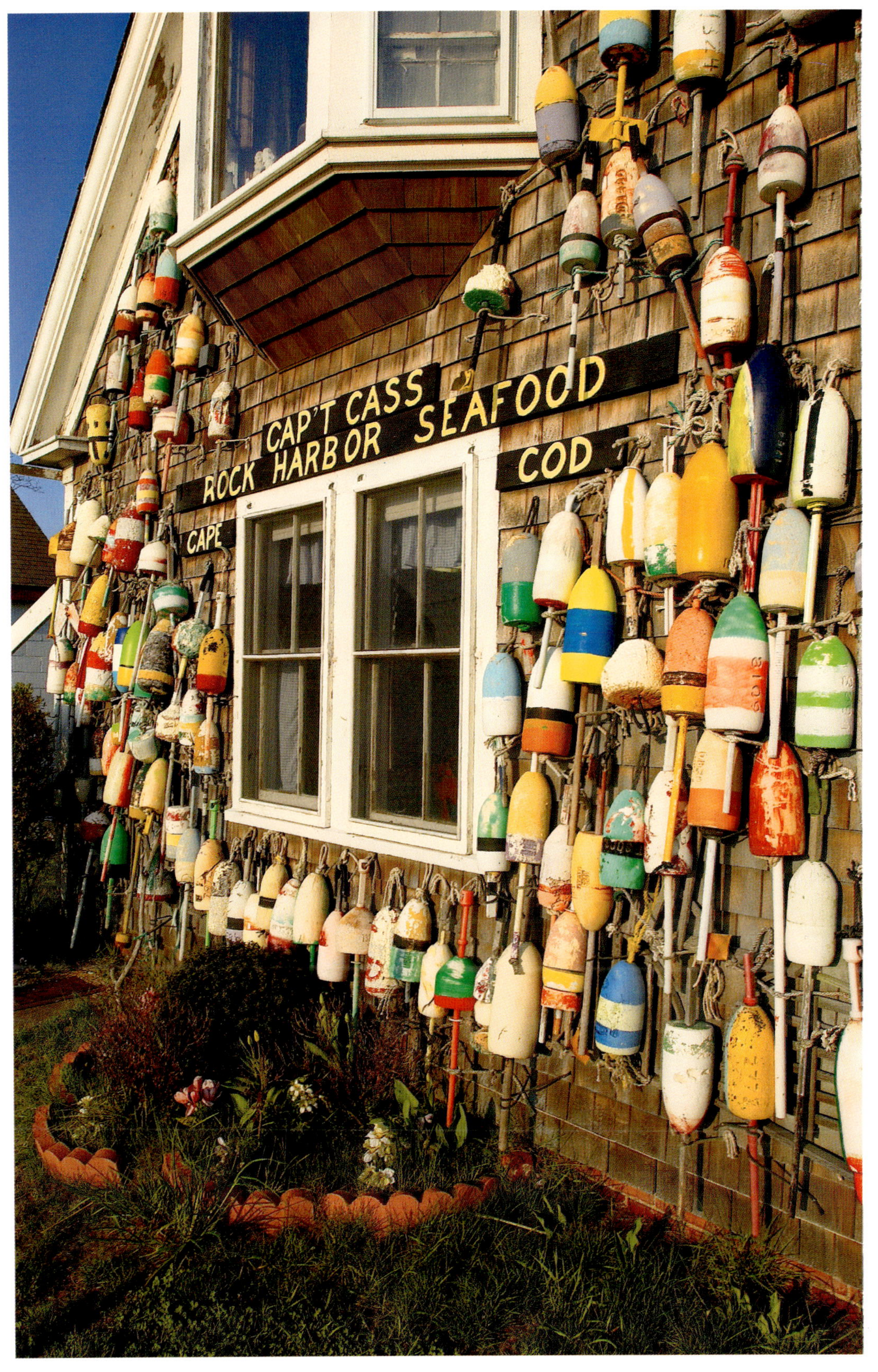

43 **Rock Harbor, Orleans**

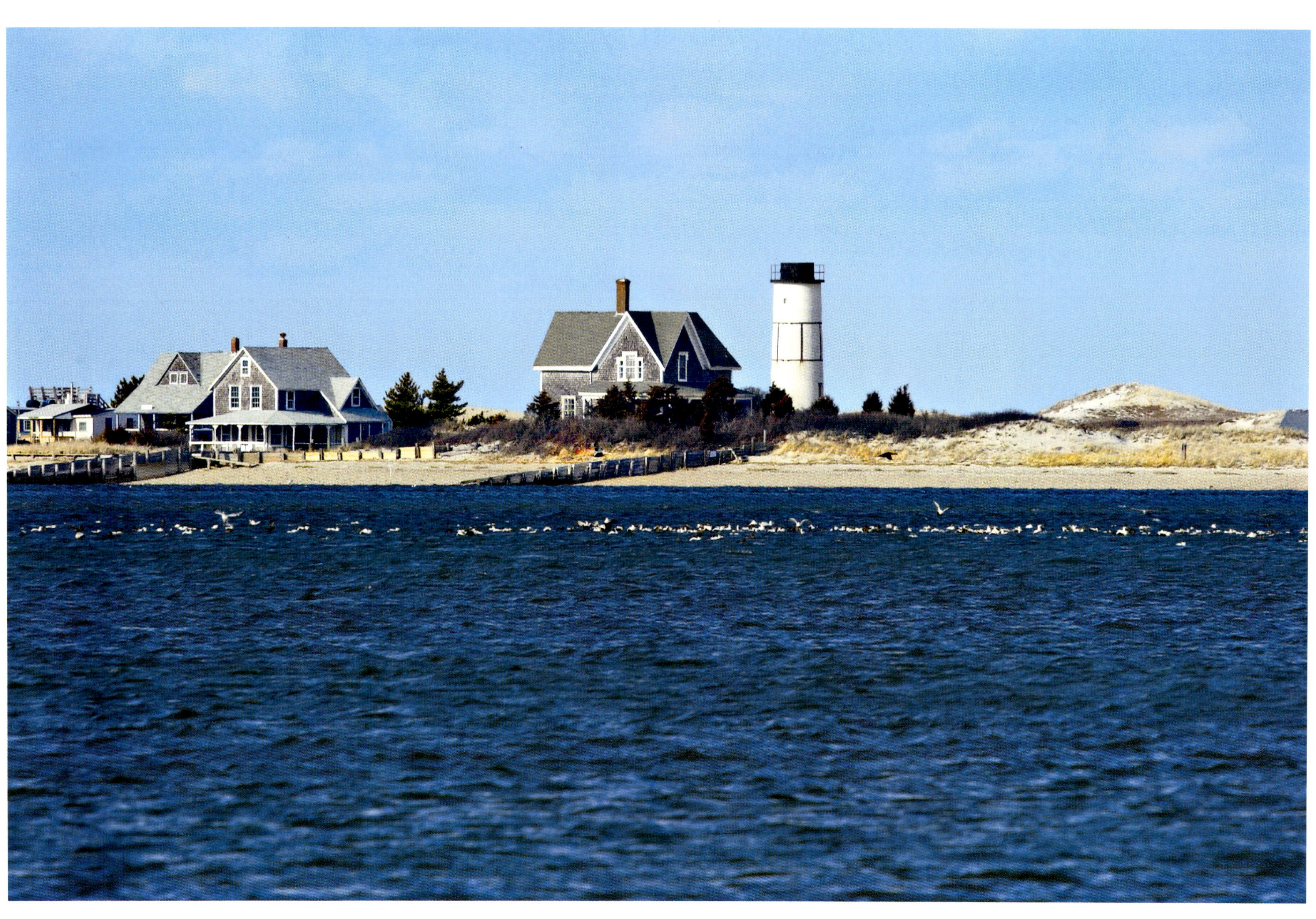

Sandy Neck Light, Barnstable

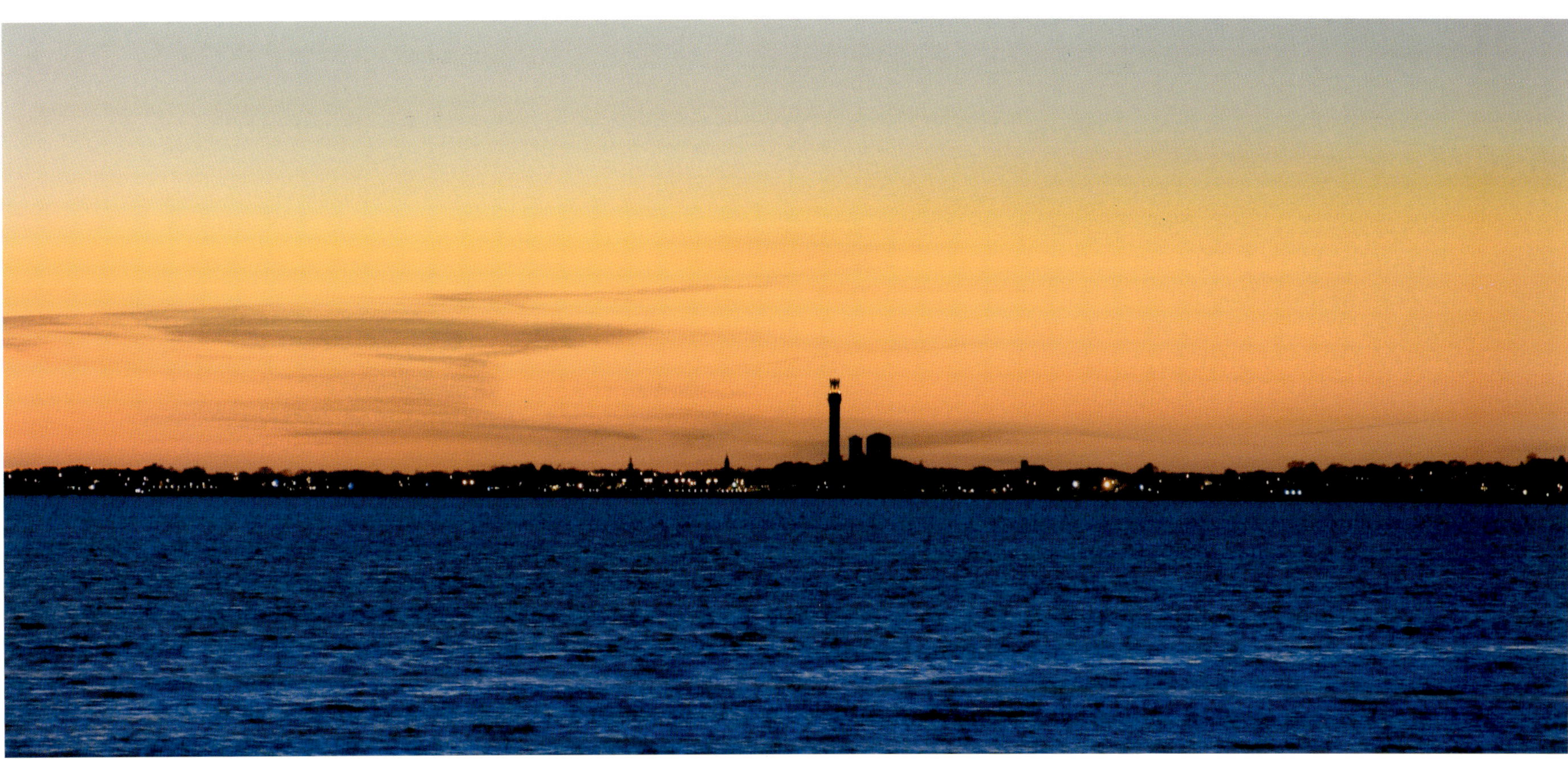

 Sunset from East End, Provincetown

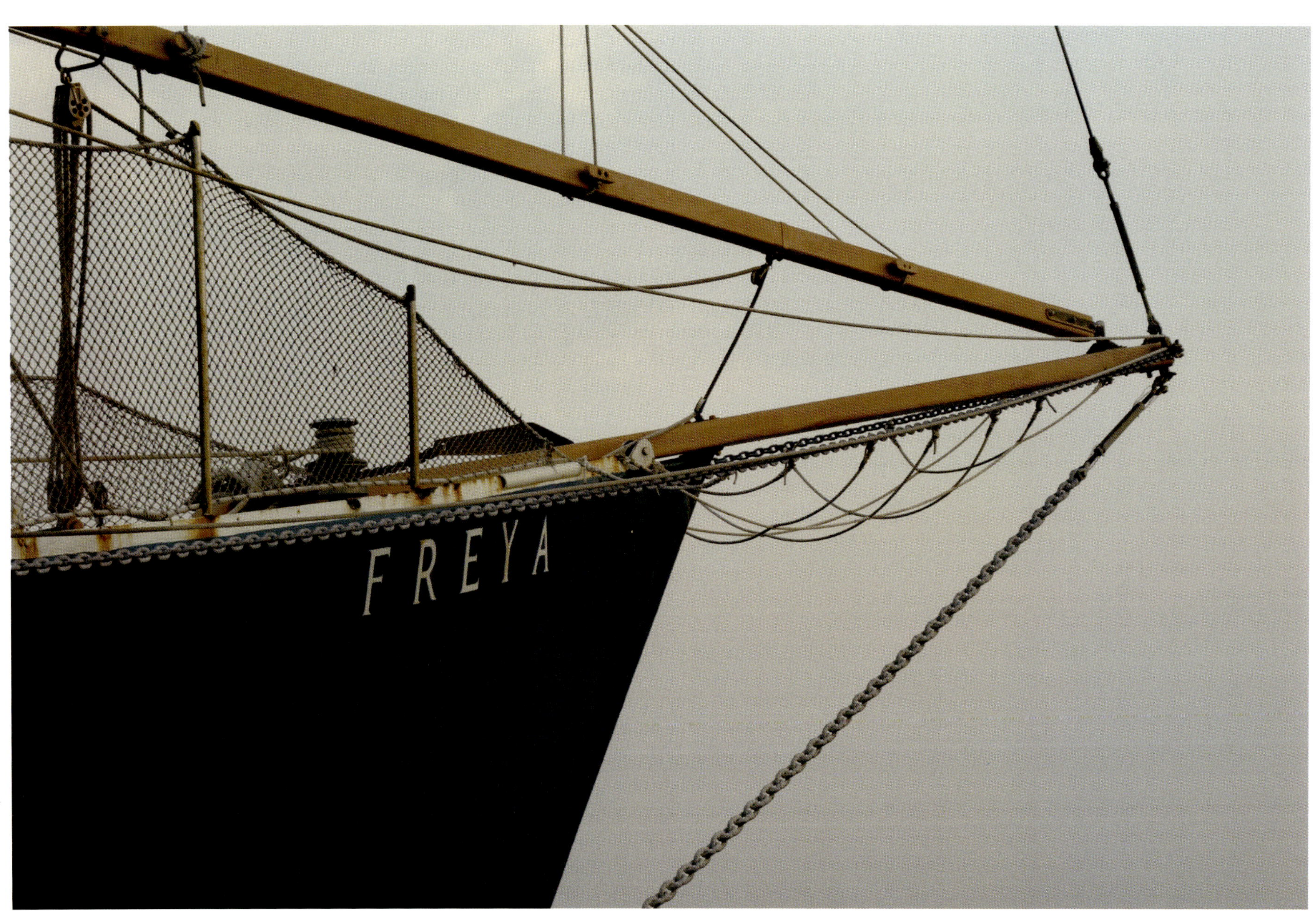

Sesuit Harbor Boat Yard, East Dennis

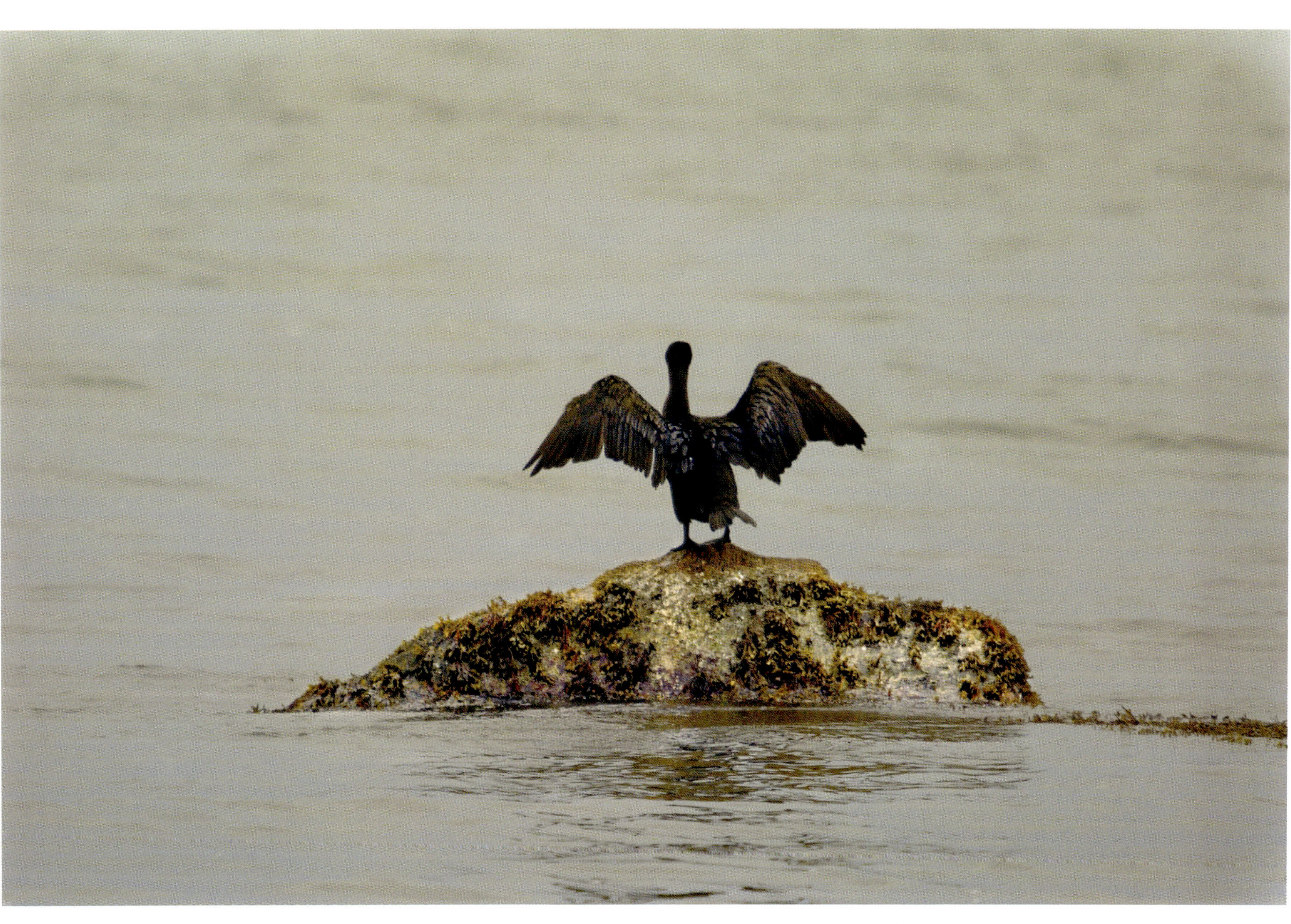

47 **Cormorant, Craigville Beach, Barnstable**

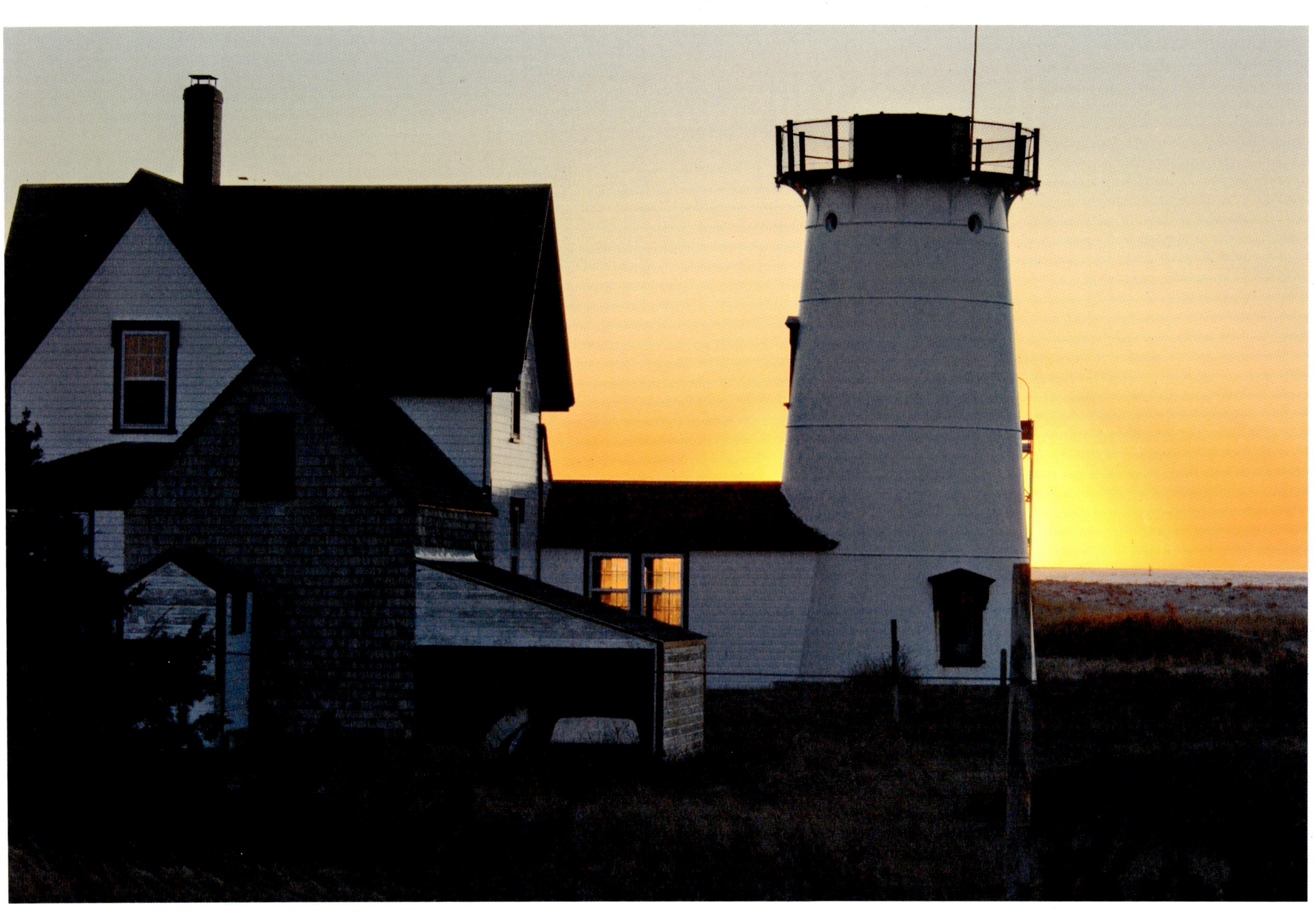

Stage Harbor Light, Chatham

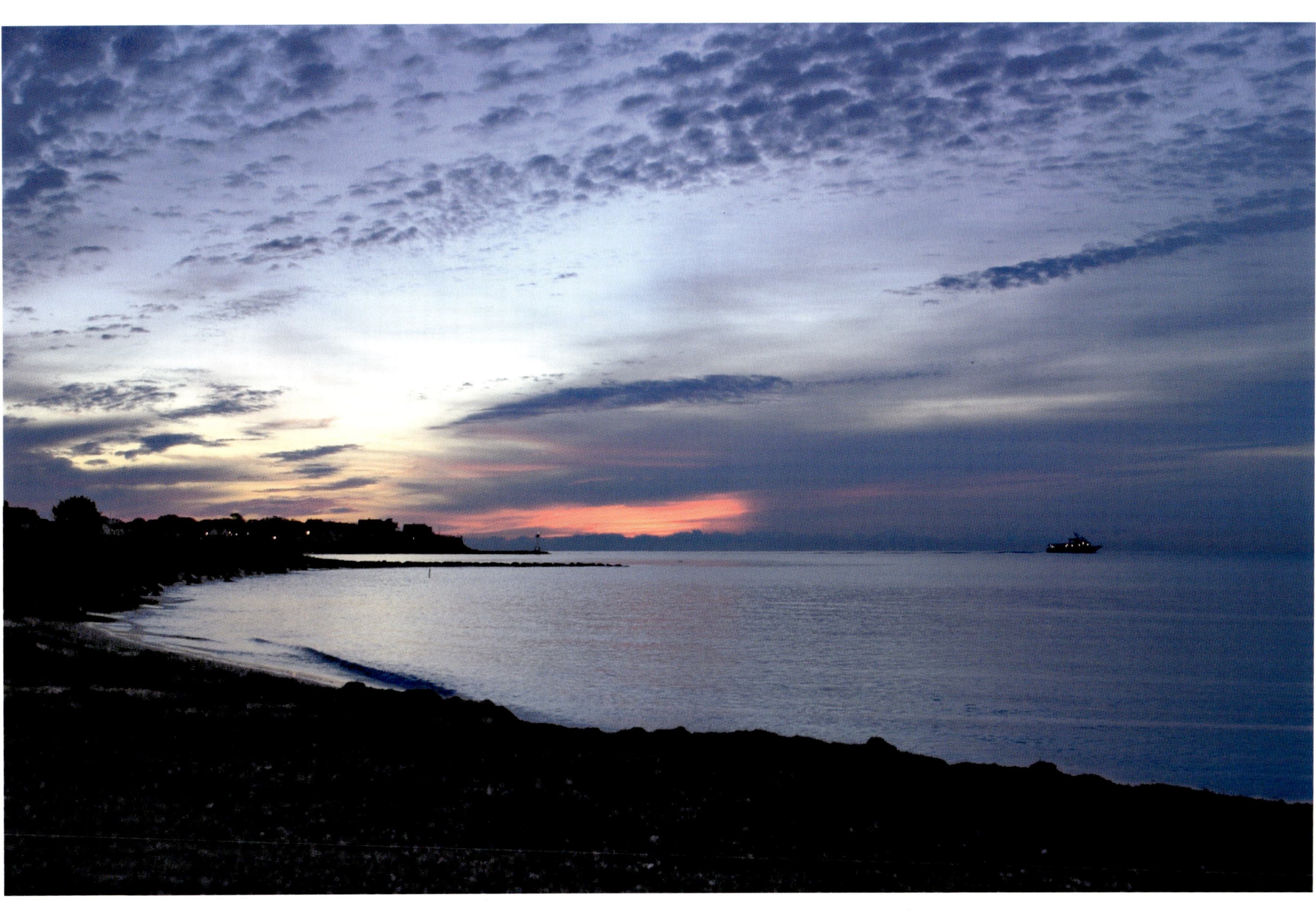

49 **Early Morning Ferry from Cape Cod to Martha's Vineyard**

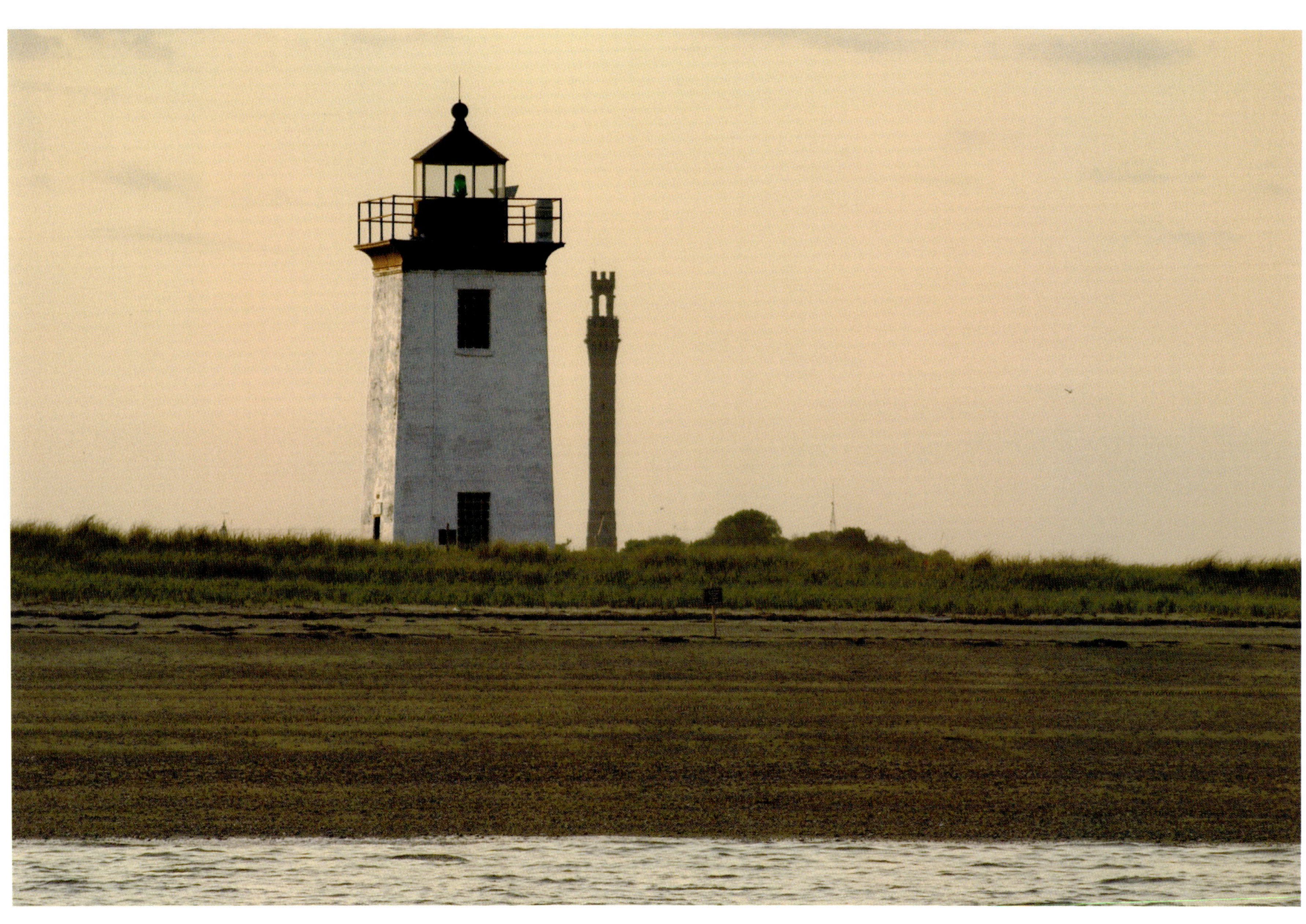

Long Point Light Dwarfs Pilgrim Monument, Provincetown

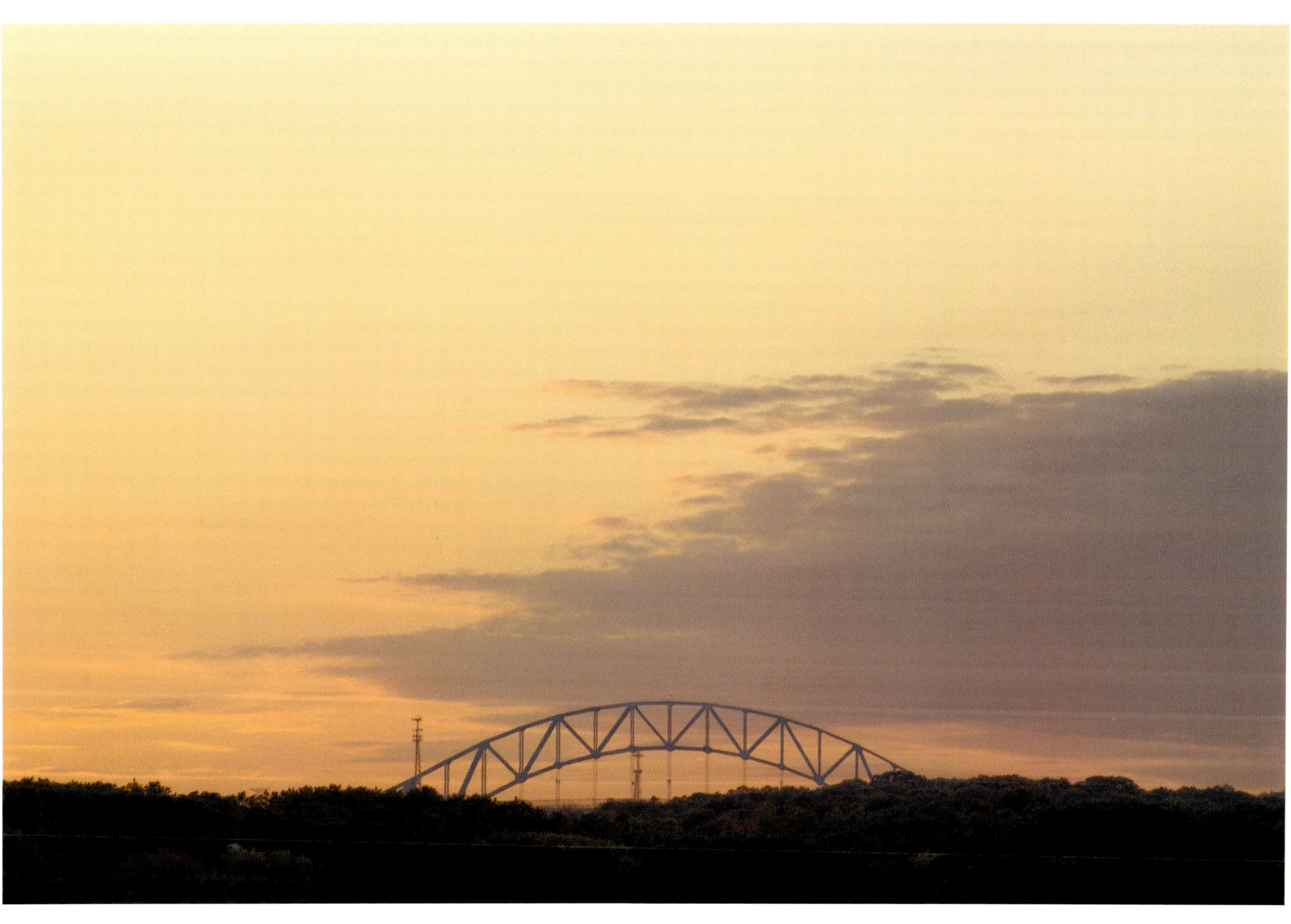

 Sagamore Bridge at Sunset, Sagamore

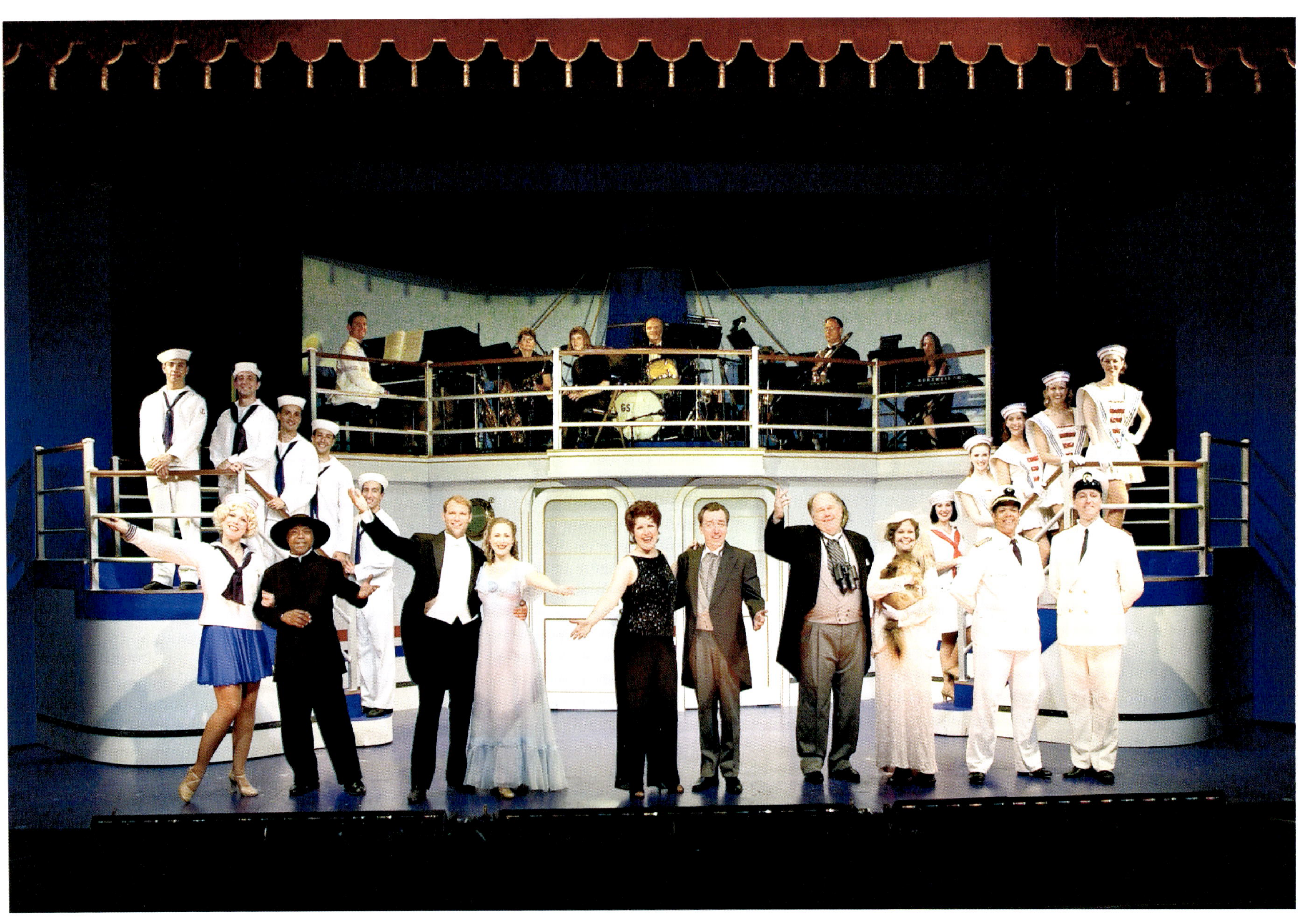

"Anything Goes" Cast, Cape Playhouse, Dennis

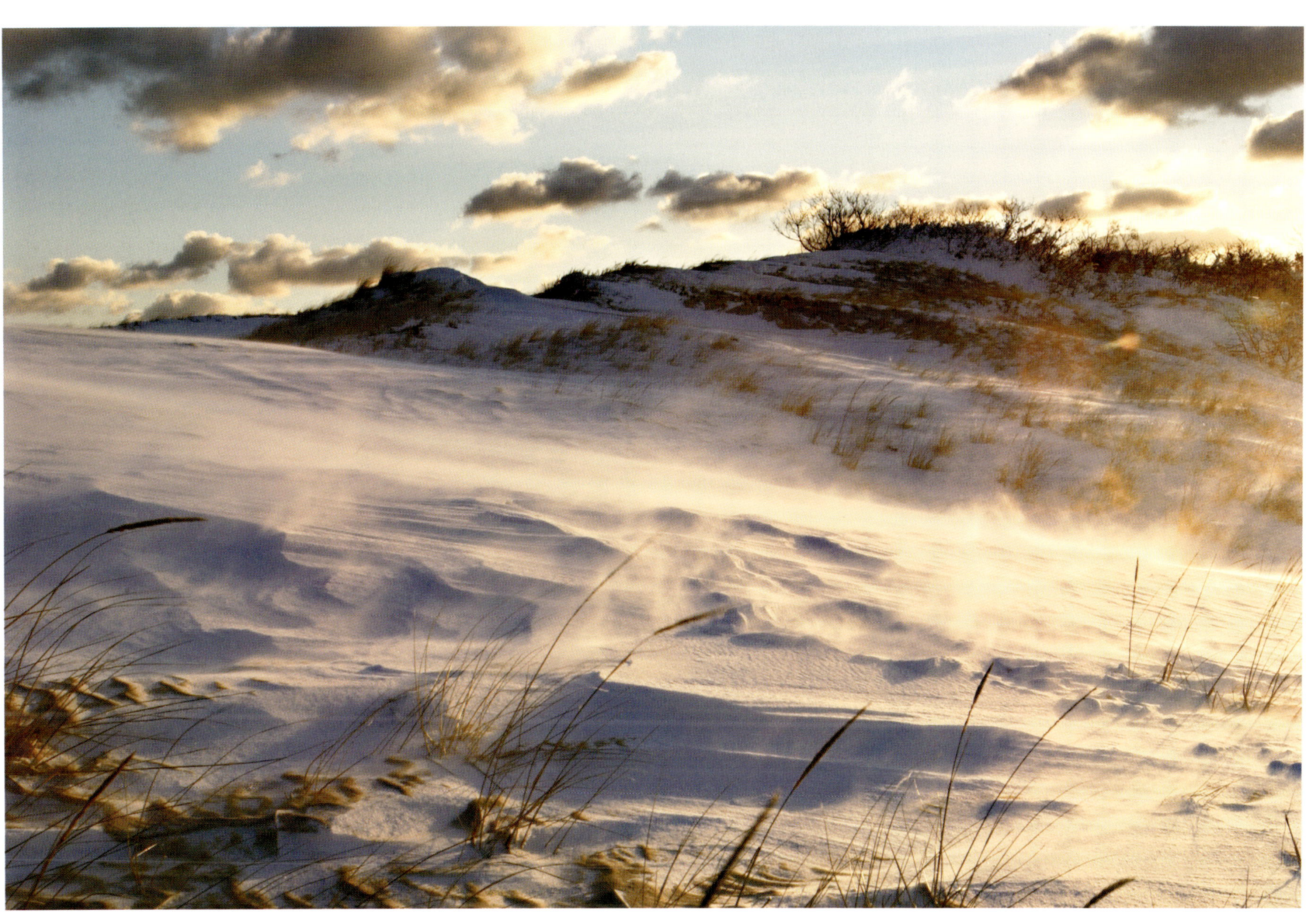

53 **Snow on the Dunes at Sunrise, Provincetown**

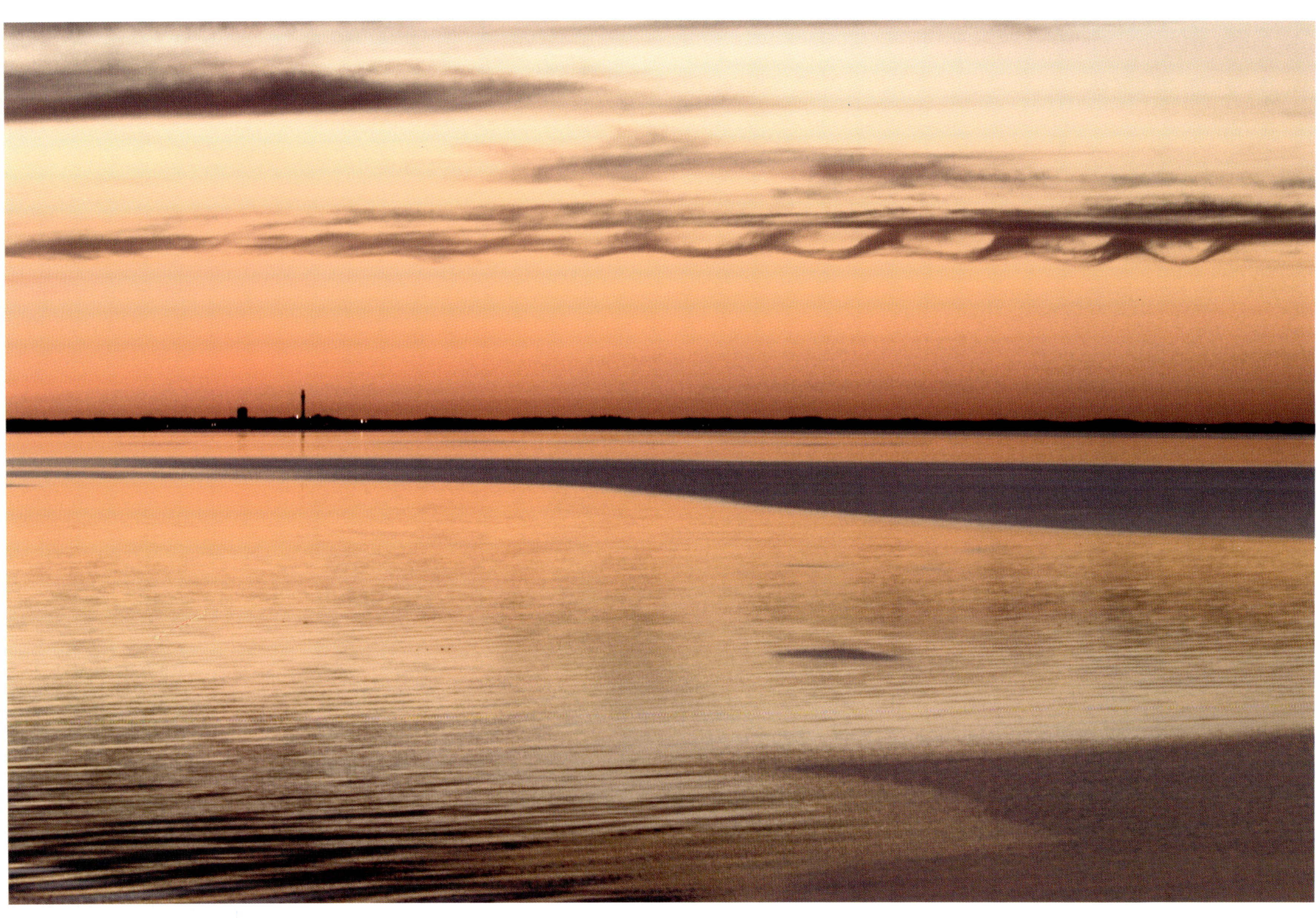

Sunset, Truro

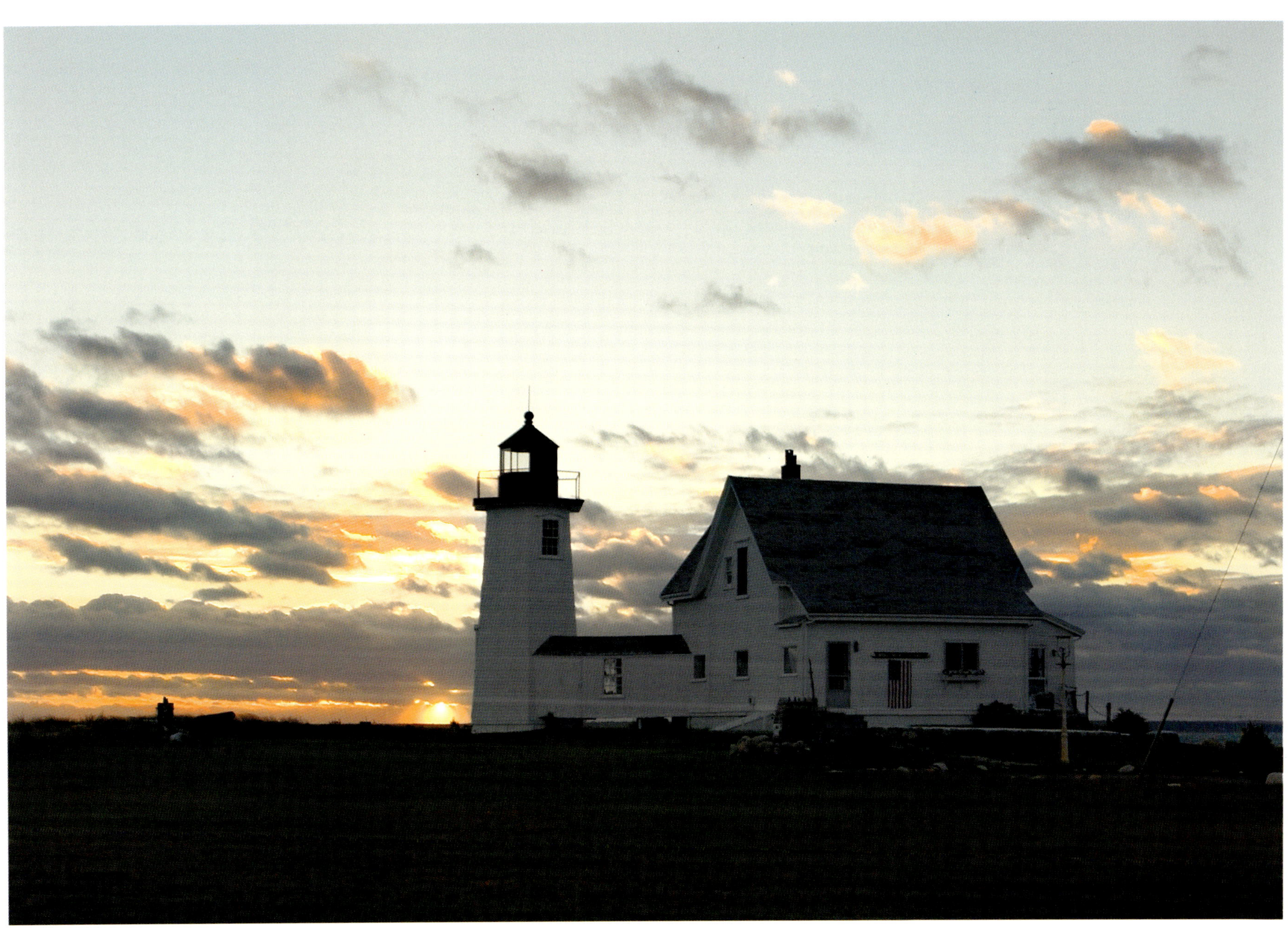

 Wings Neck Light, Bourne

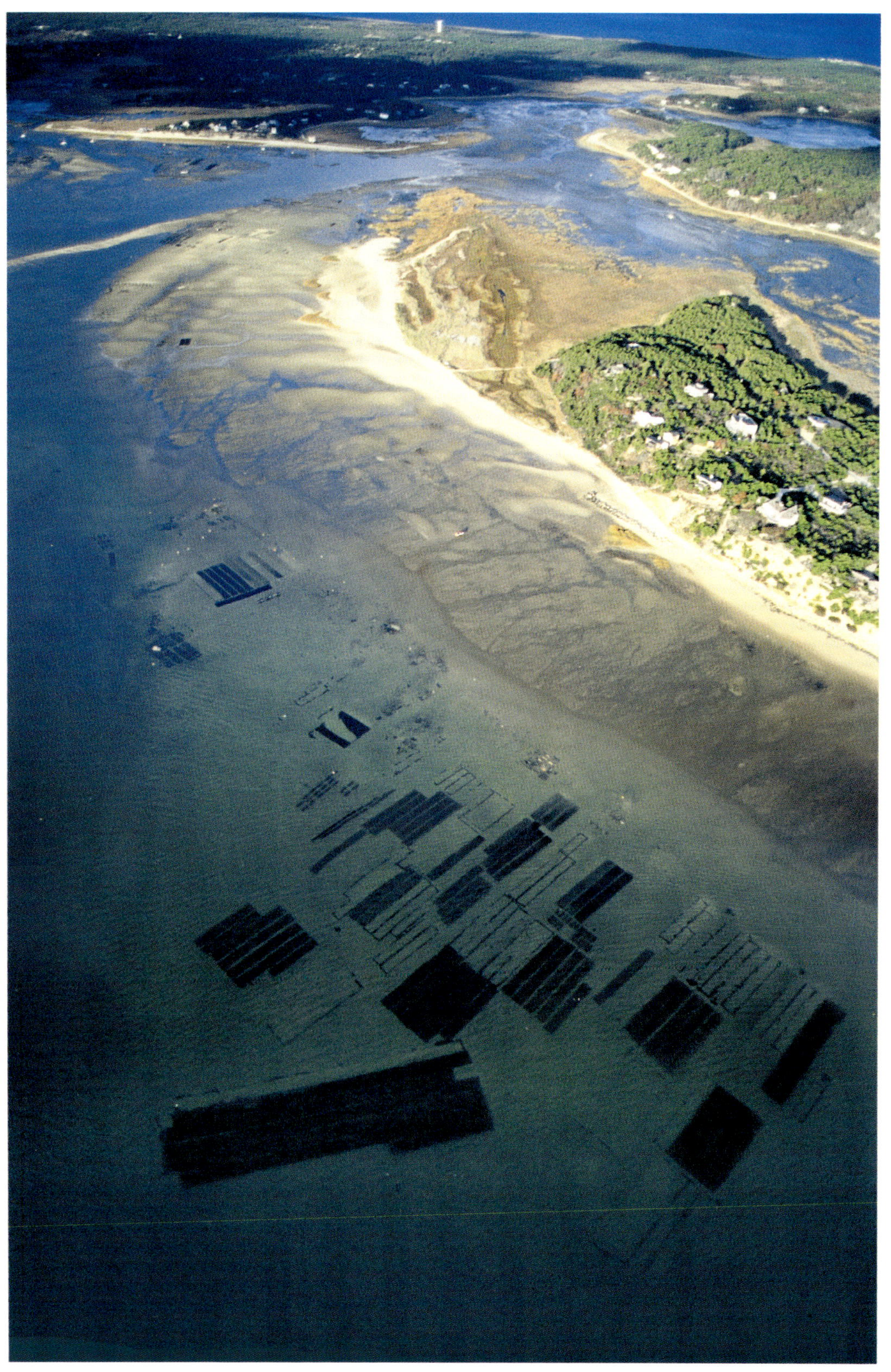

Aerial View Oyster Beds, Wellfleet

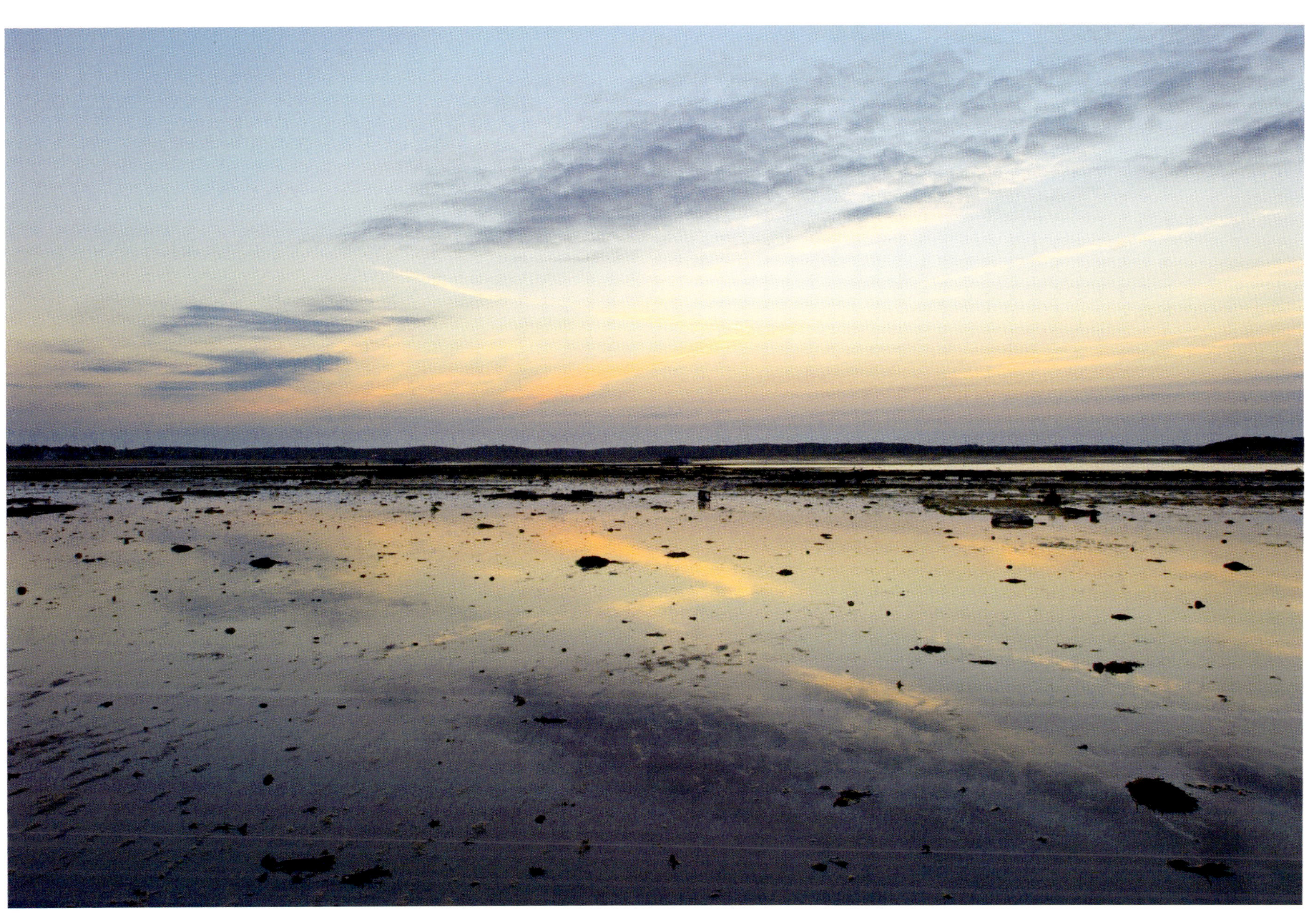

 Clam and Oyster Aquaculture Beds, Wellfleet

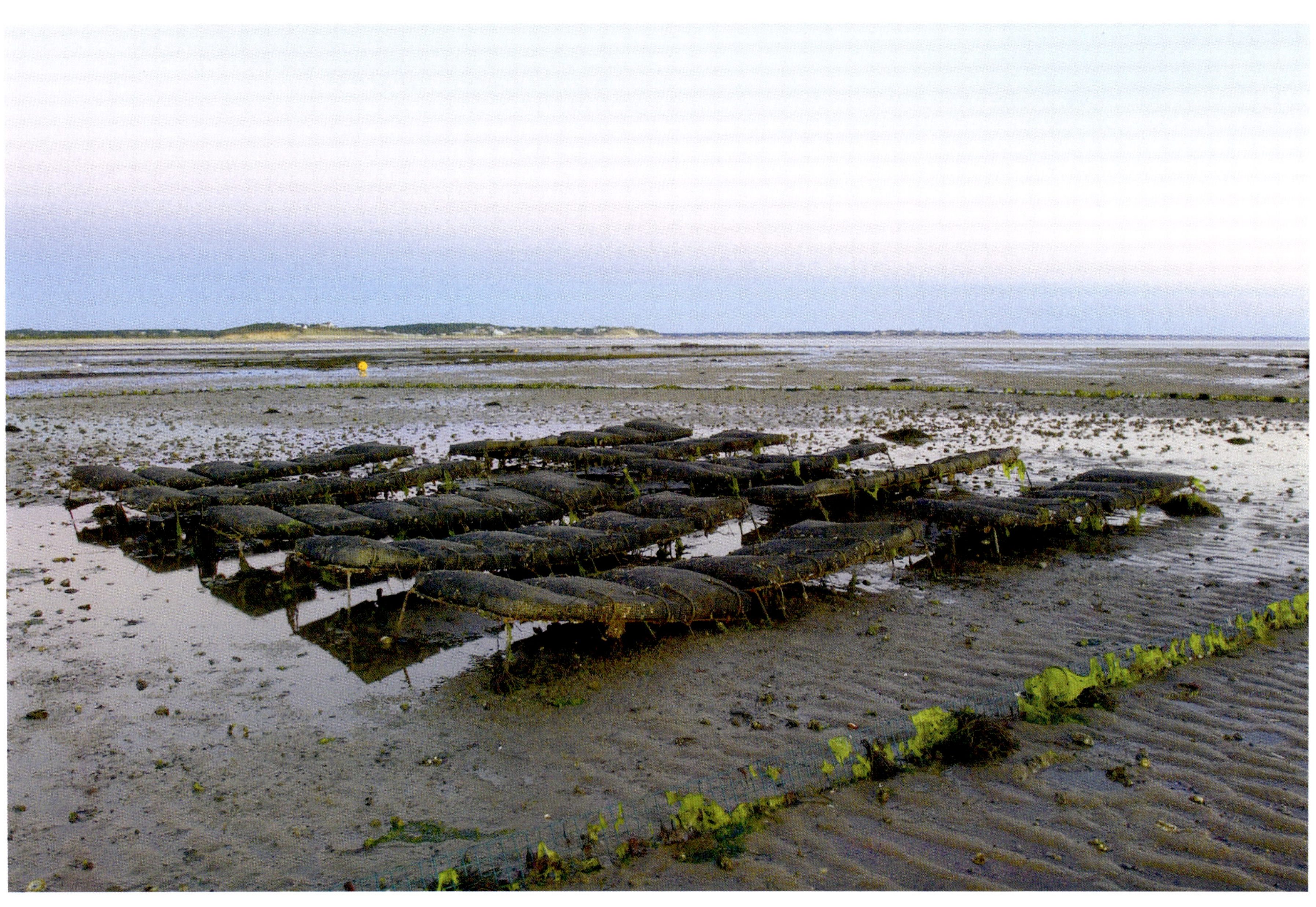

Oyster Beds, Wellfleet

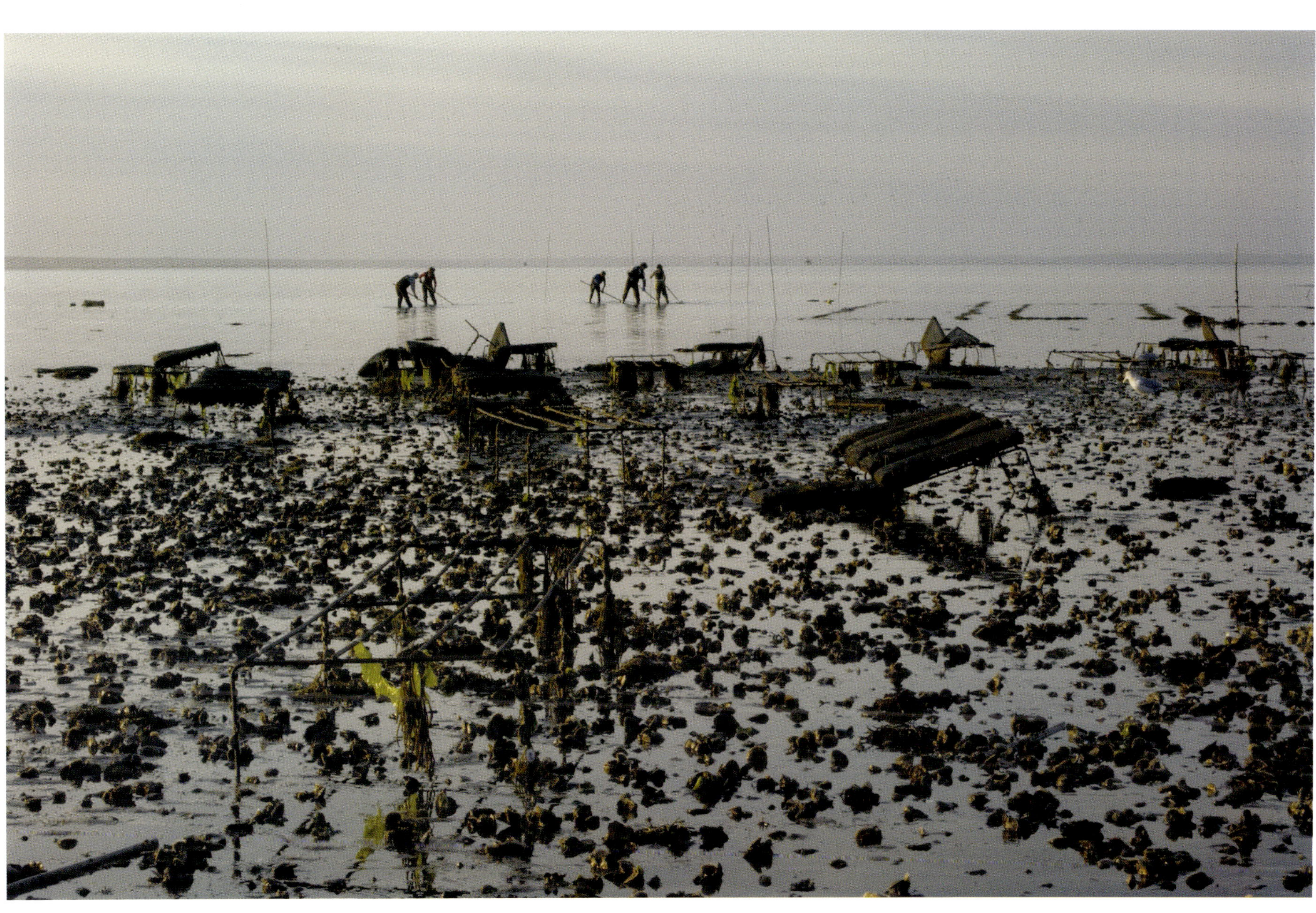

 Clam and Oyster Beds, Wellfleet

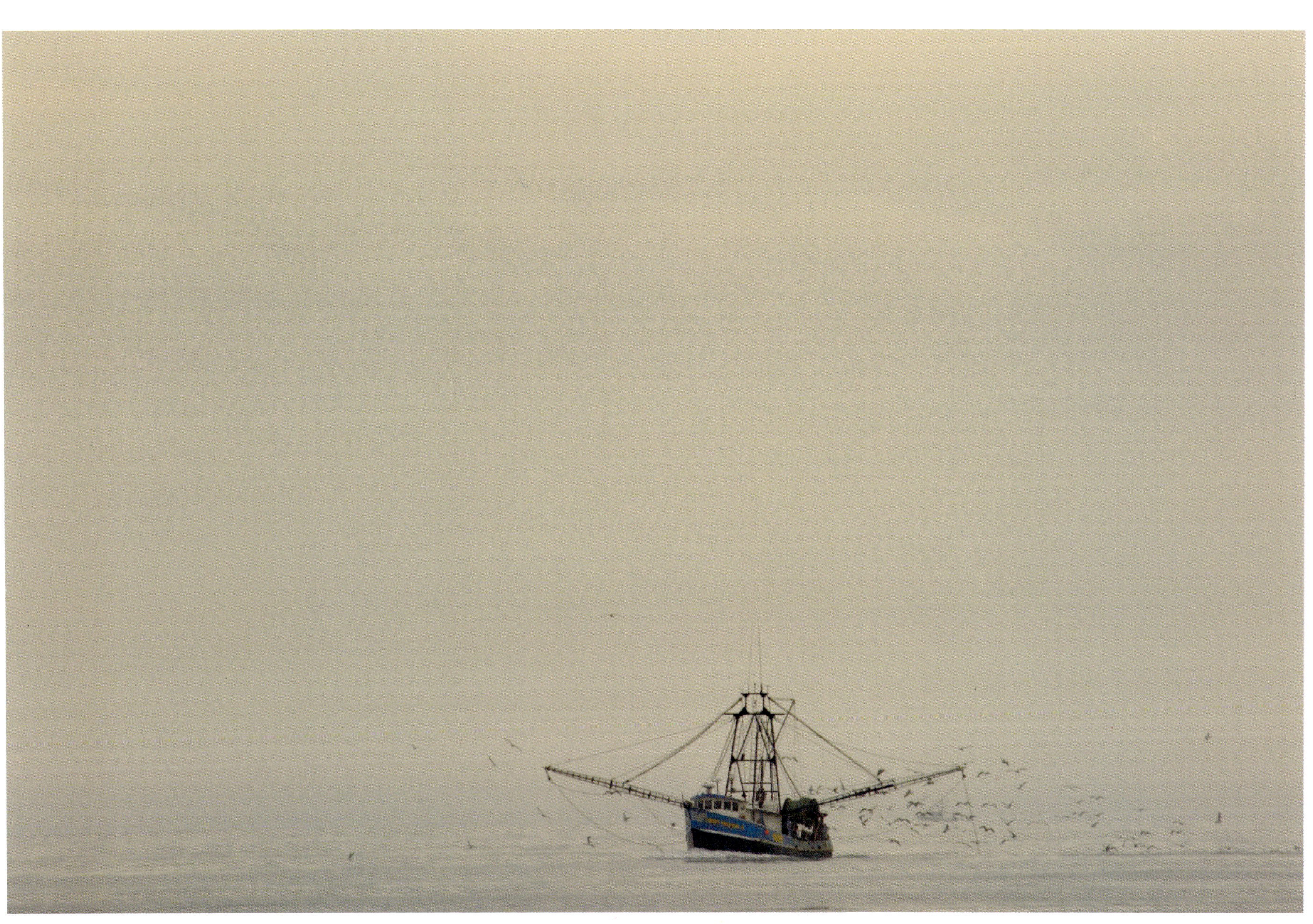

Jersey Princess II, Scalloping off Race Point, Provincetown

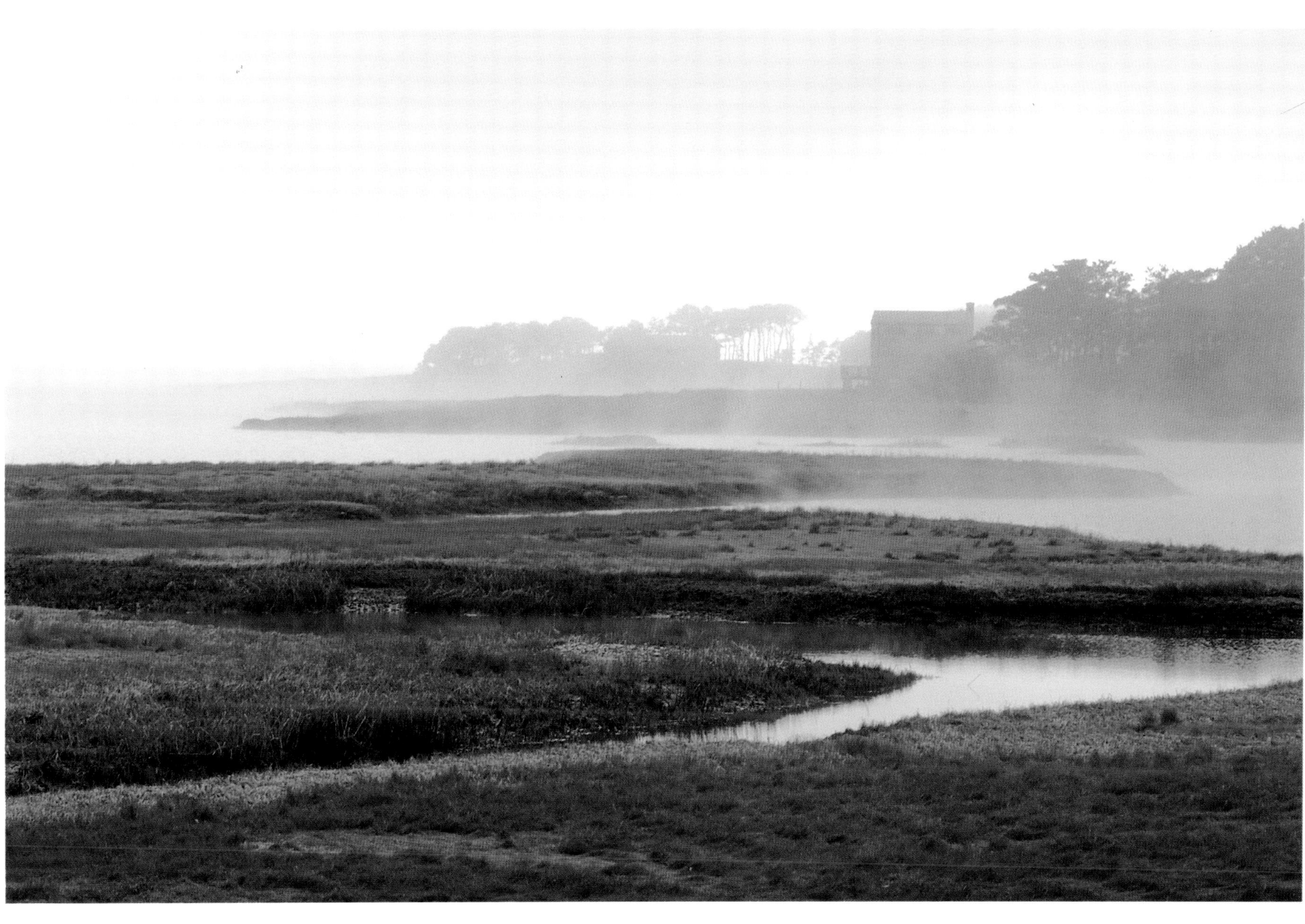

 Black Fish Creek, Wellfleet

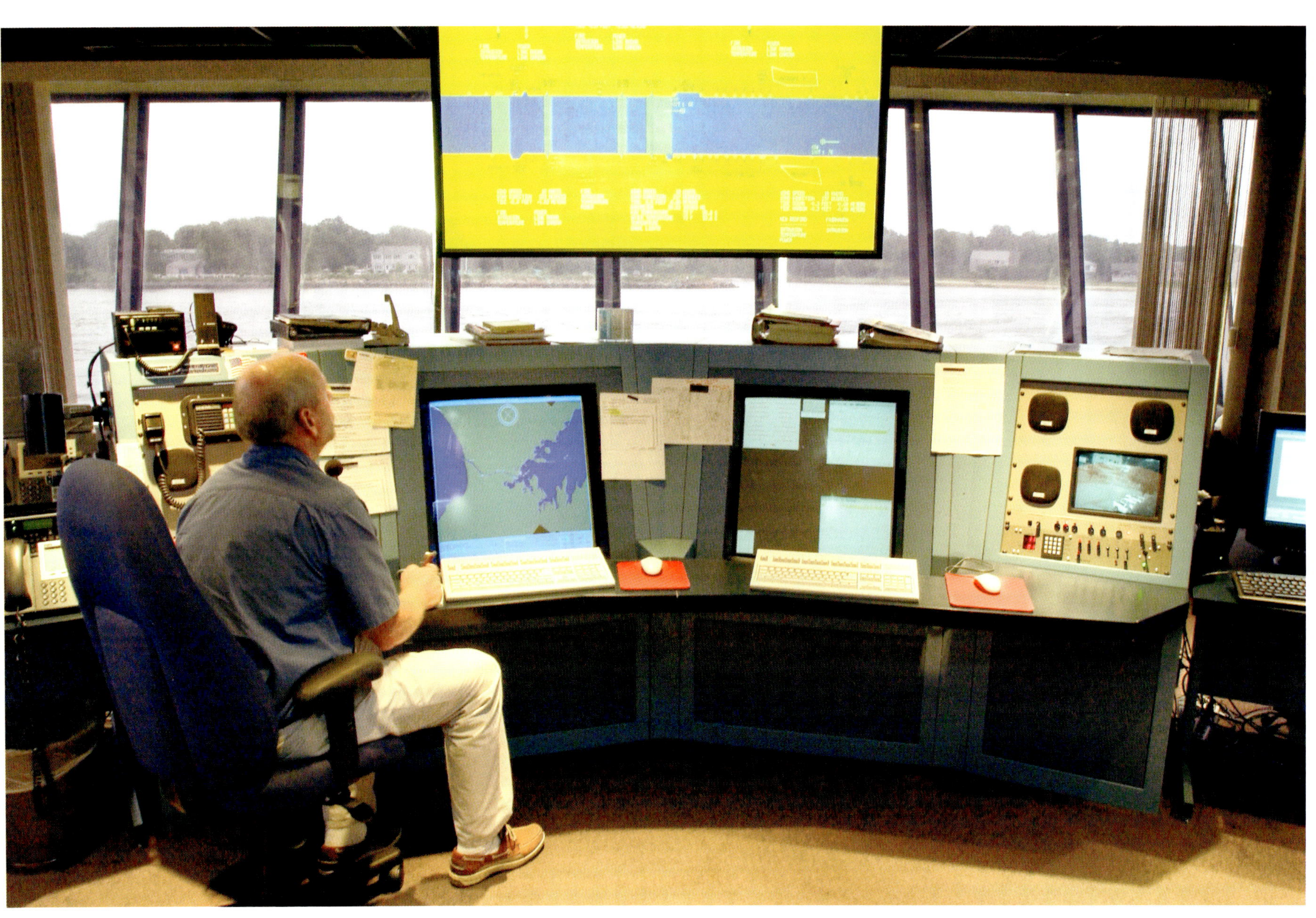

Cape Cod Canal Control Center, Bourne

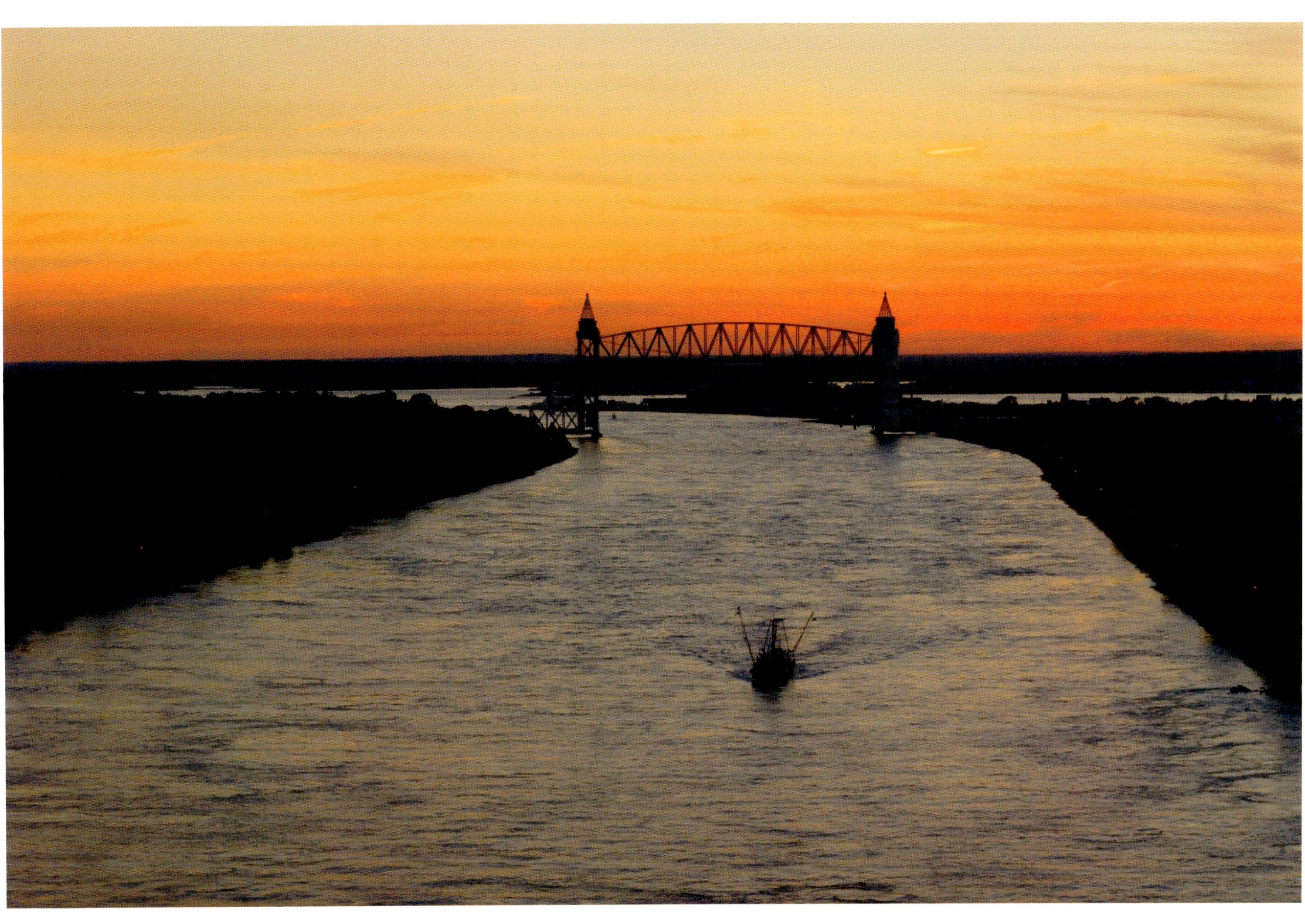

63 Cape Cod Canal, Railroad Bridge, Bourne

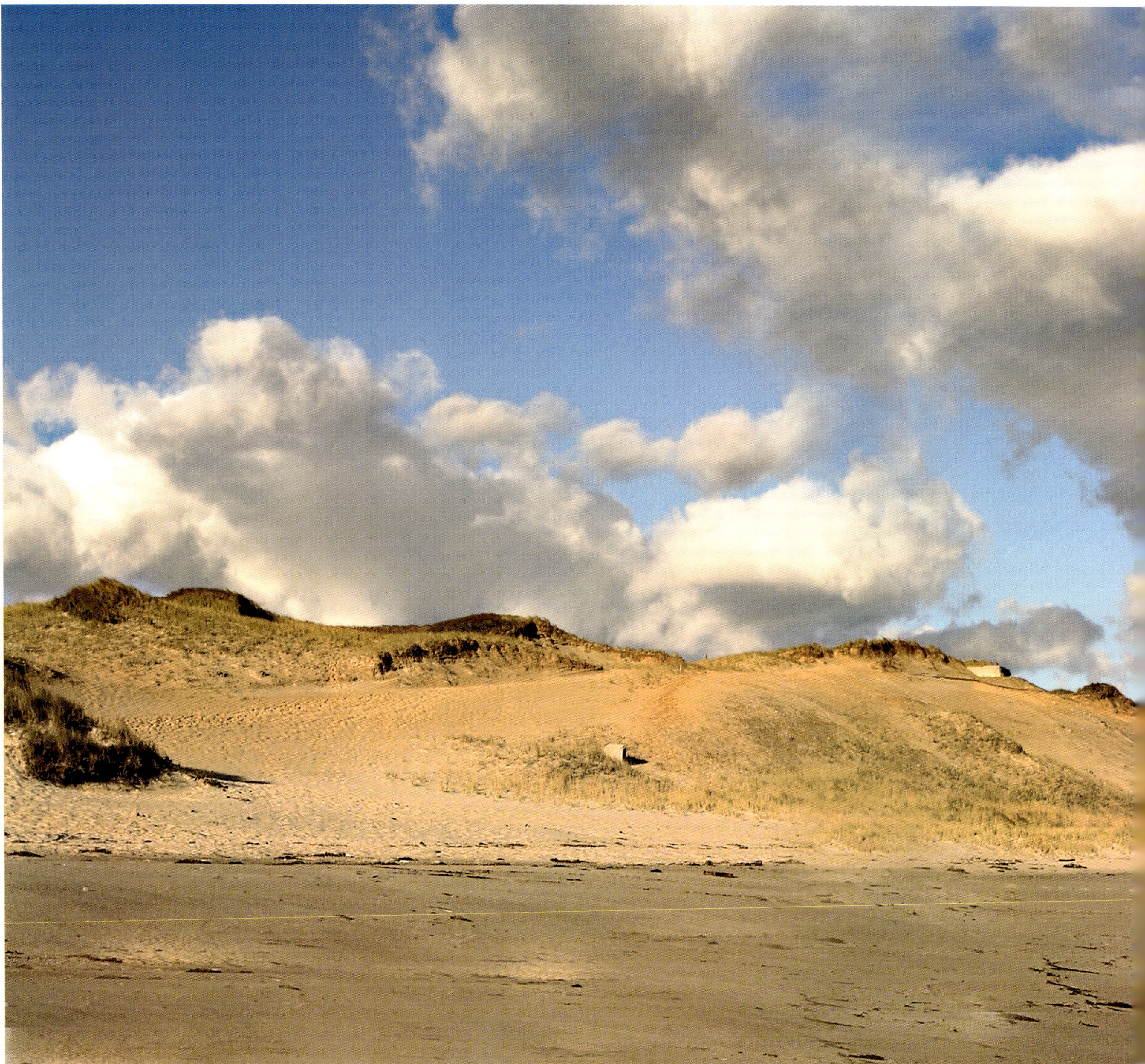

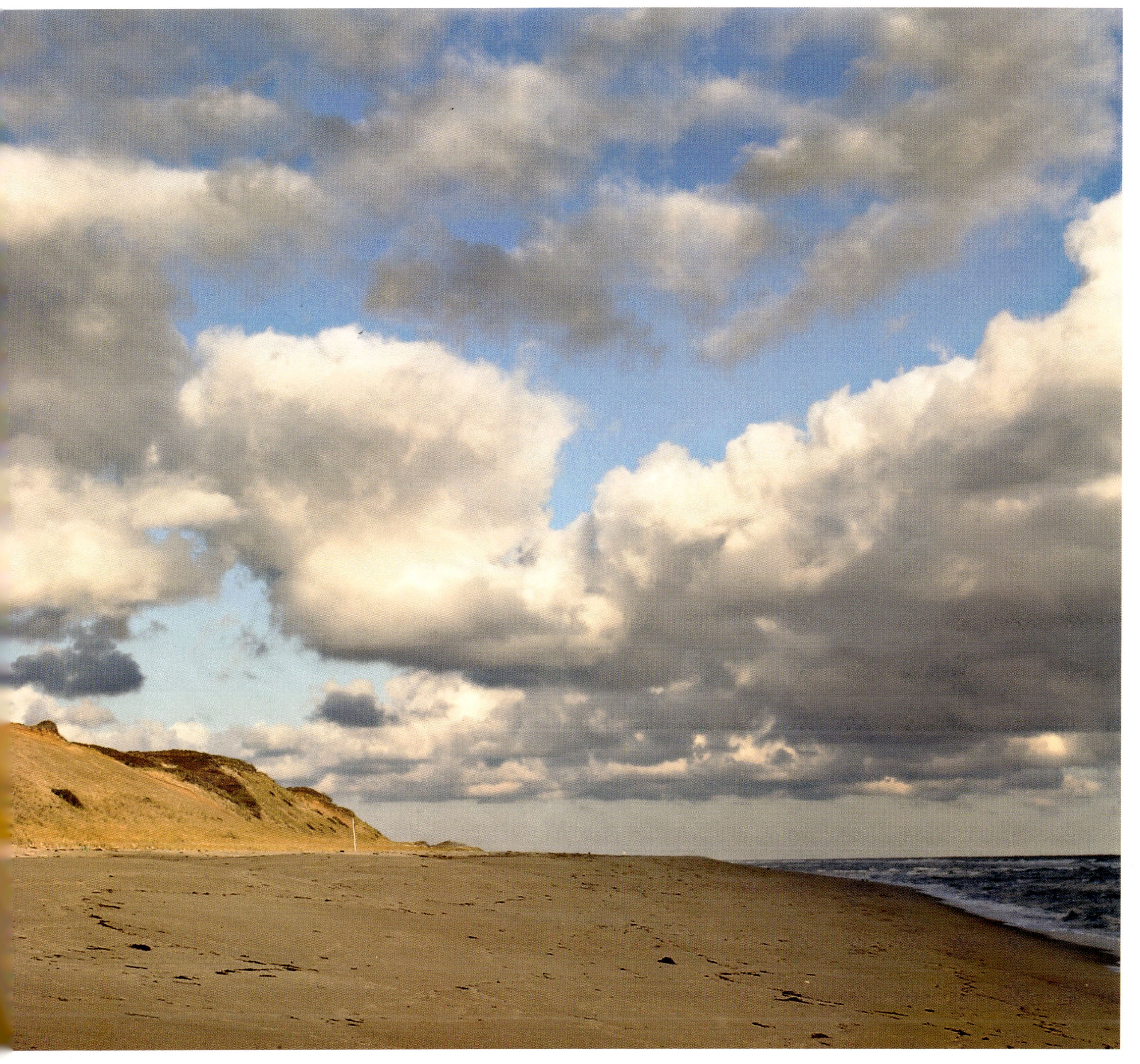

Ballston Beach on a Clear Crisp Autumn Day, Truro

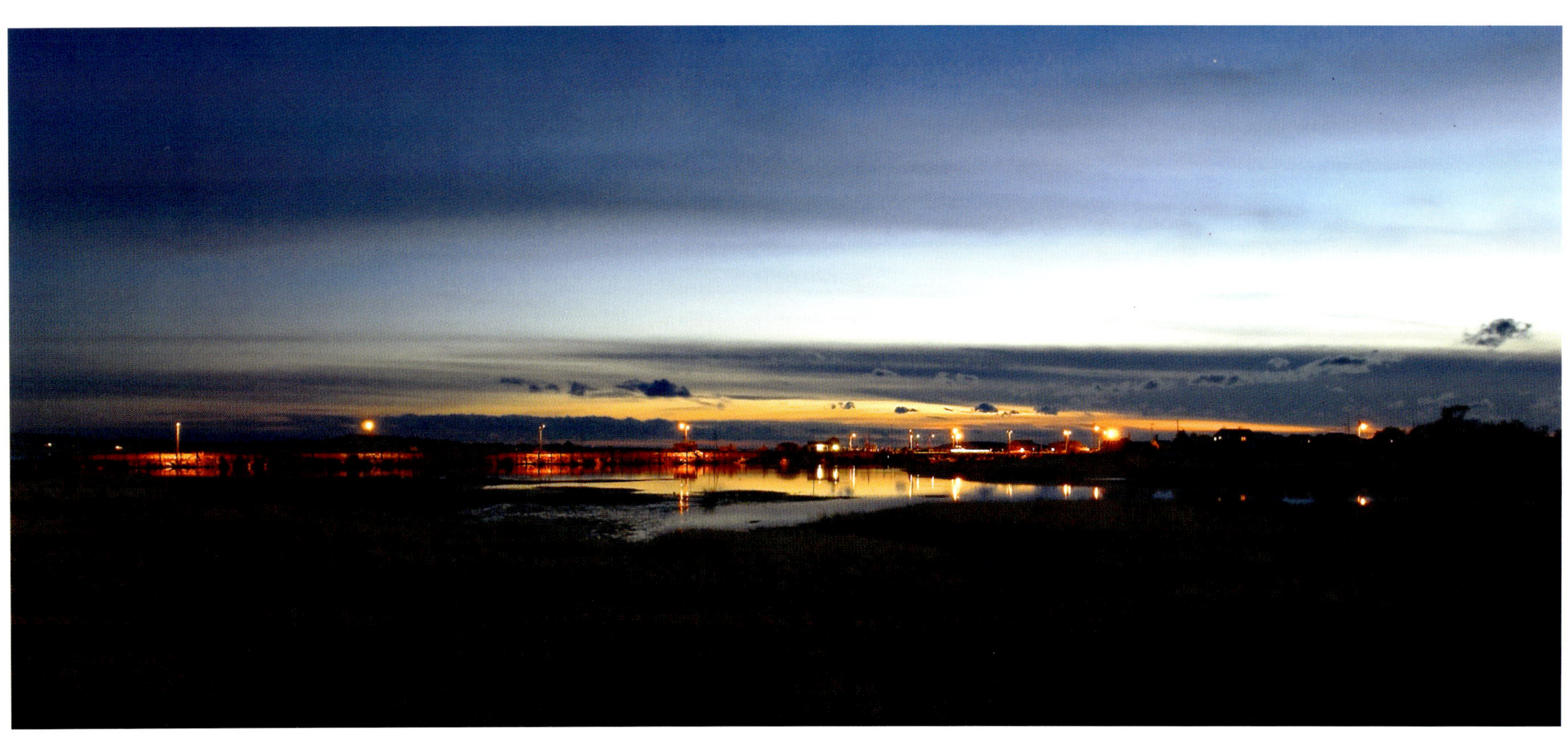

Sunset, Wellfleet Harbor

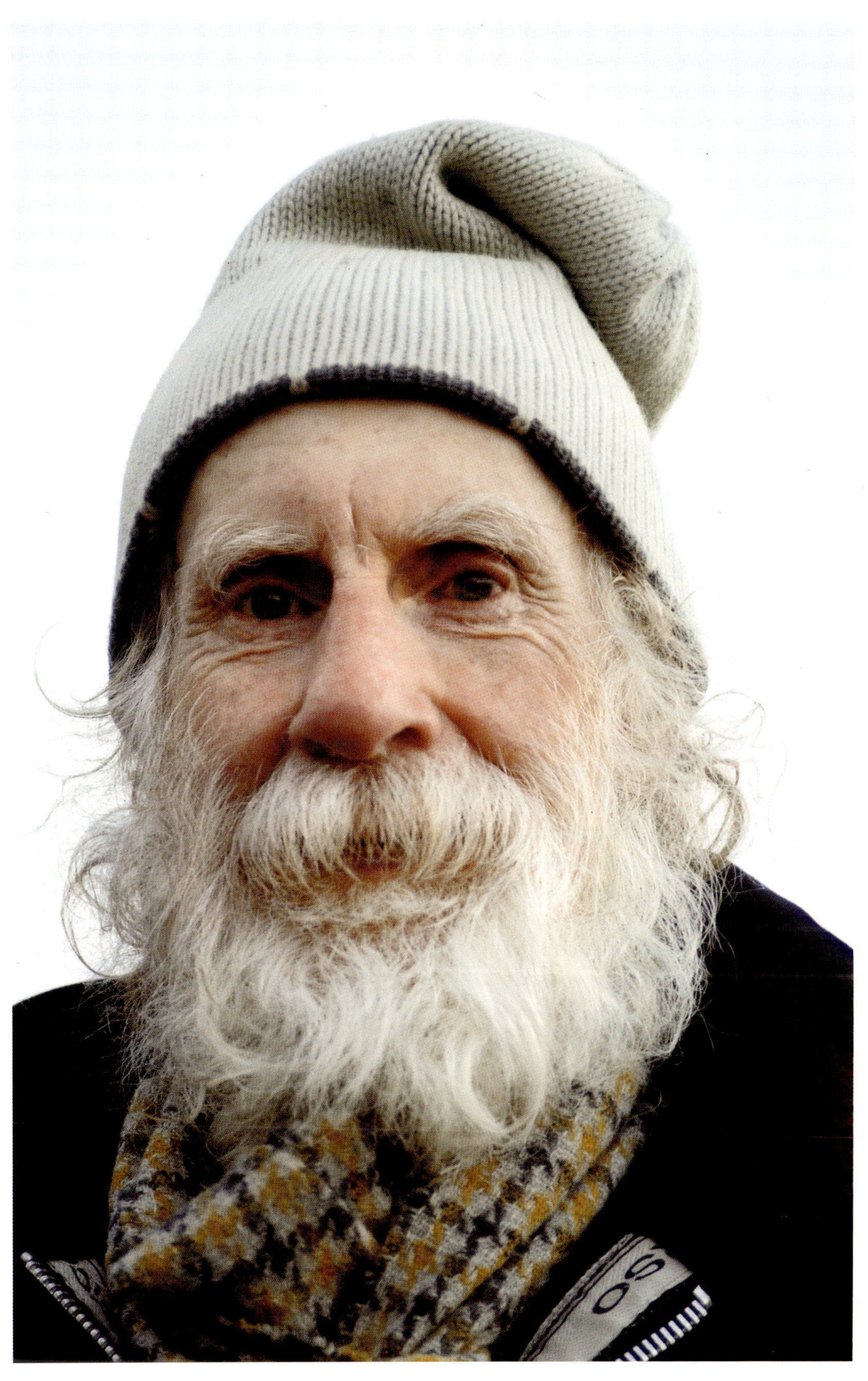

 John Mulcahy Artist, Wellfleet

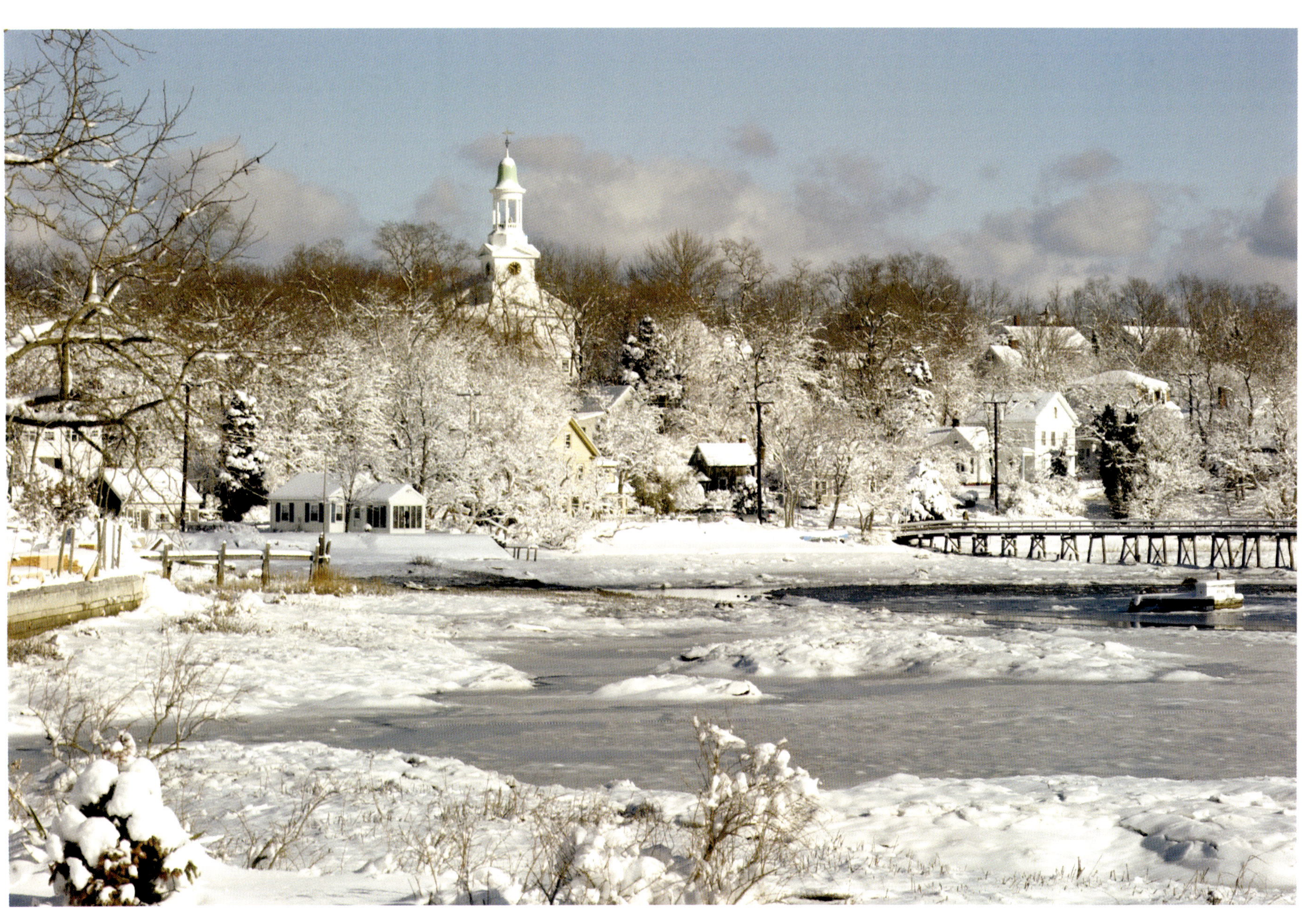

Duck Creek and Uncle Tim's Bridge, Wellfleet

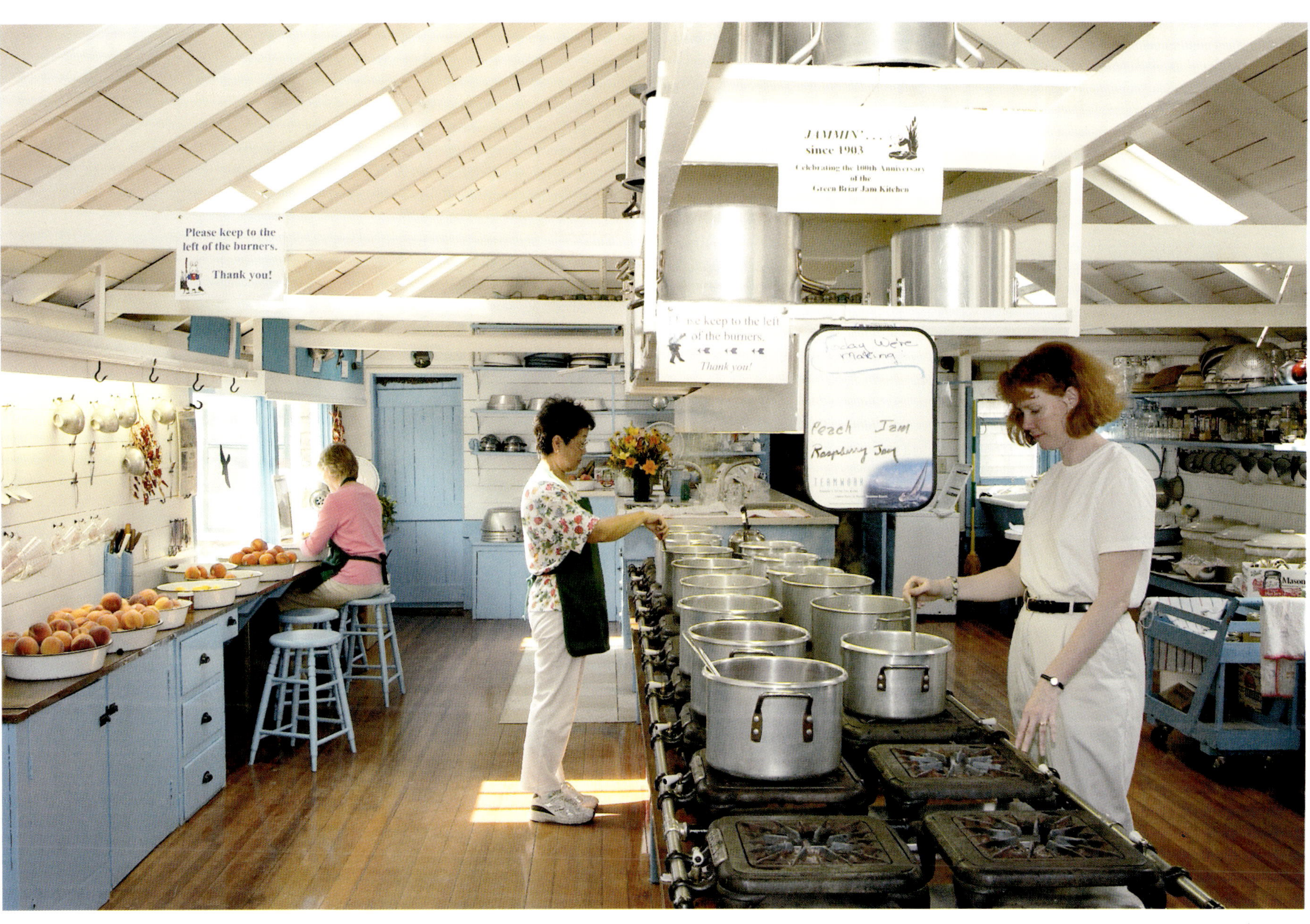

 Green Briar Jam Kitchen, Sandwich

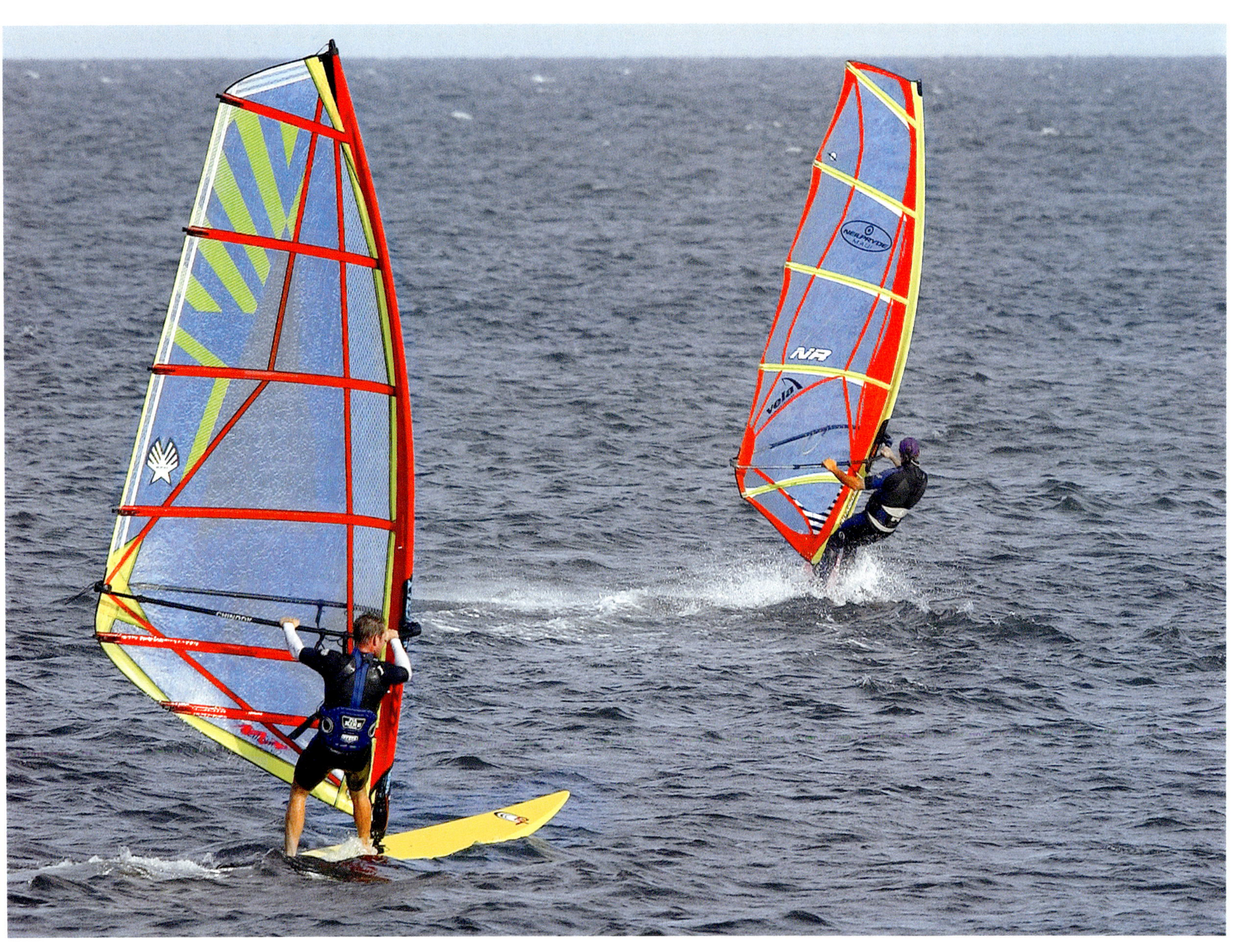

Windsurfing, West Dennis

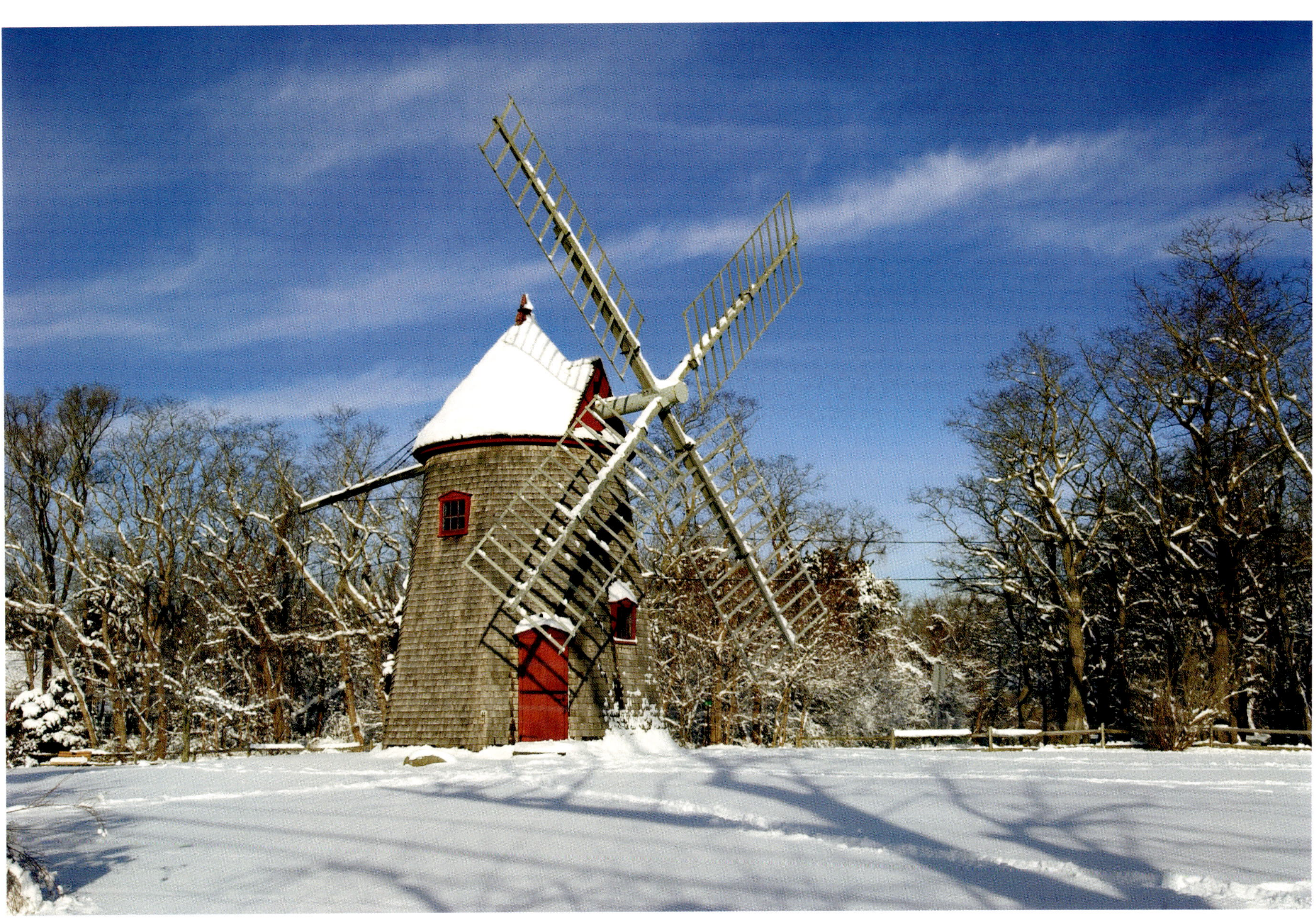

 Windmill Park, Eastham

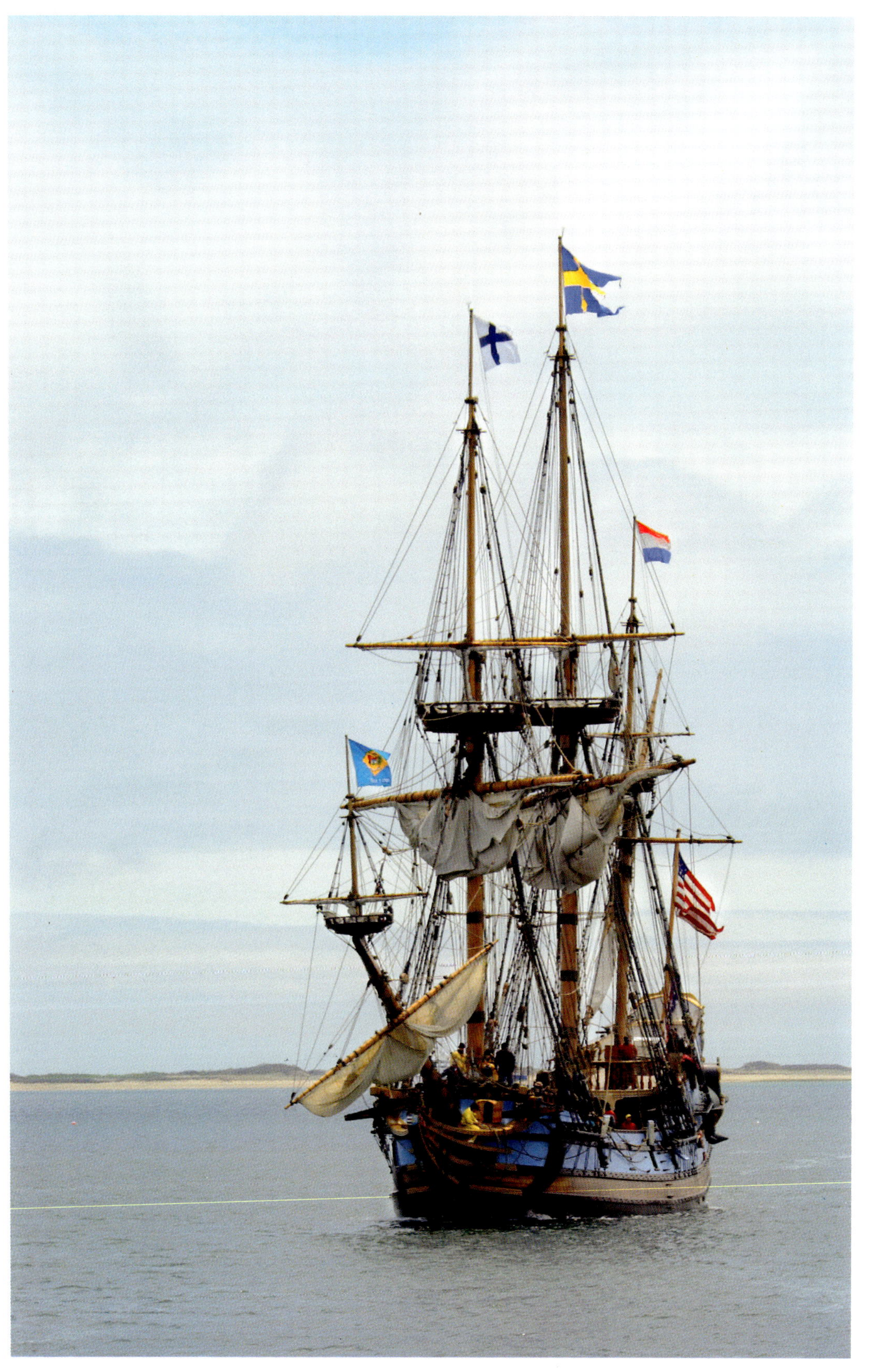

Tall Ship Kalmar Nyckel at Sail, Provincetown

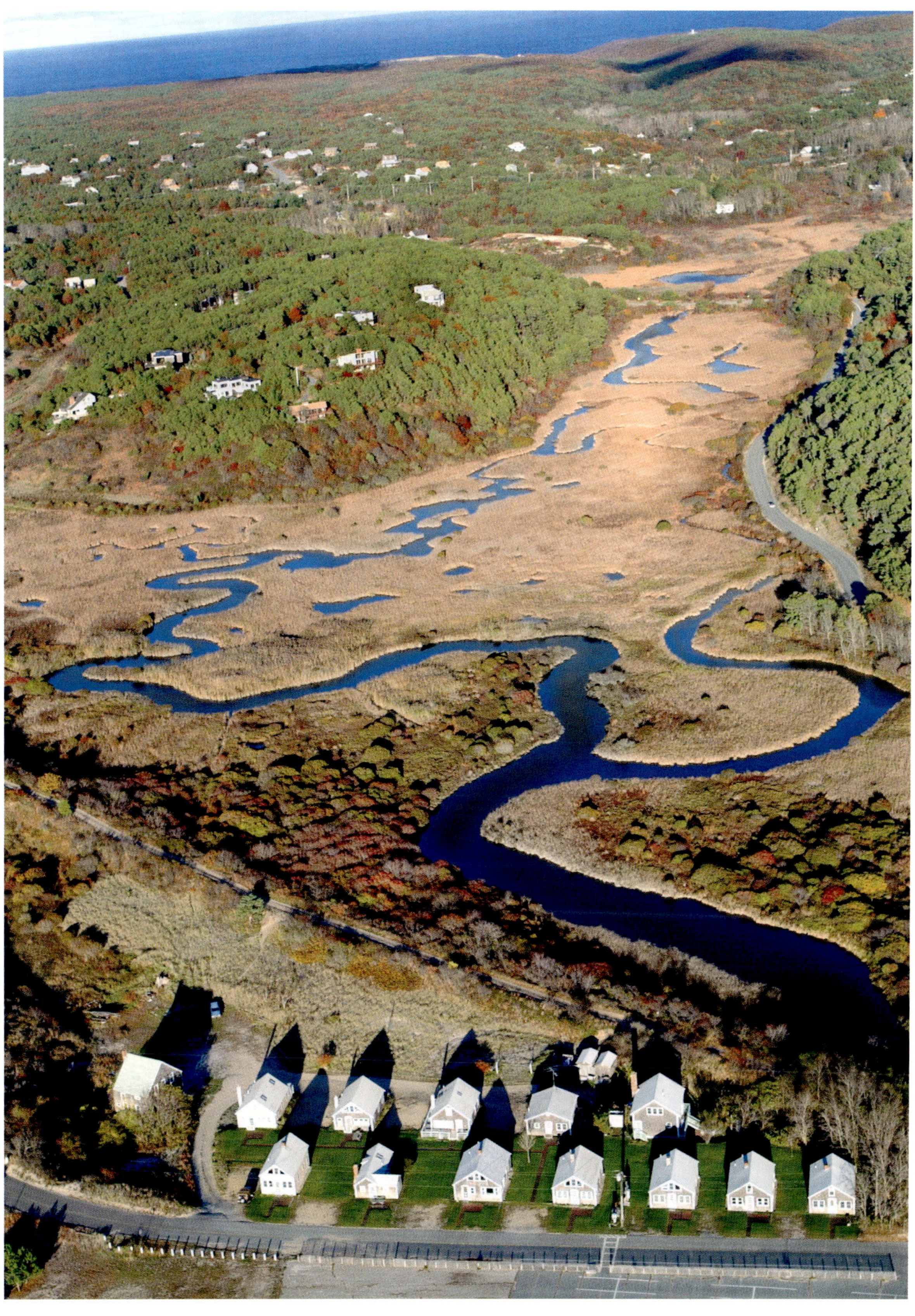

 Little Pamet River, Truro

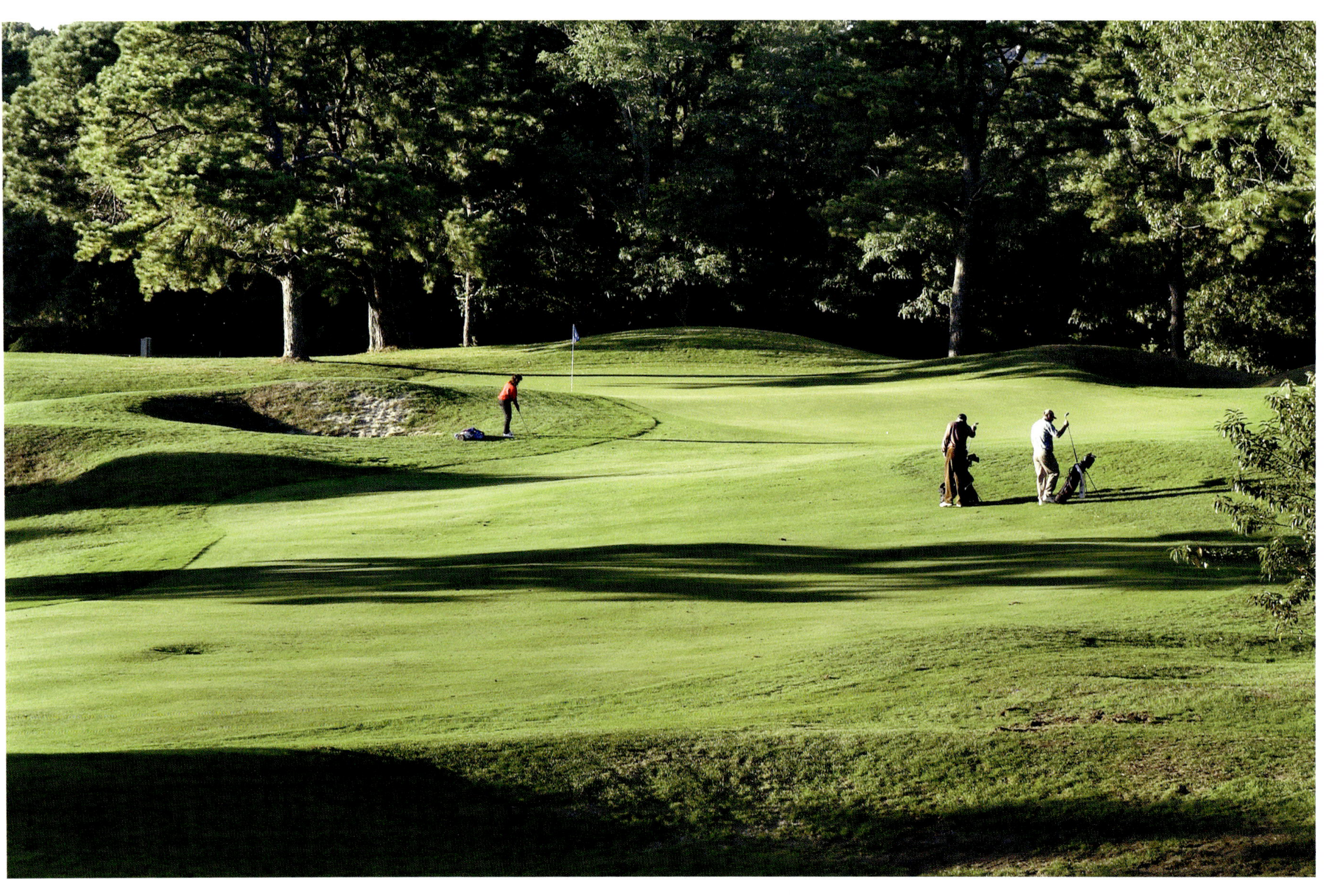

Ocean Edge Golf Club, Brewster

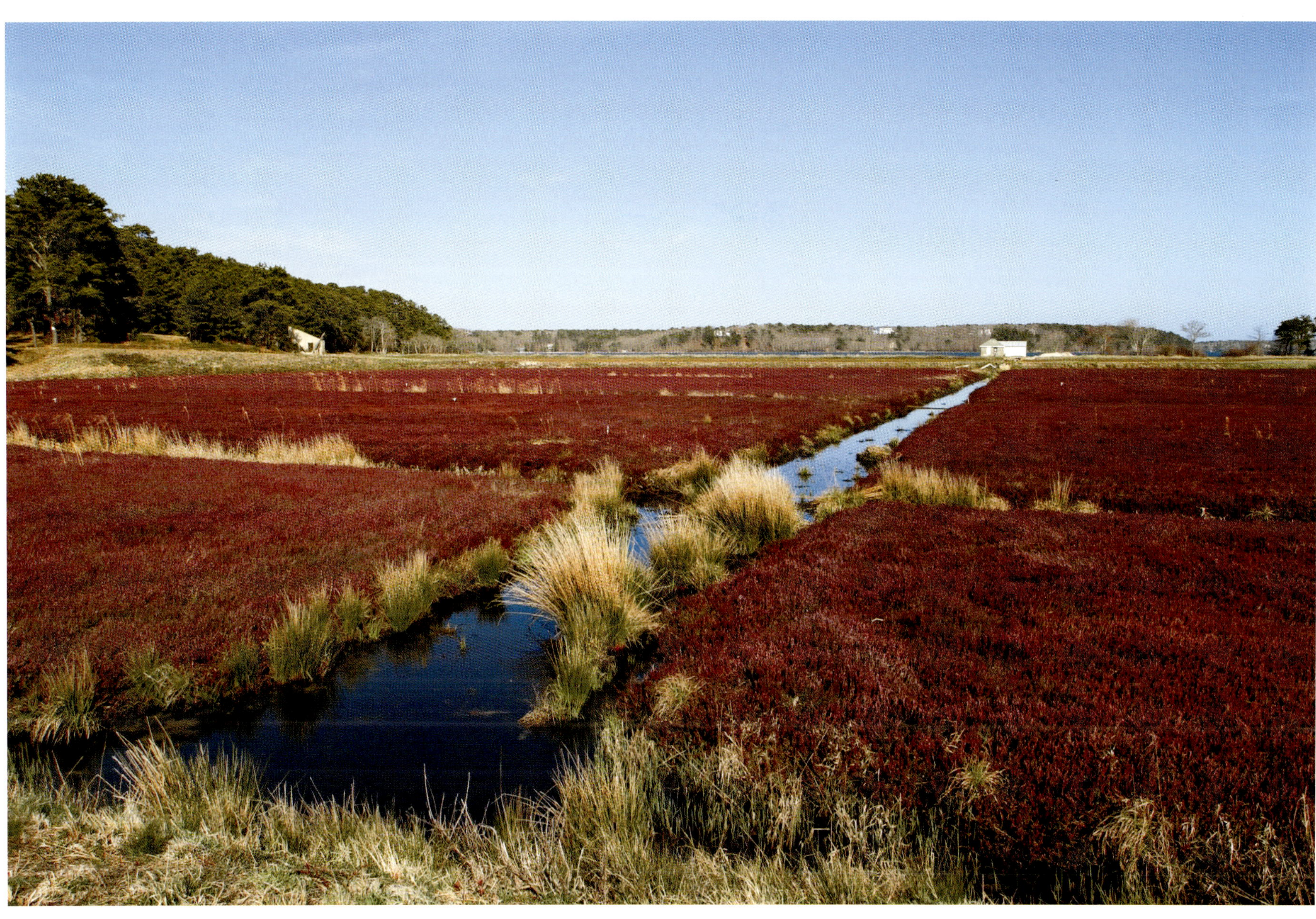

 Cranberry Bog, Brewster

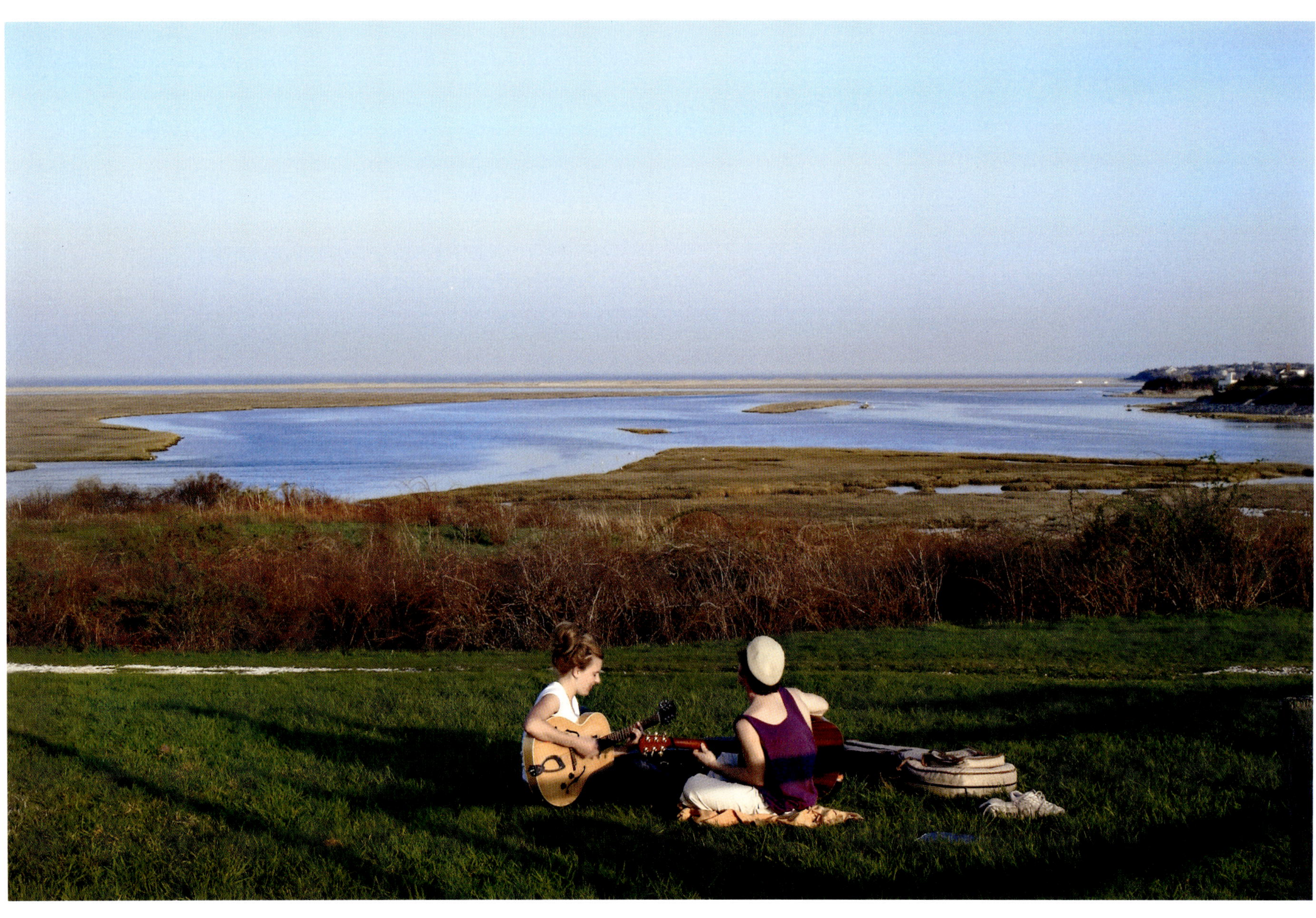

Fort Hill, Eastham

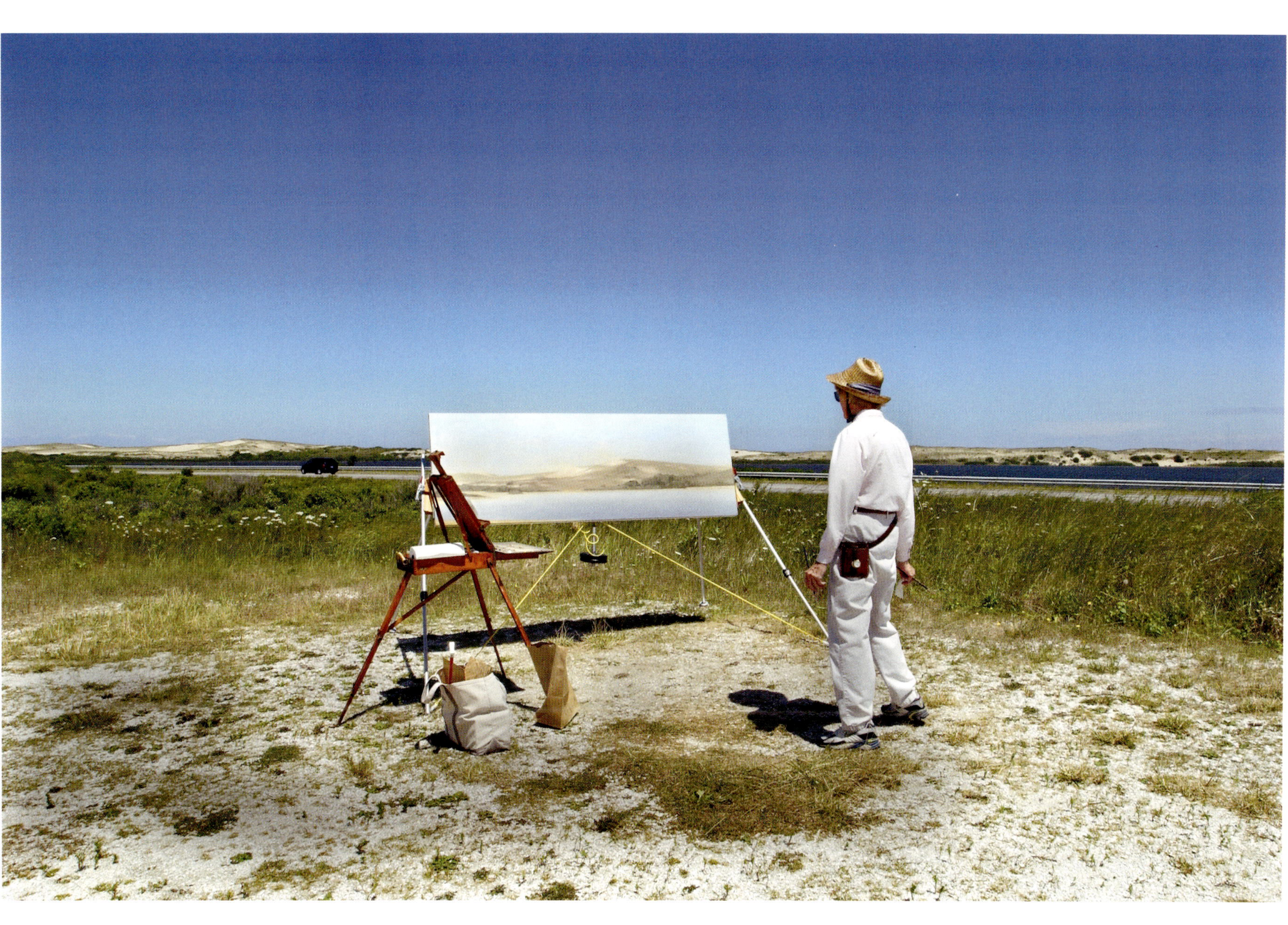

77 **Artist Anne MacAdam at Her Easel, North Truro**

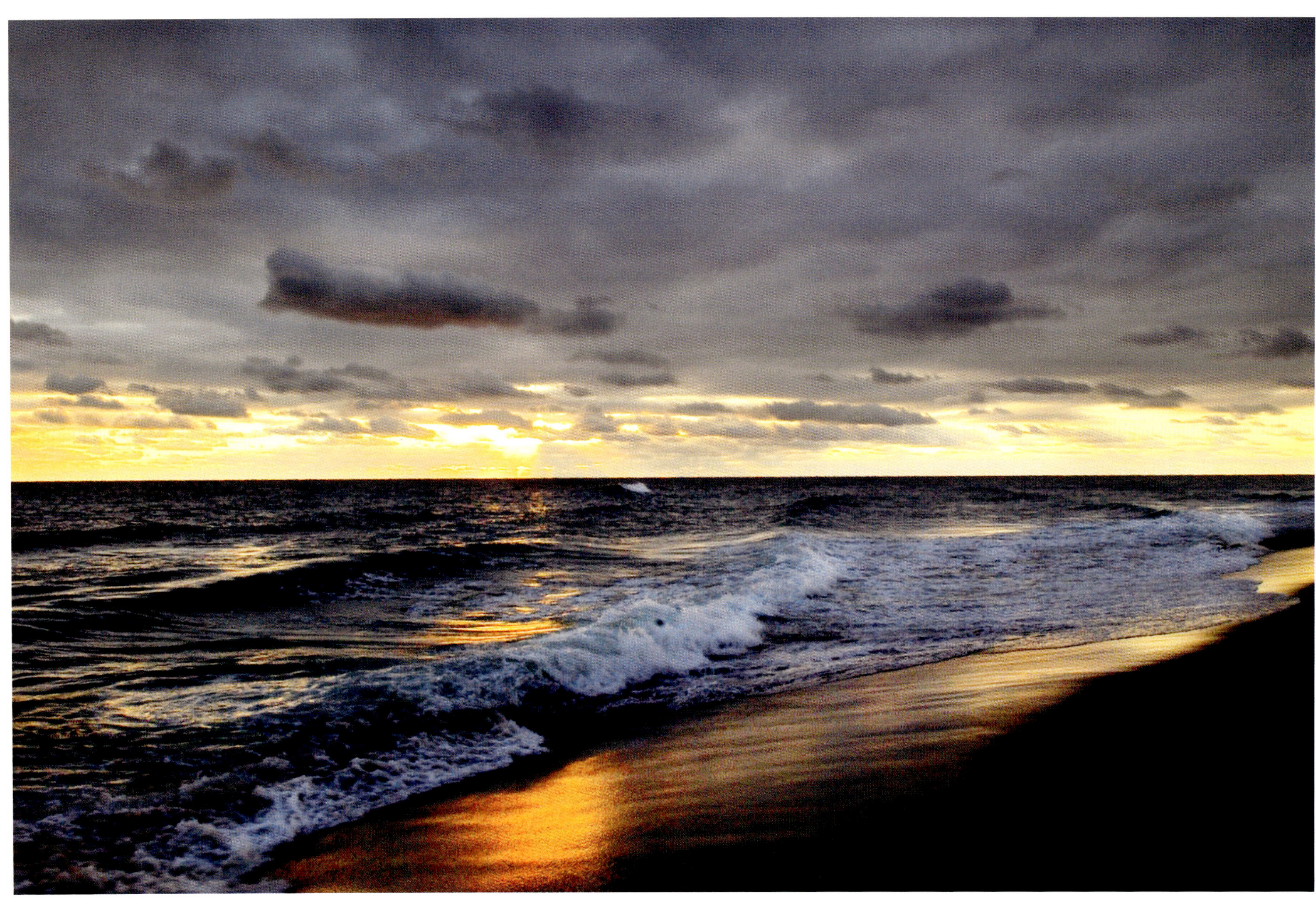

Sunrise Nauset Beach, Eastham

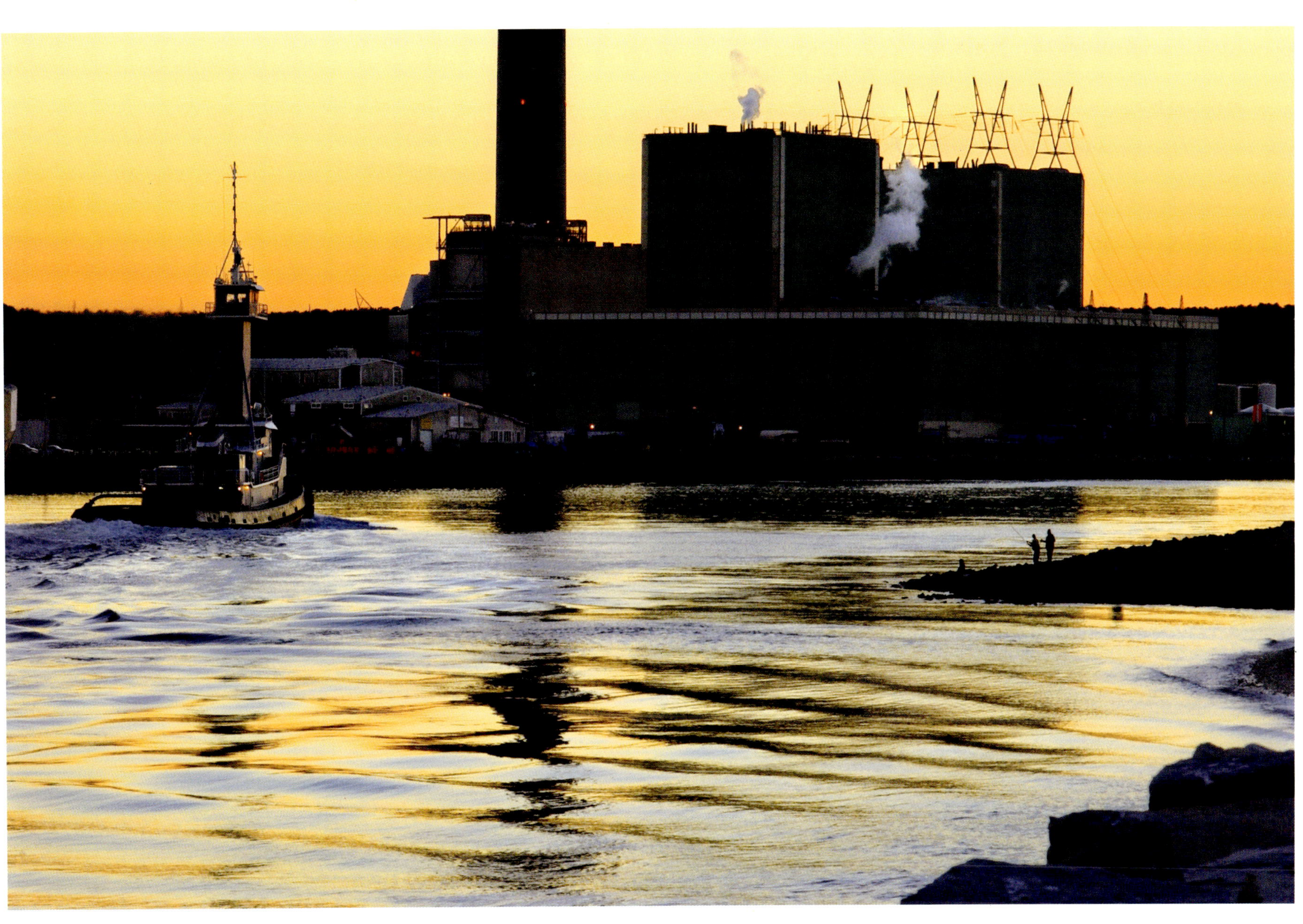

79 Cape Cod Canal from Scusset Harbor, Sagamore

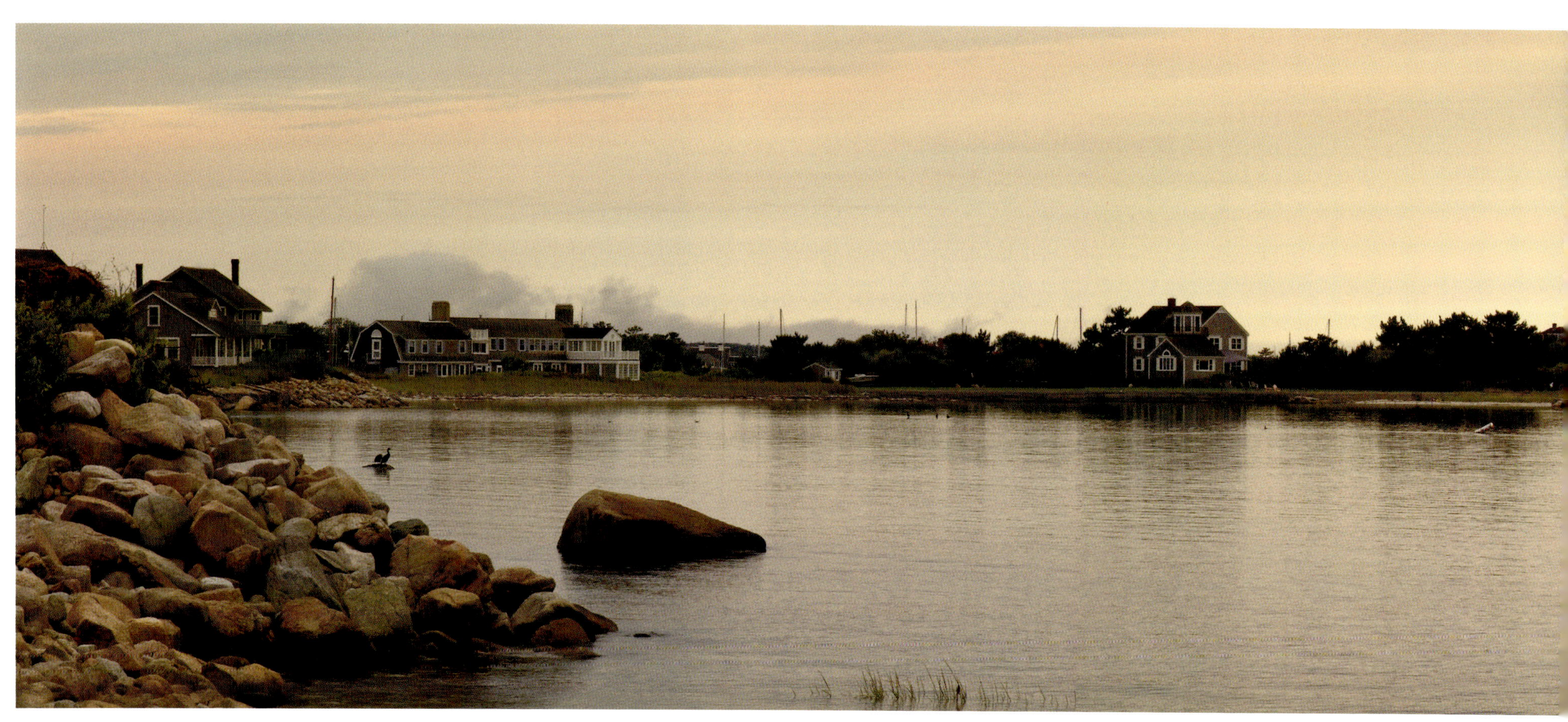

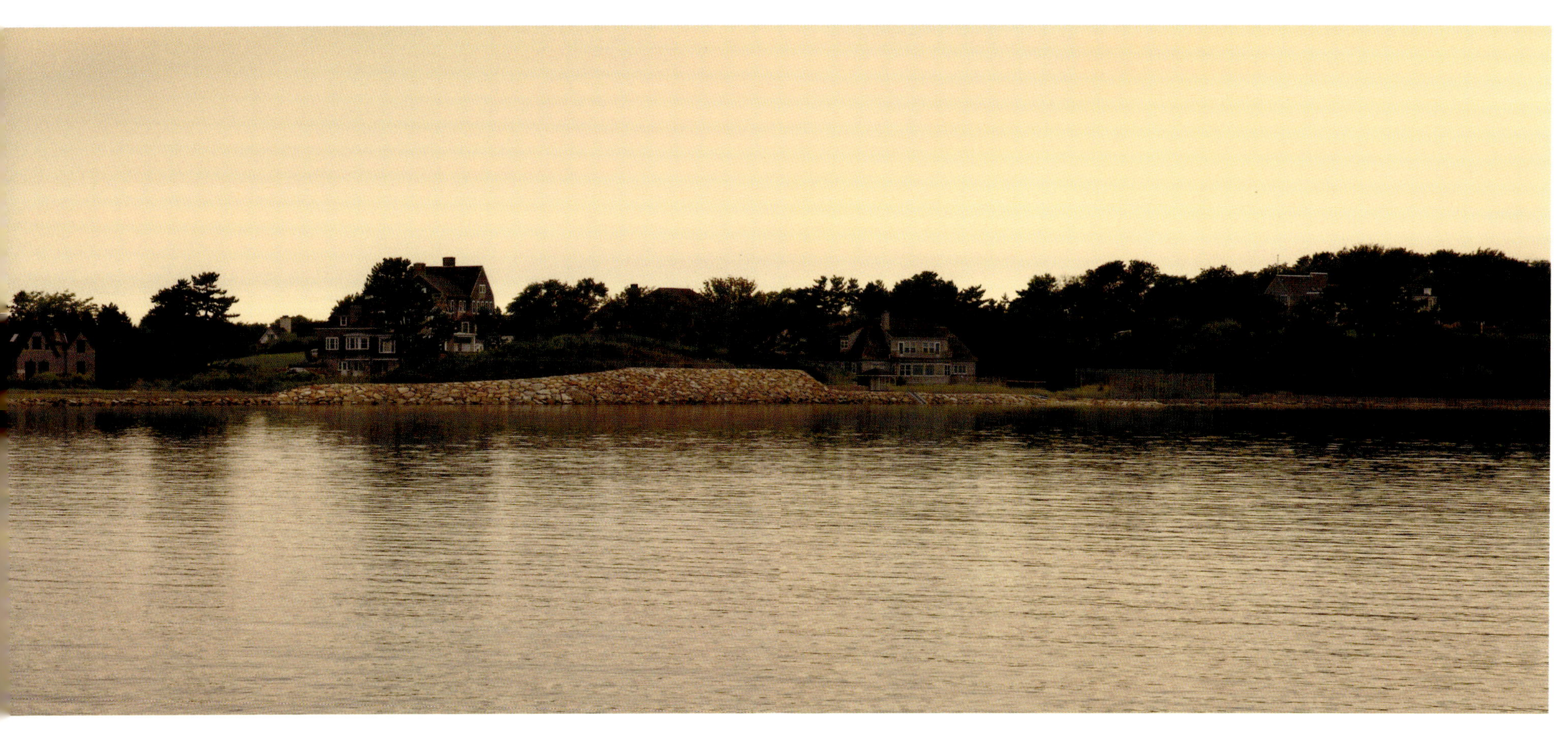

Great Harbor from Penzance Point, Woods Hole

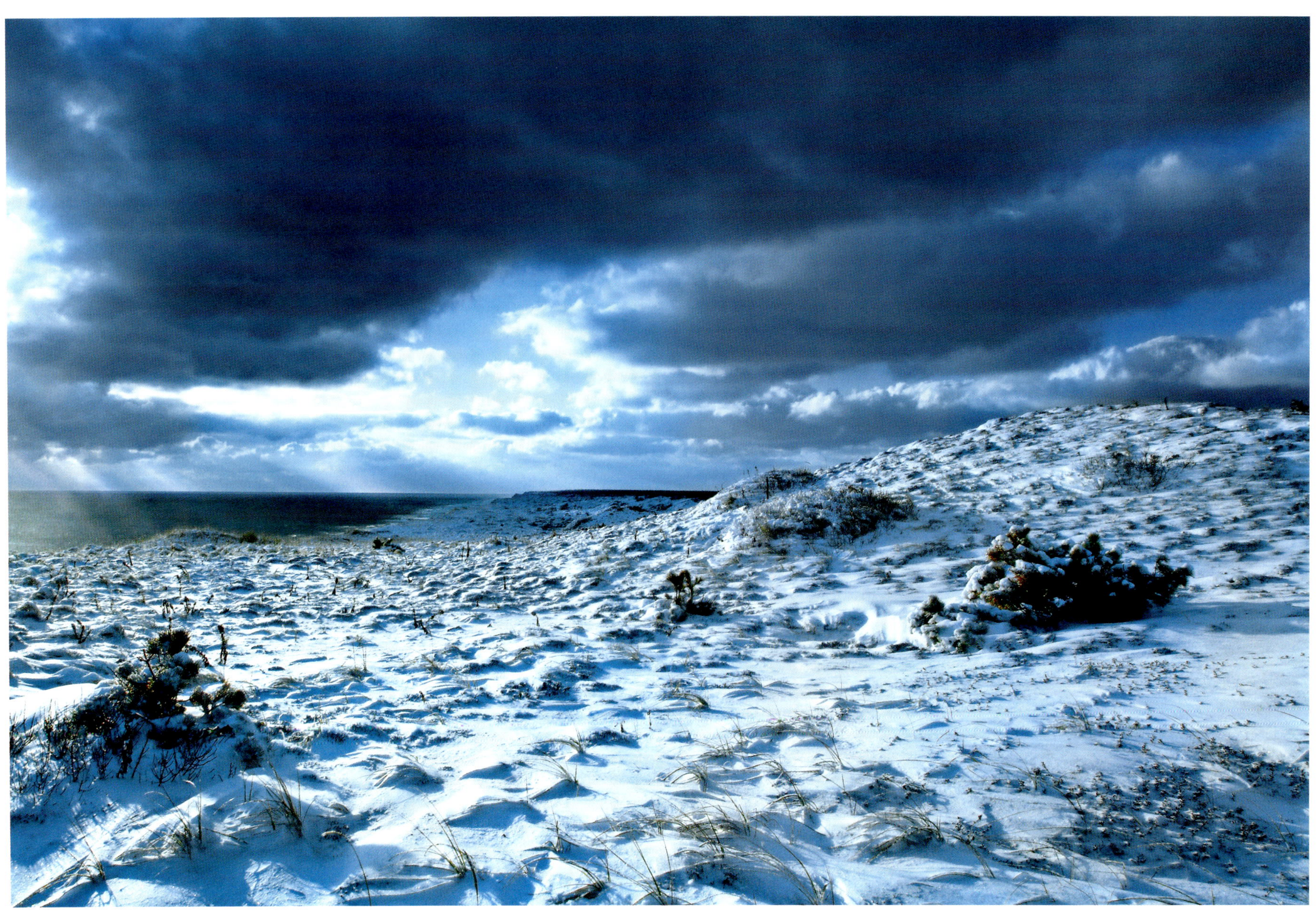

Below Zero, A Frozen Morning at Marconi Station, Wellfleet

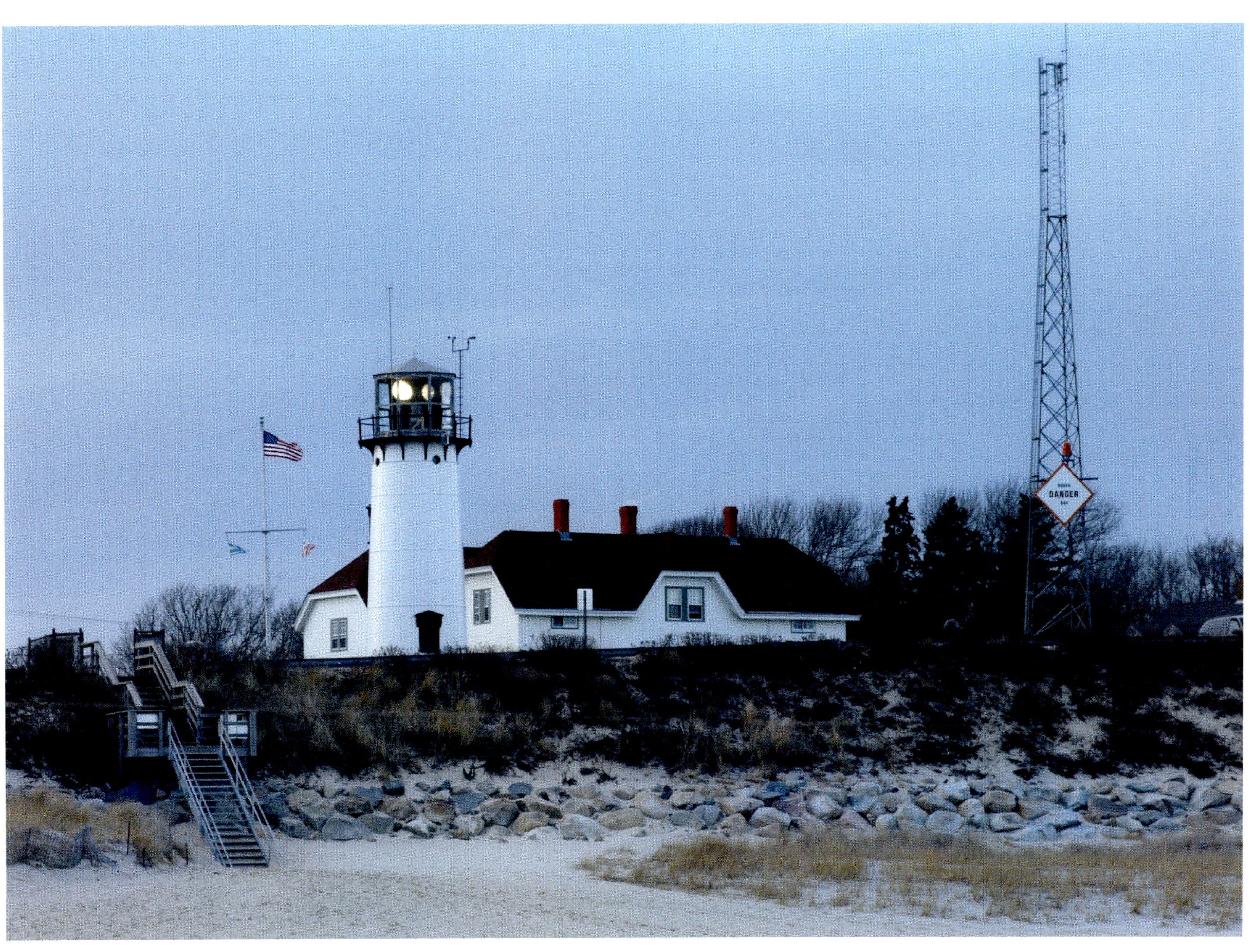

 Chatham Light, Chatham

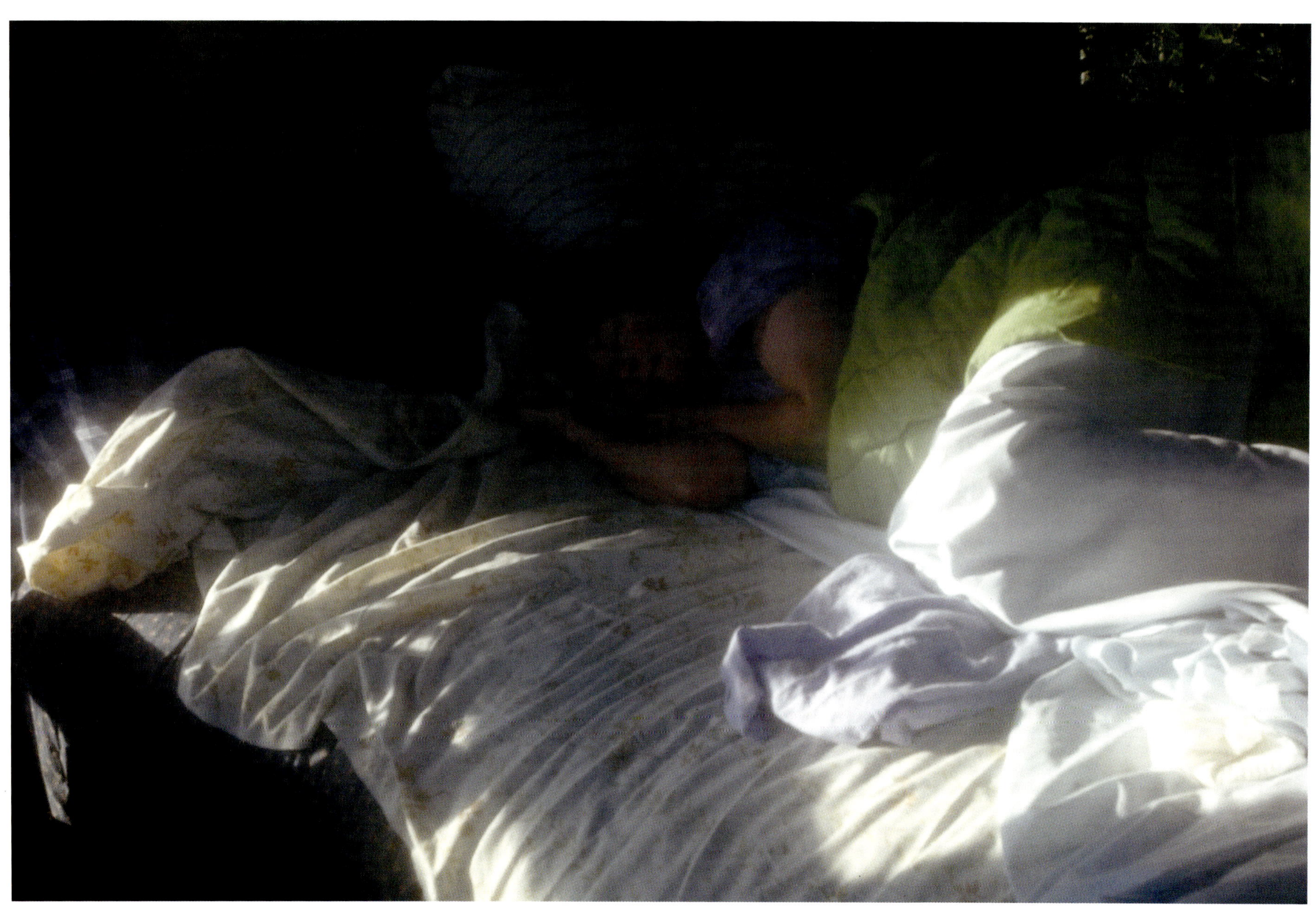

Gail Dreaming on the Dunes, Harry Kemp Dune Shack, Provincetown

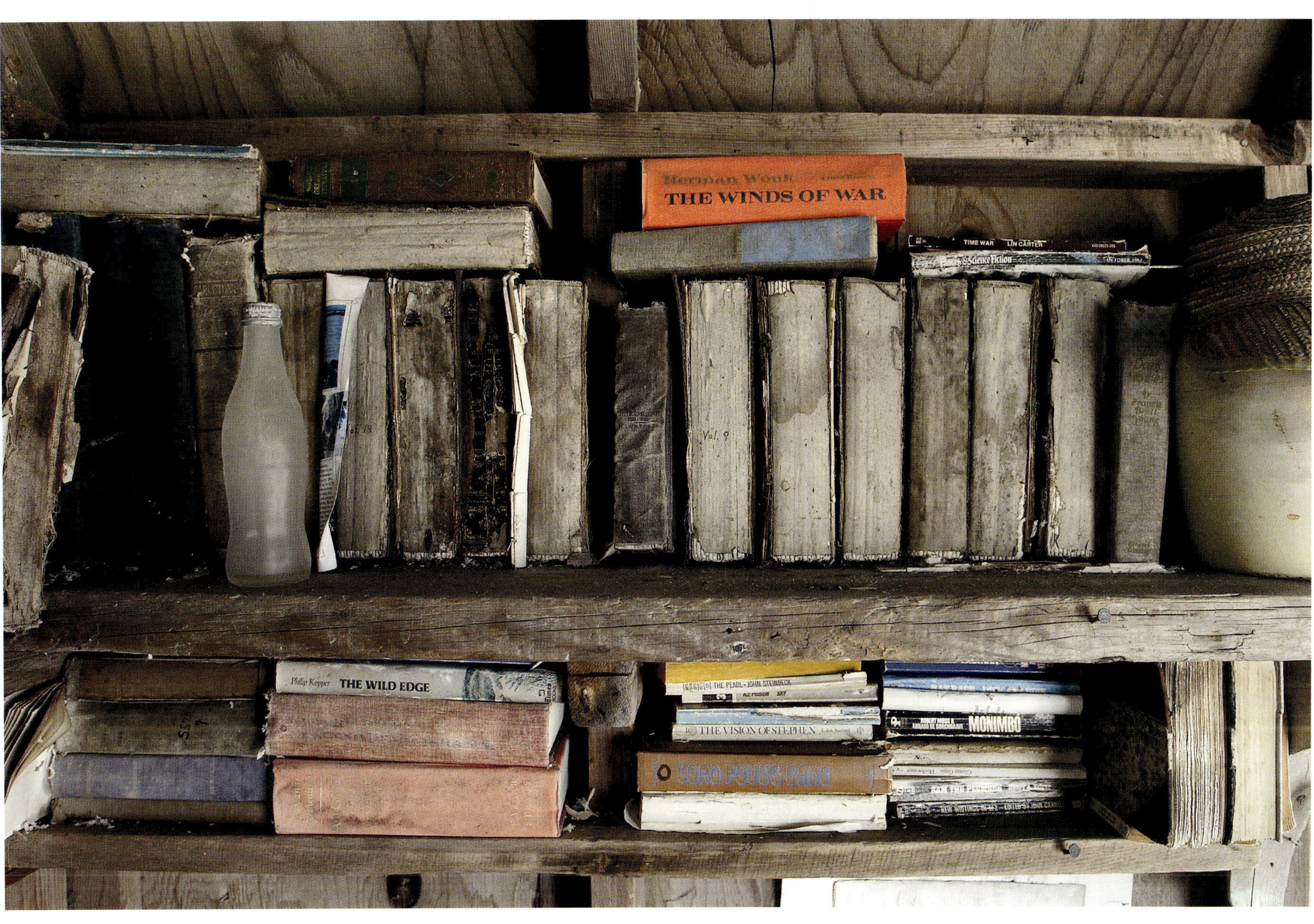

 Book Shelves, Harry Kemps' "Poet of the Dunes" Dune Shack, Provincetown

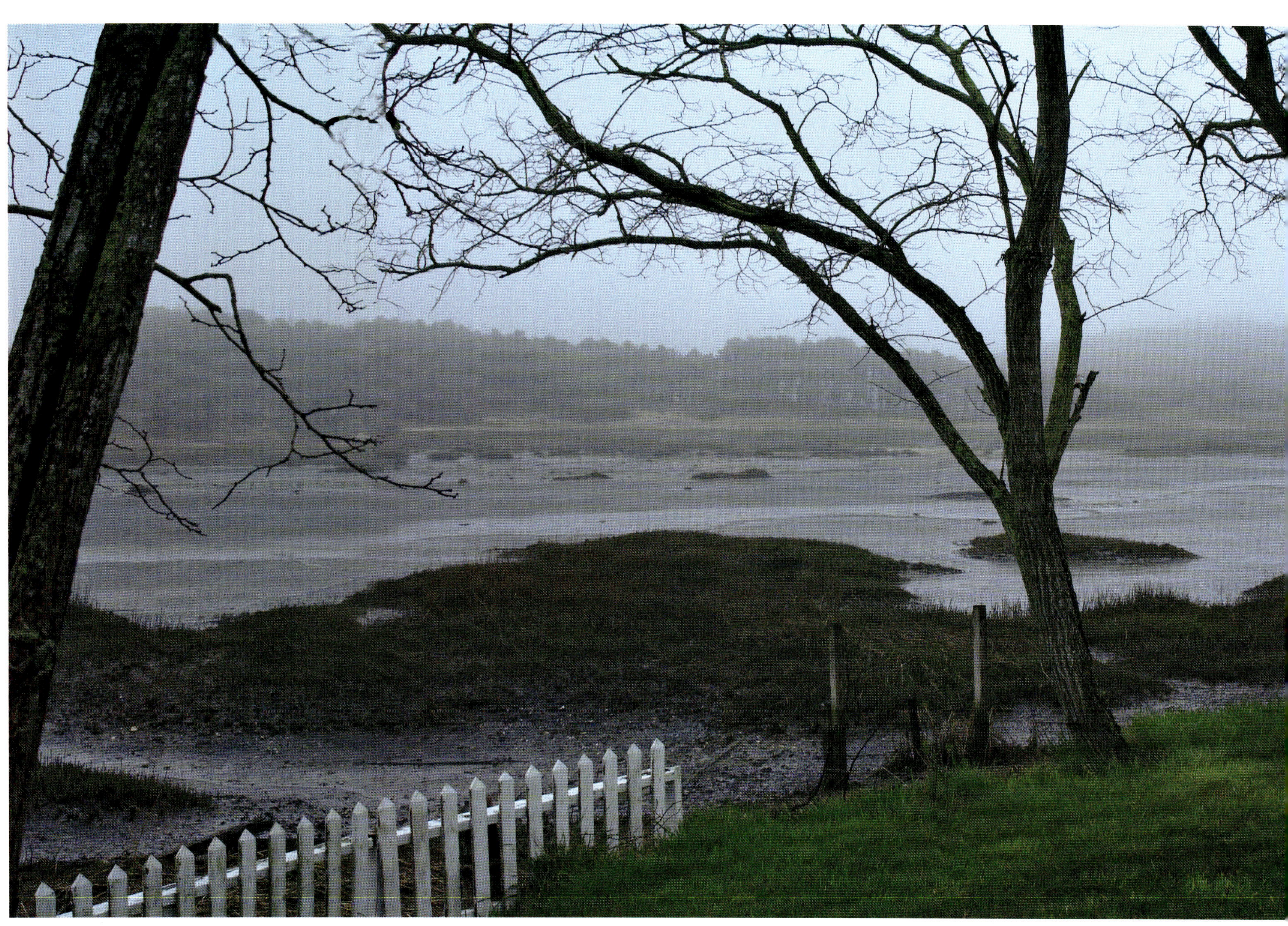

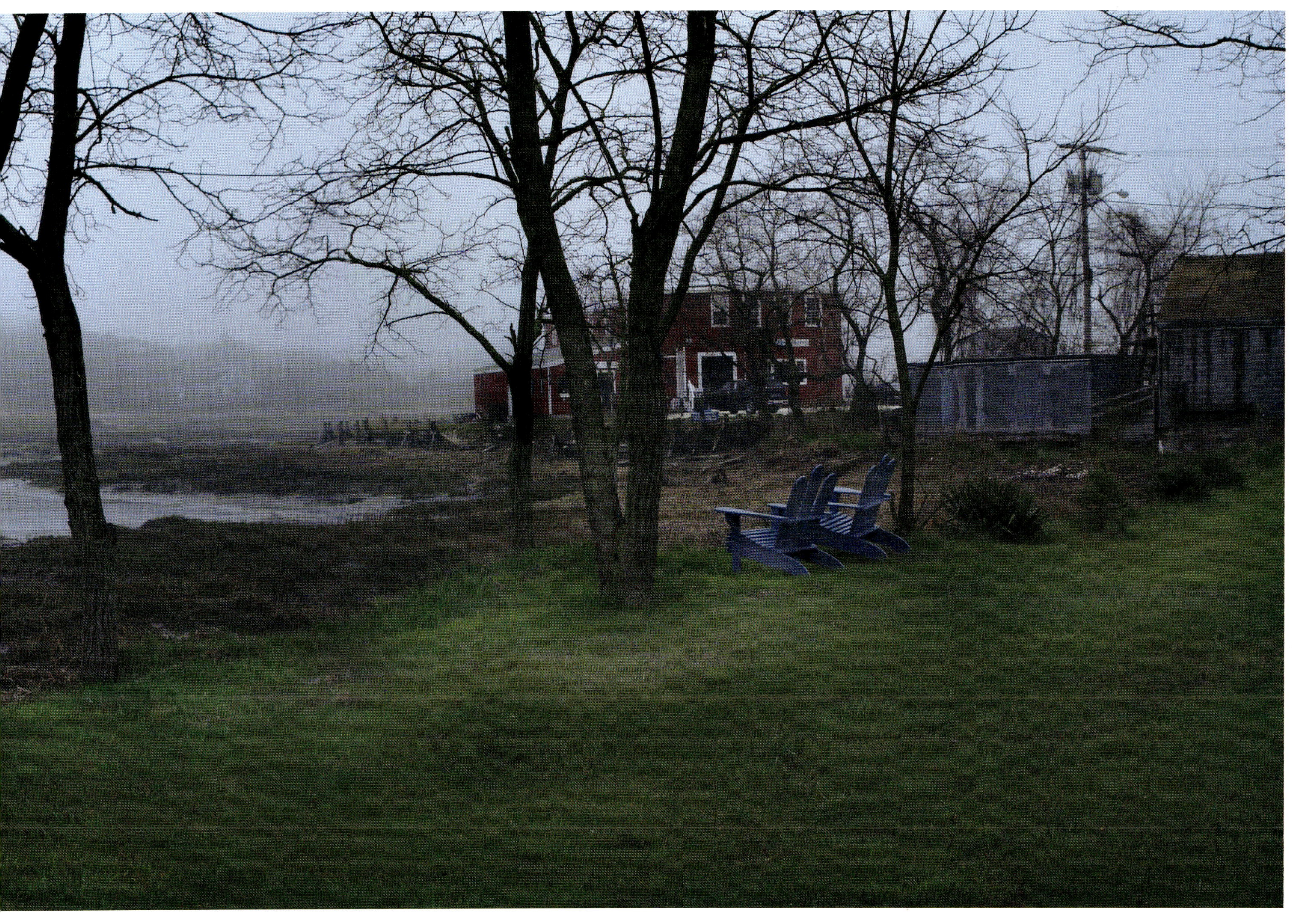

Morning, Wellfleet

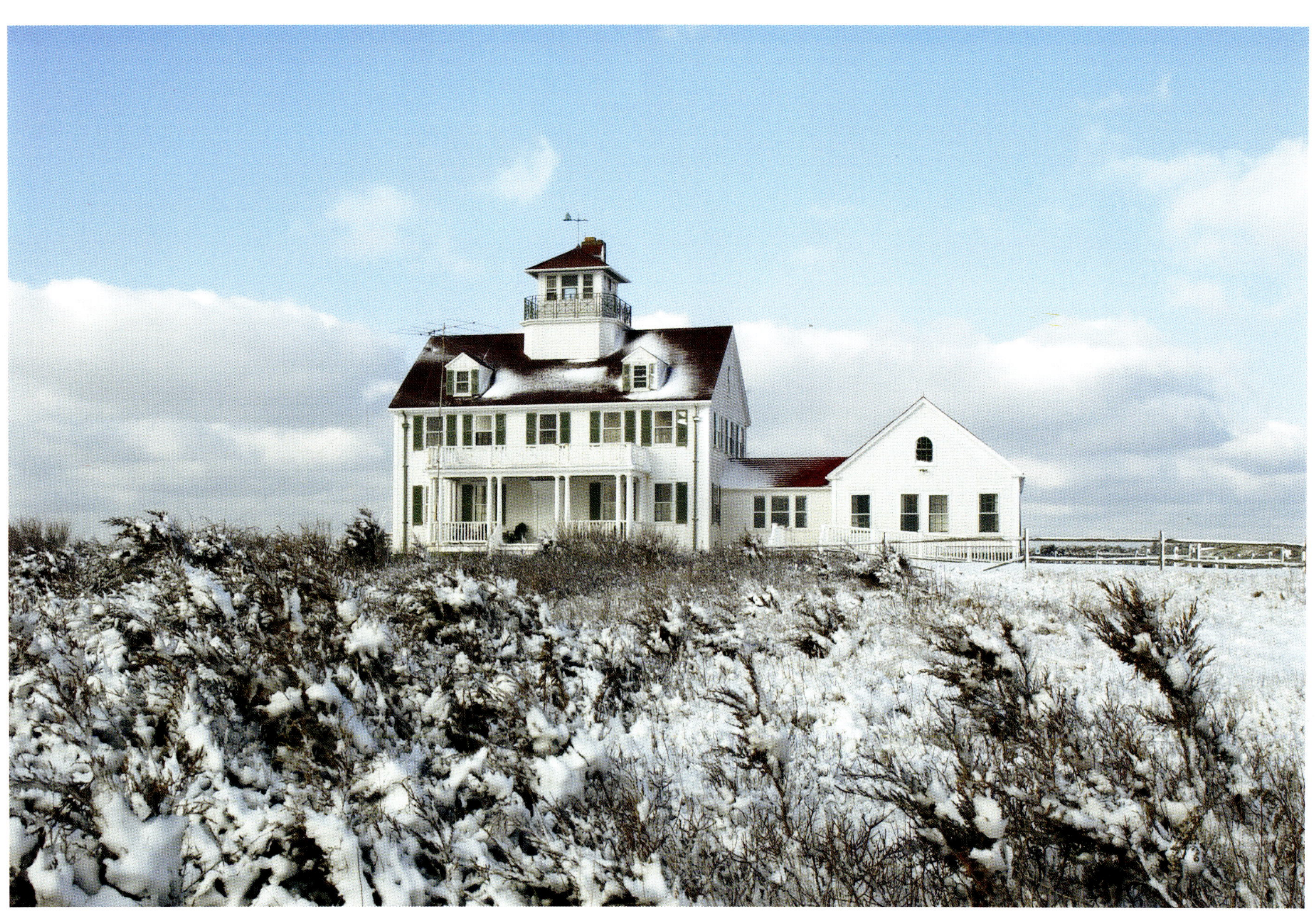

Coast Guard Station, Eastham

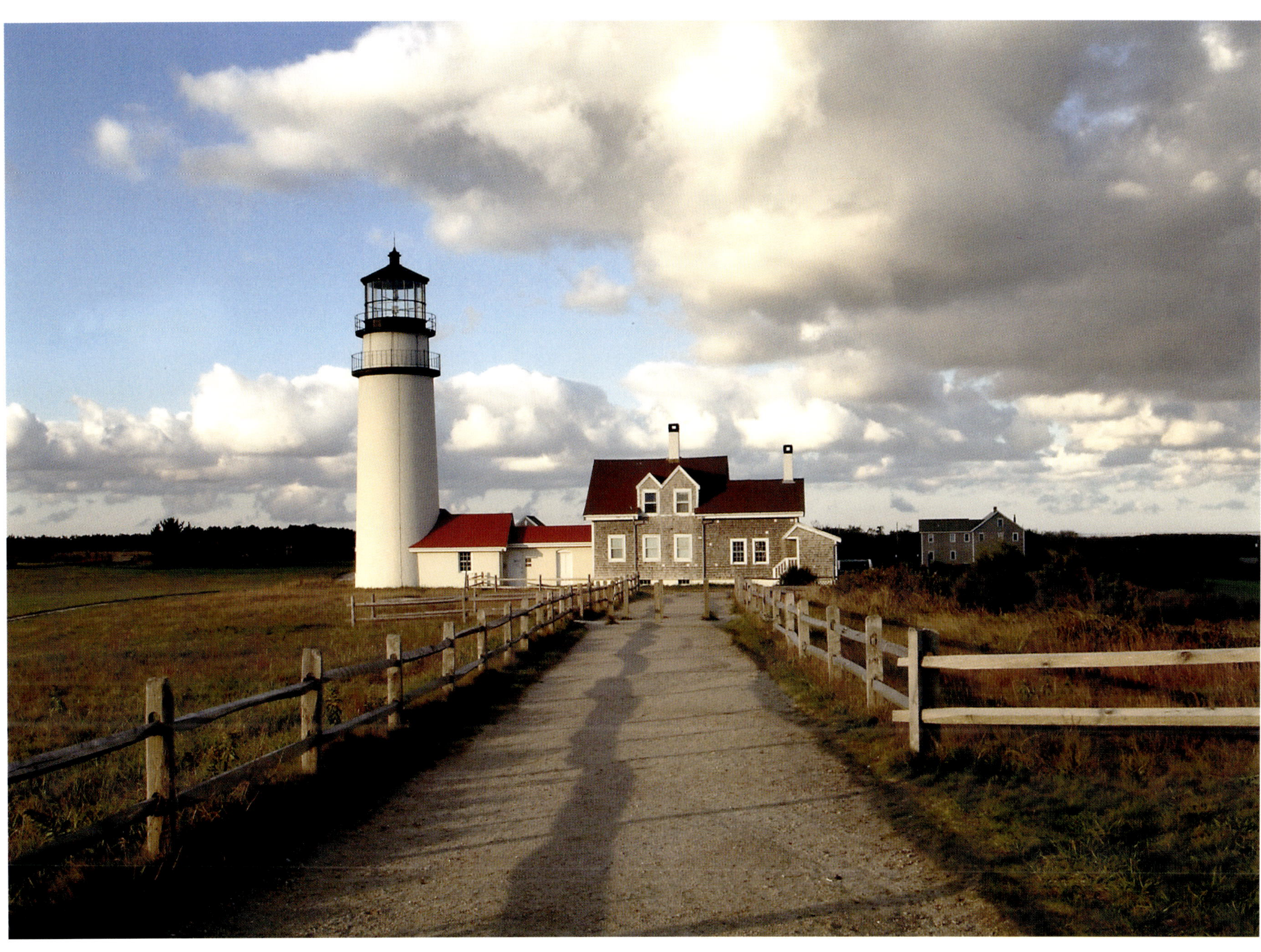

 Highland Light, Truro

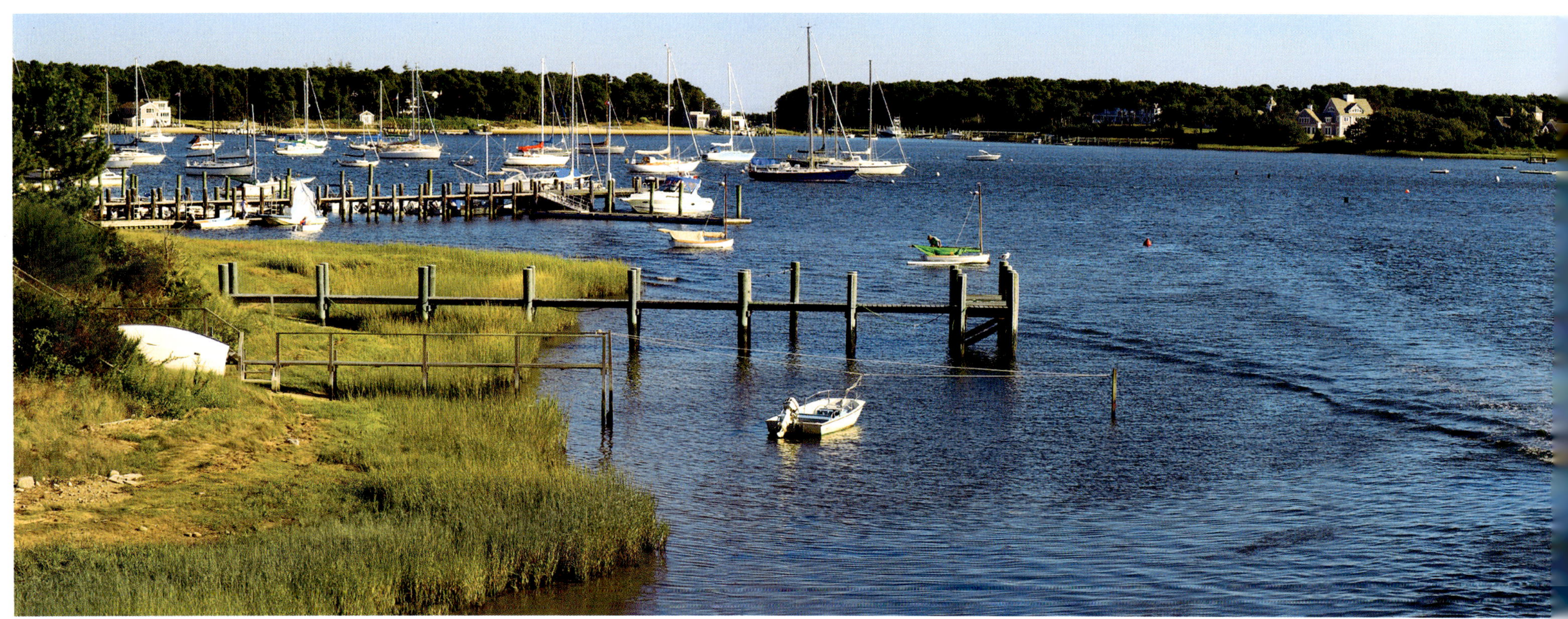

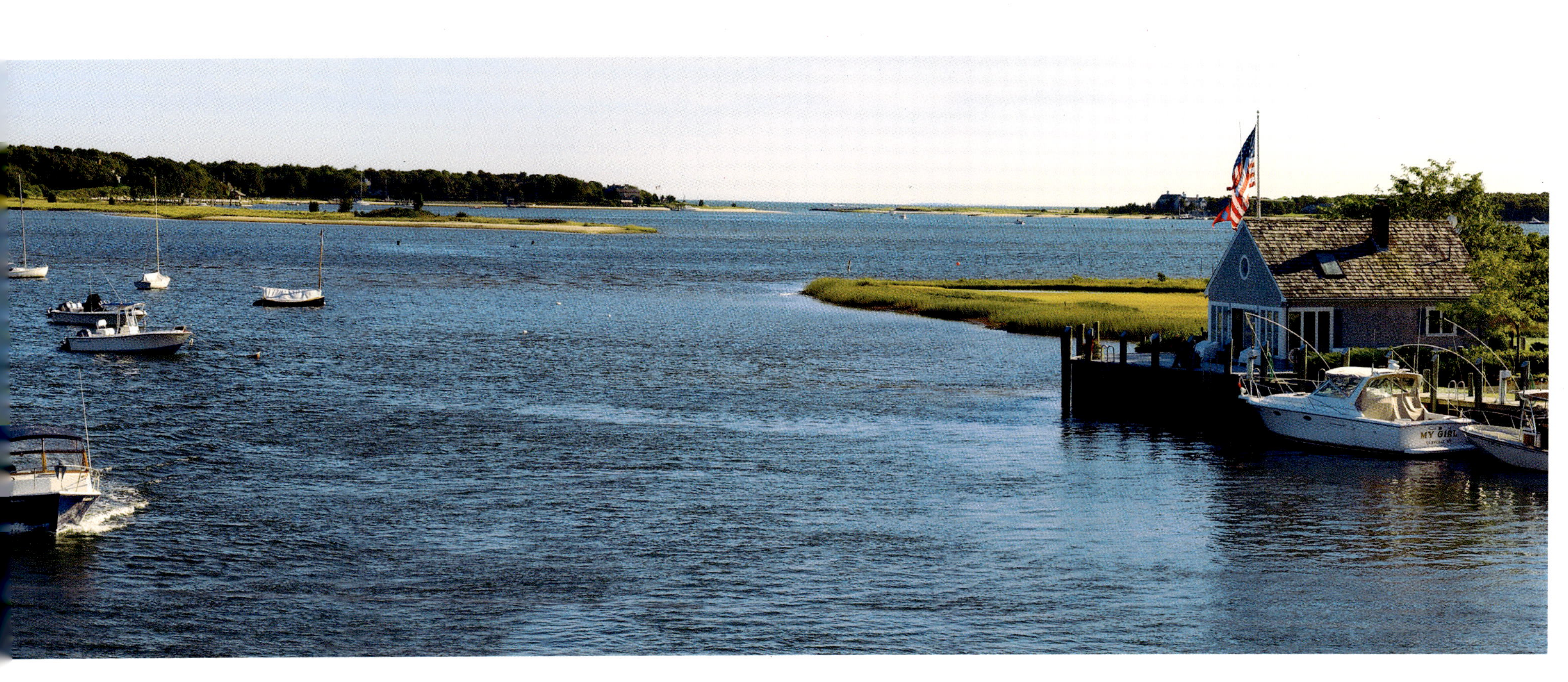

Osterville

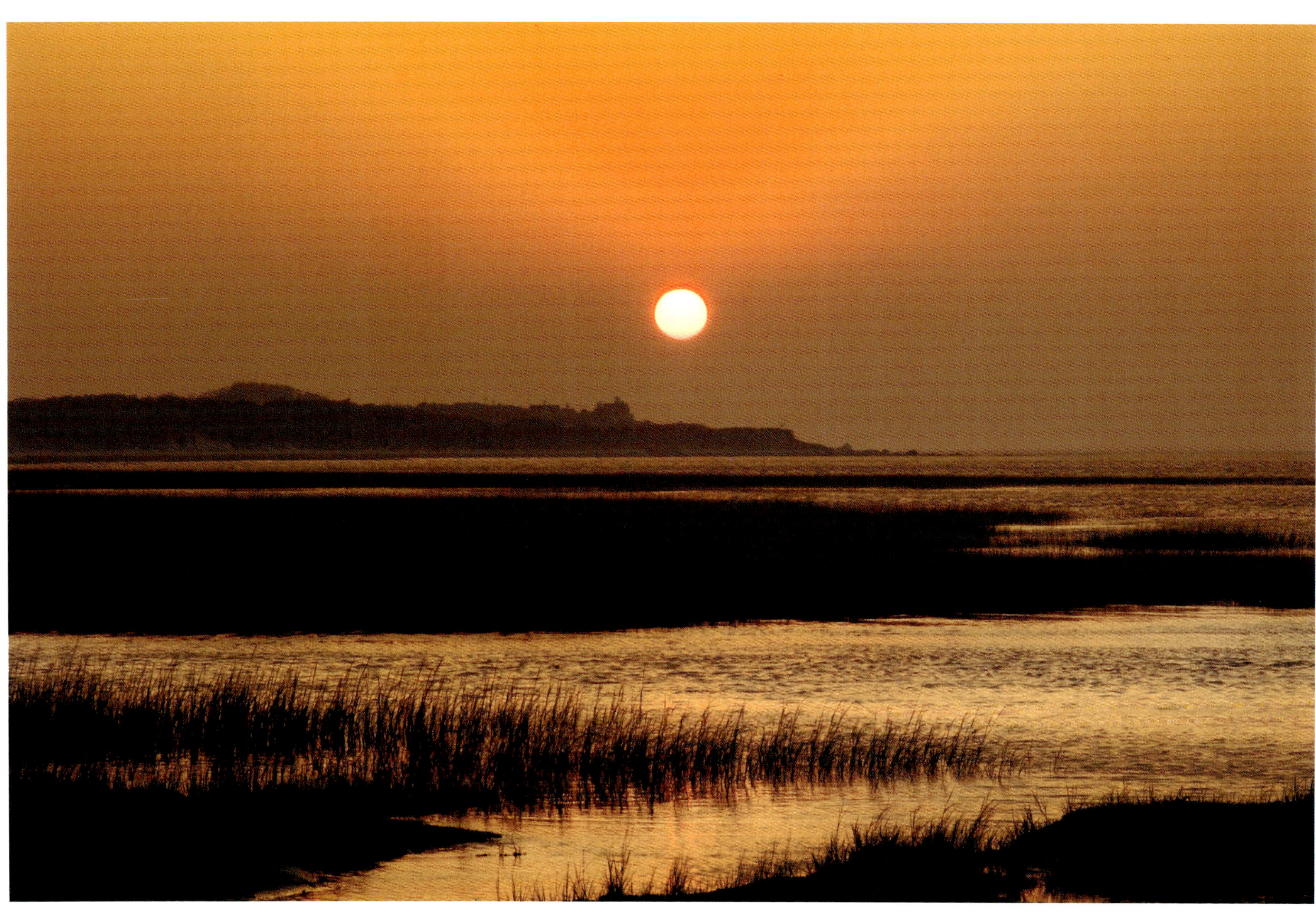

Sunrise Paine's Creek, Brewster

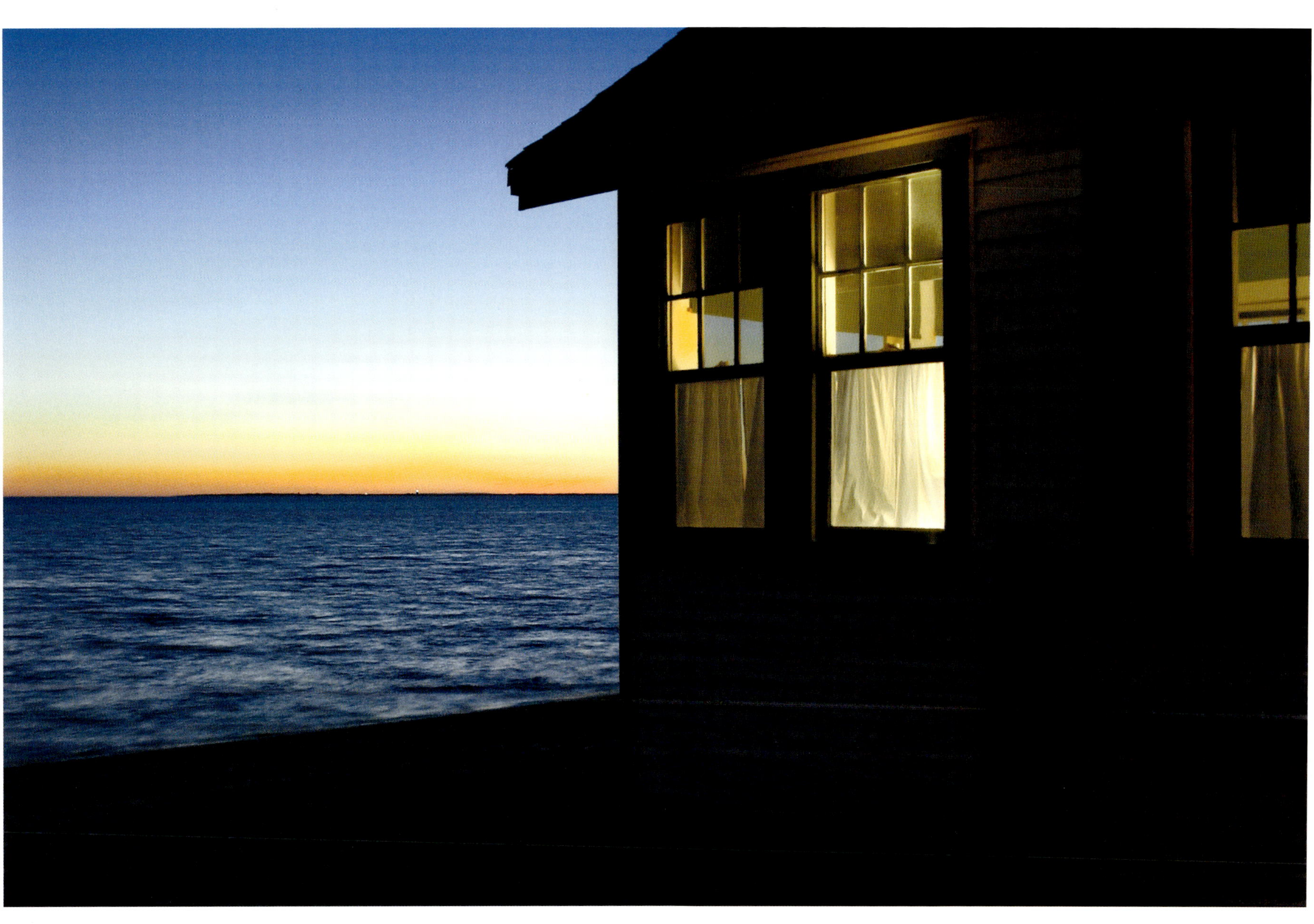

 Sunrise Days' Cottage, North Truro

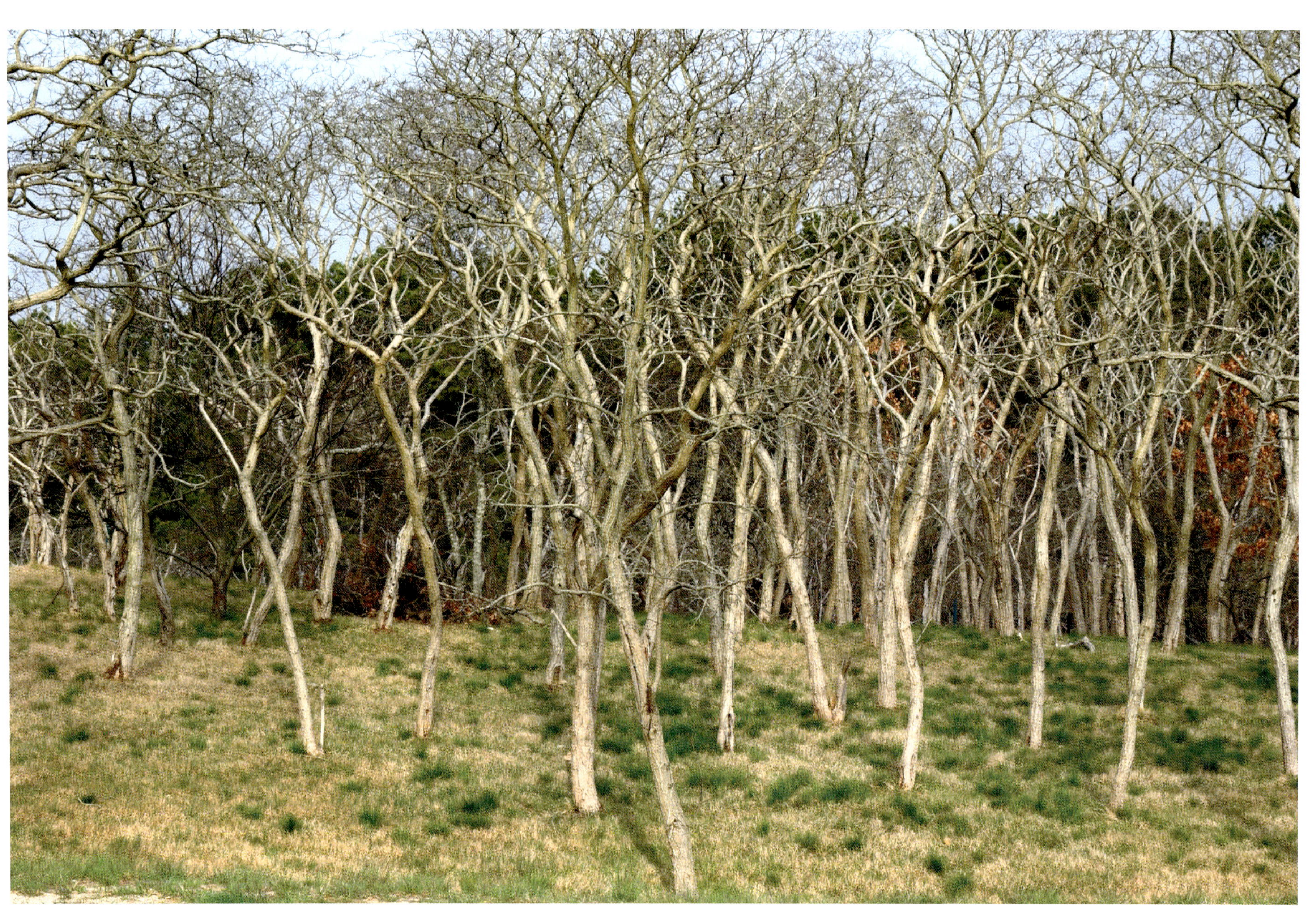

Spring, A Clutch of Black Locust Trees, Wellfleet

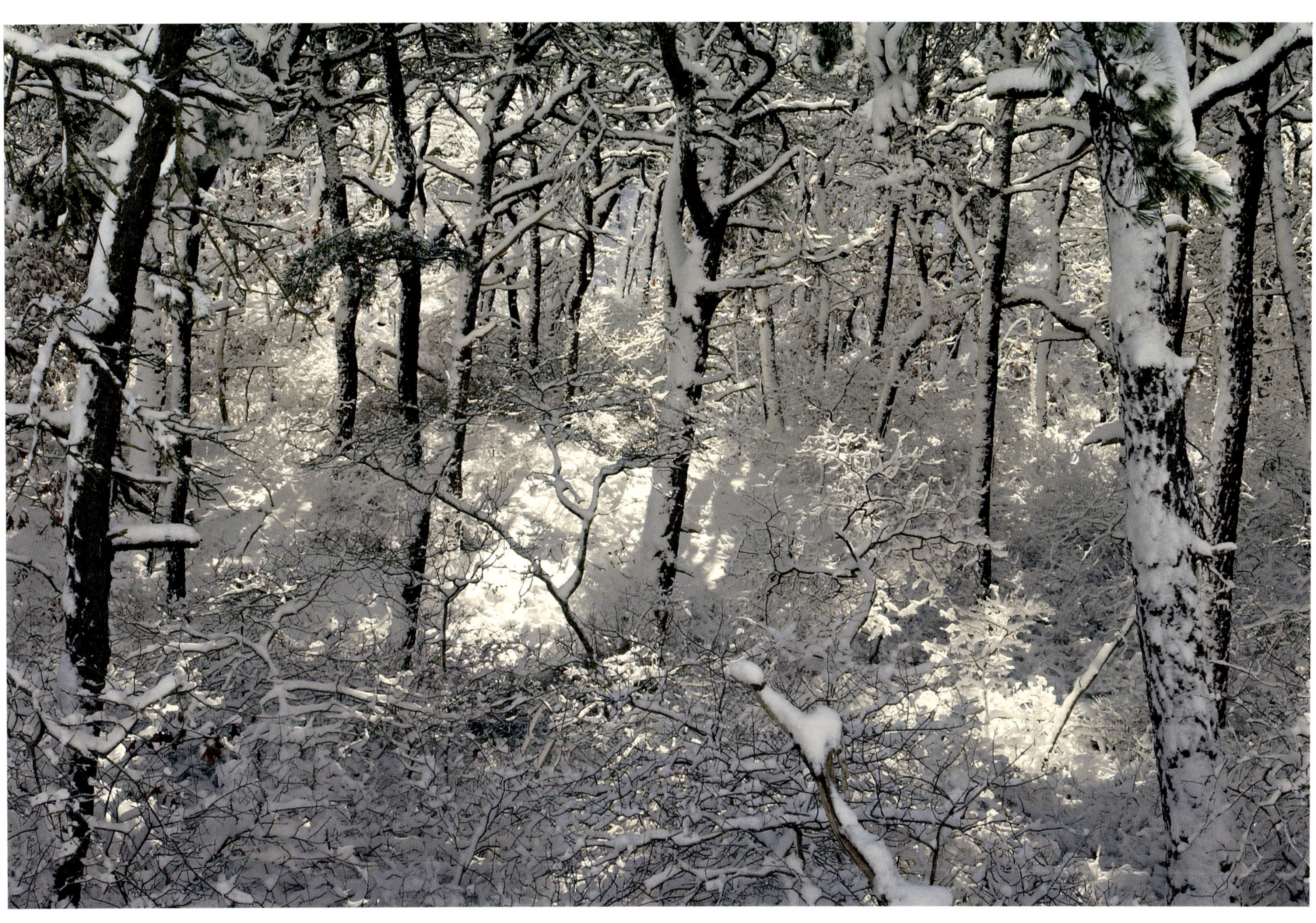

 Winter Forest, Truro

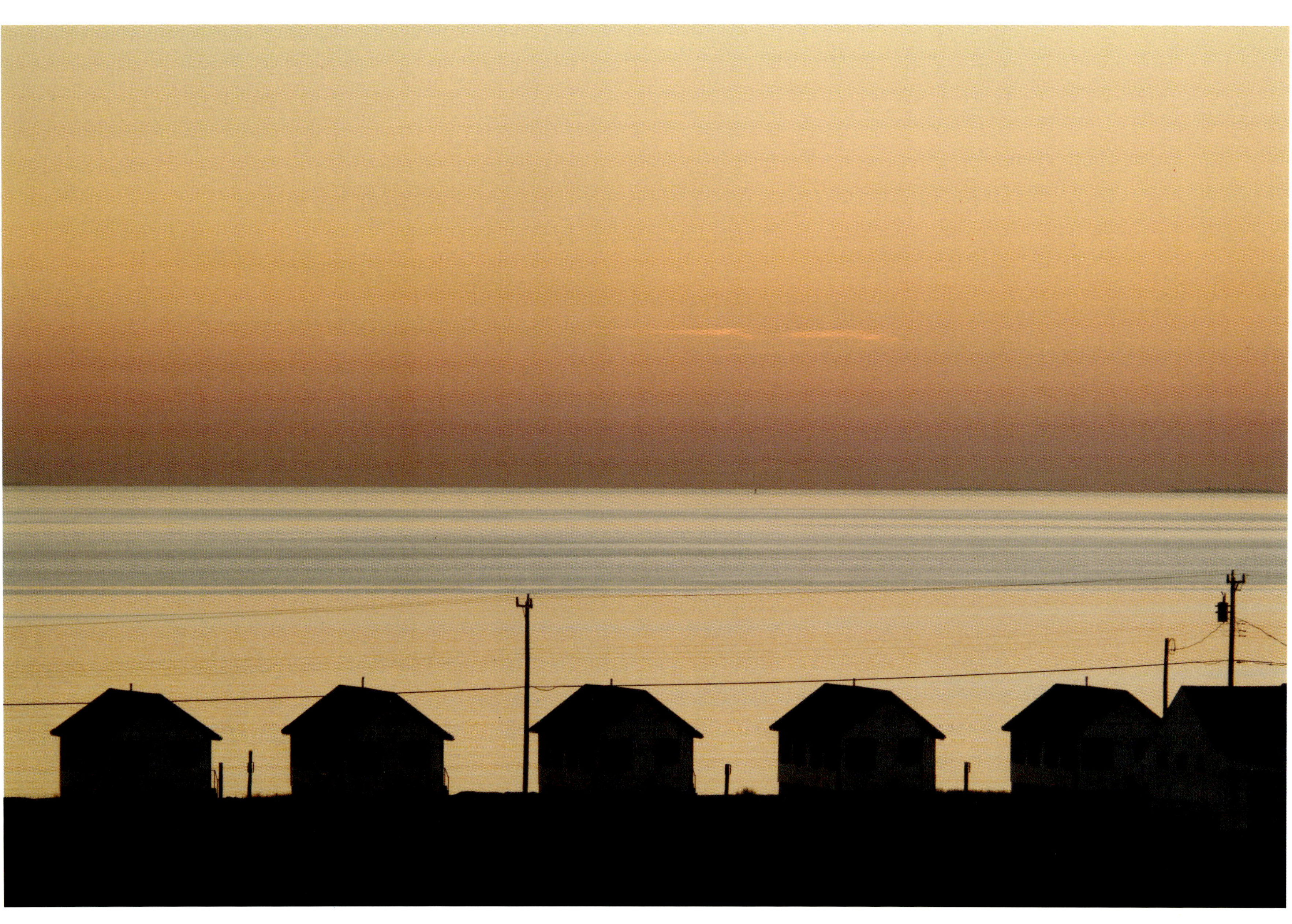

Days' Cottages, North Truro

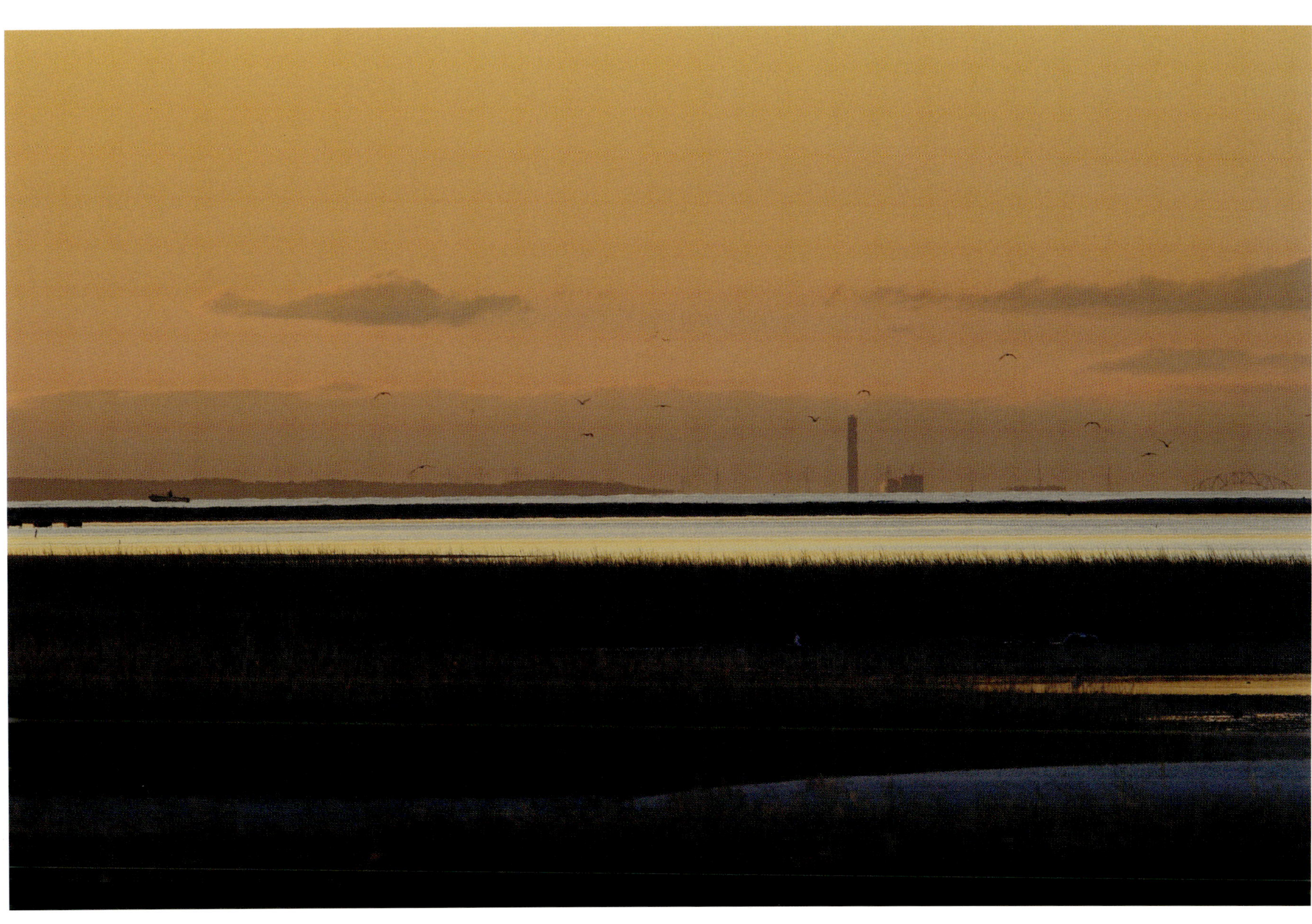

97 **View from Paine's Creek, Brewster**

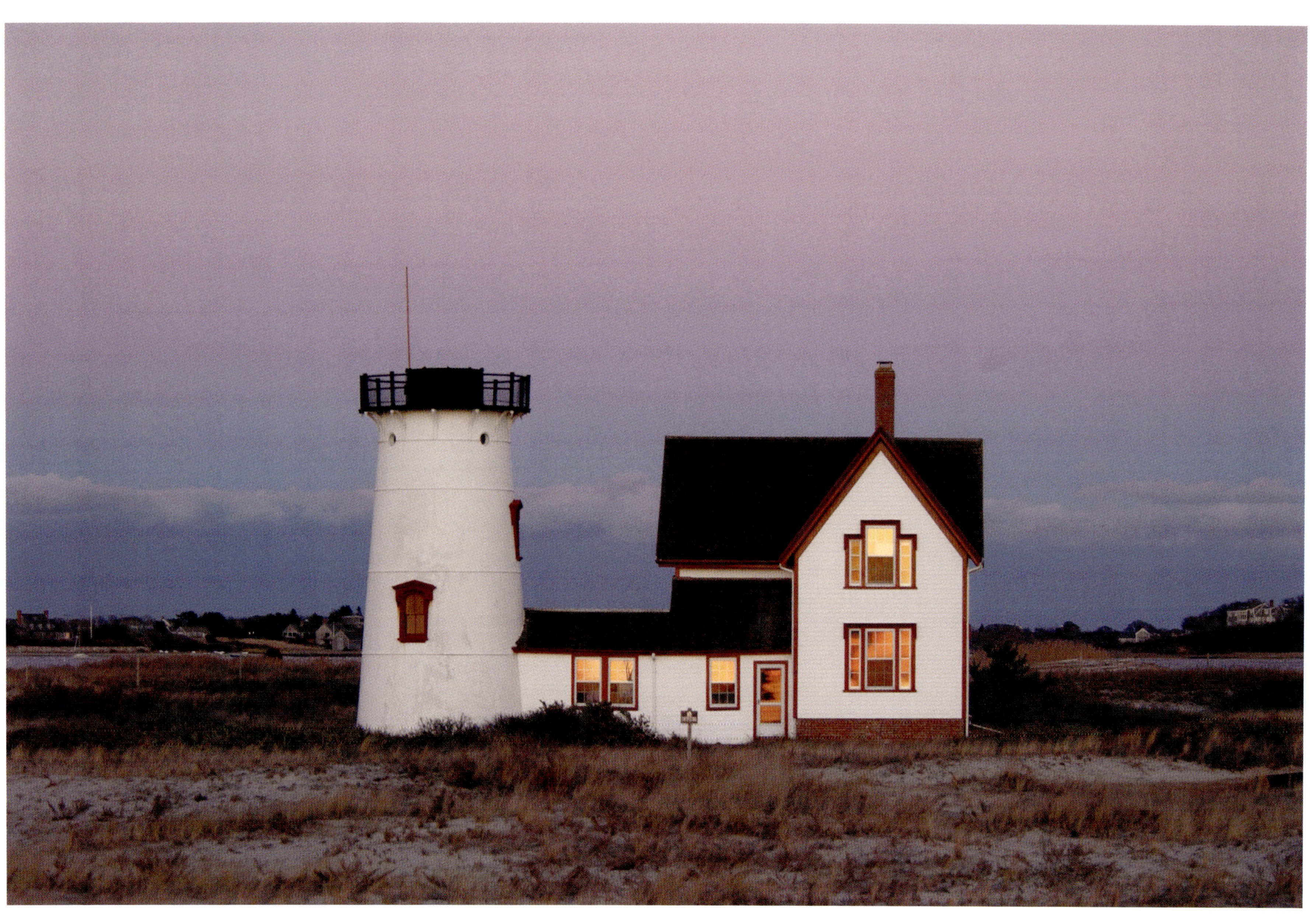

Stage Harbor Light, Chatham

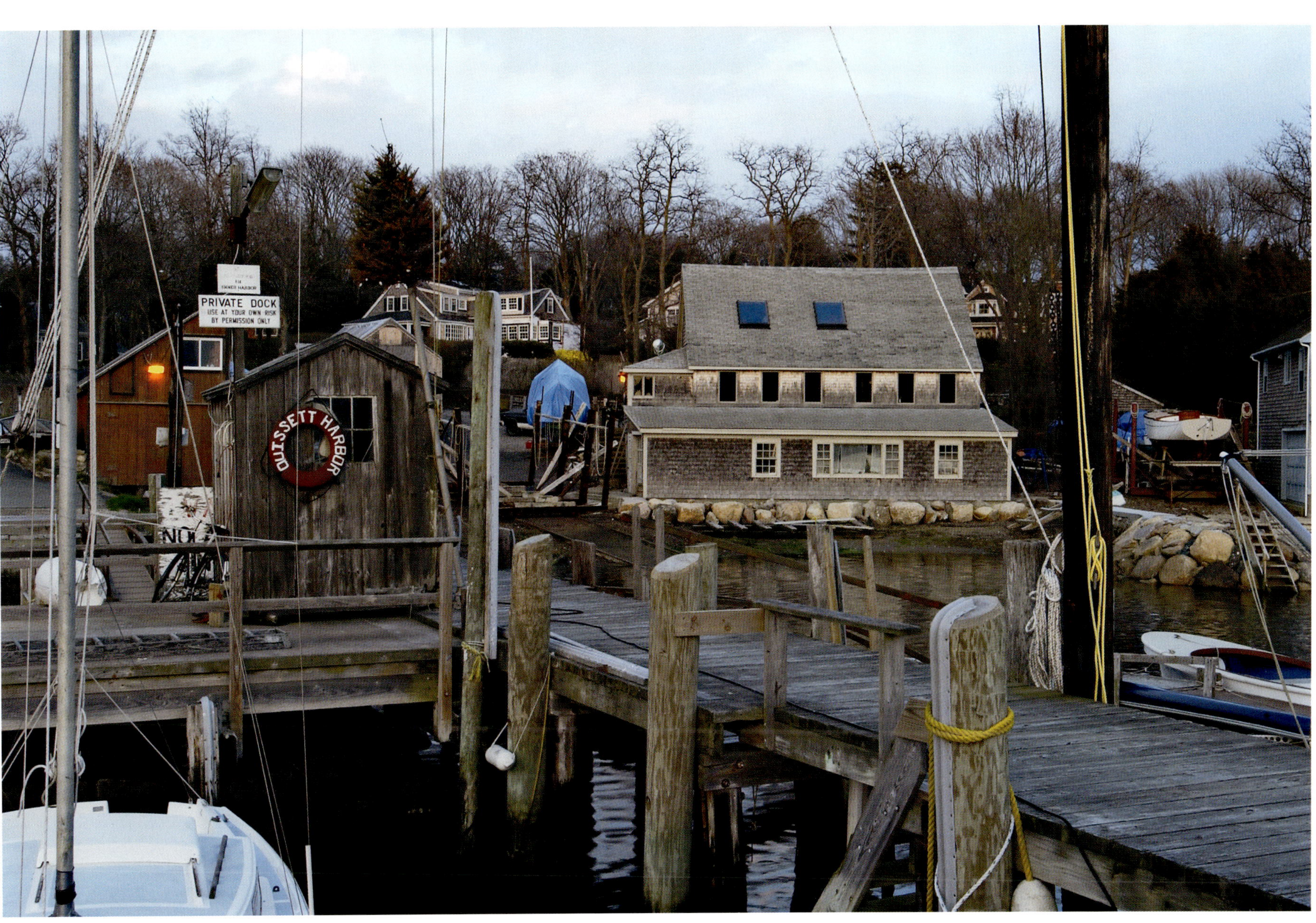

 Quissett Harbor, Woods Hole, Falmouth

Sunrise, Chatham

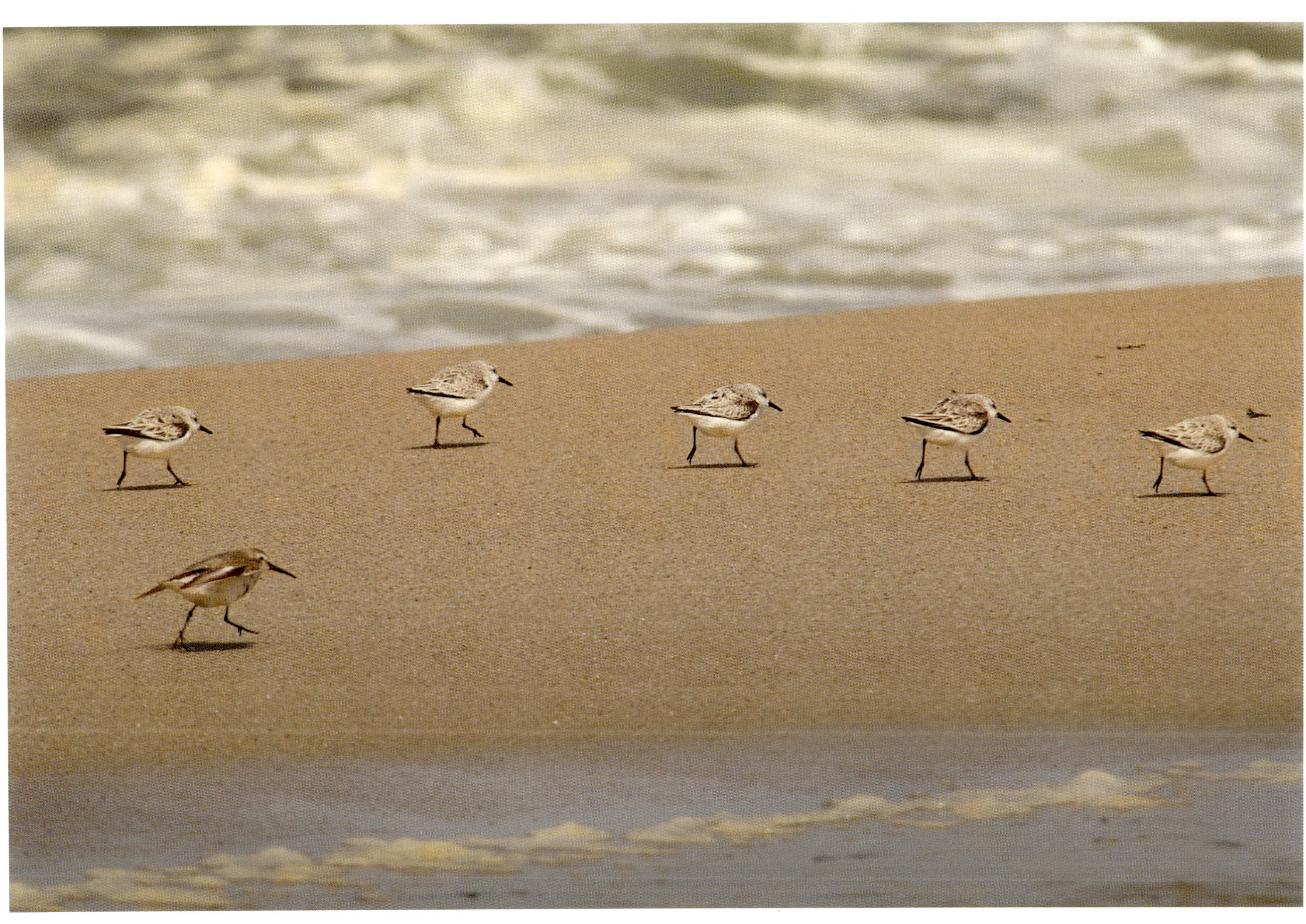

 Sand Pipers, Chatham

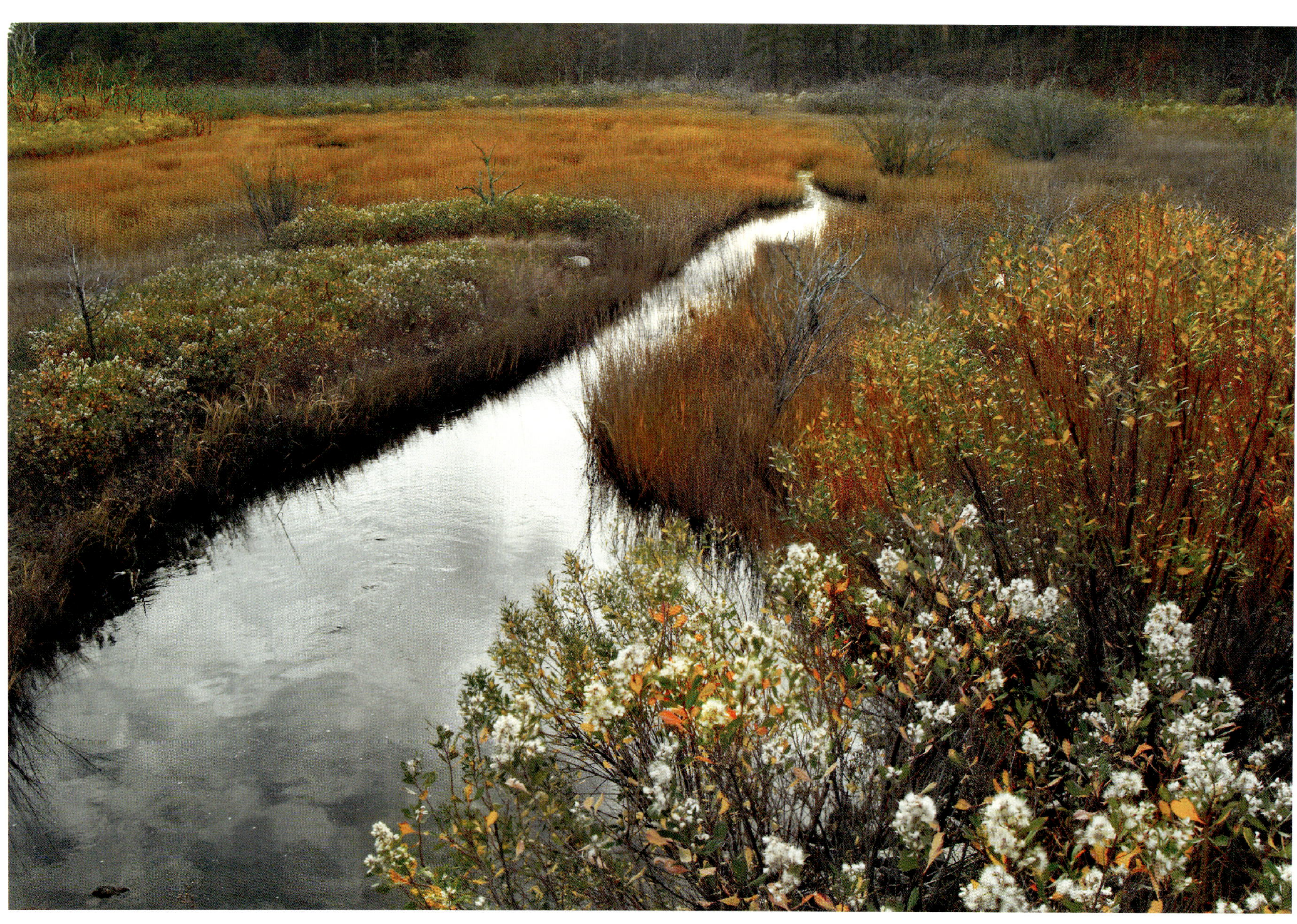

Corn Hill, Pamet River, Truro

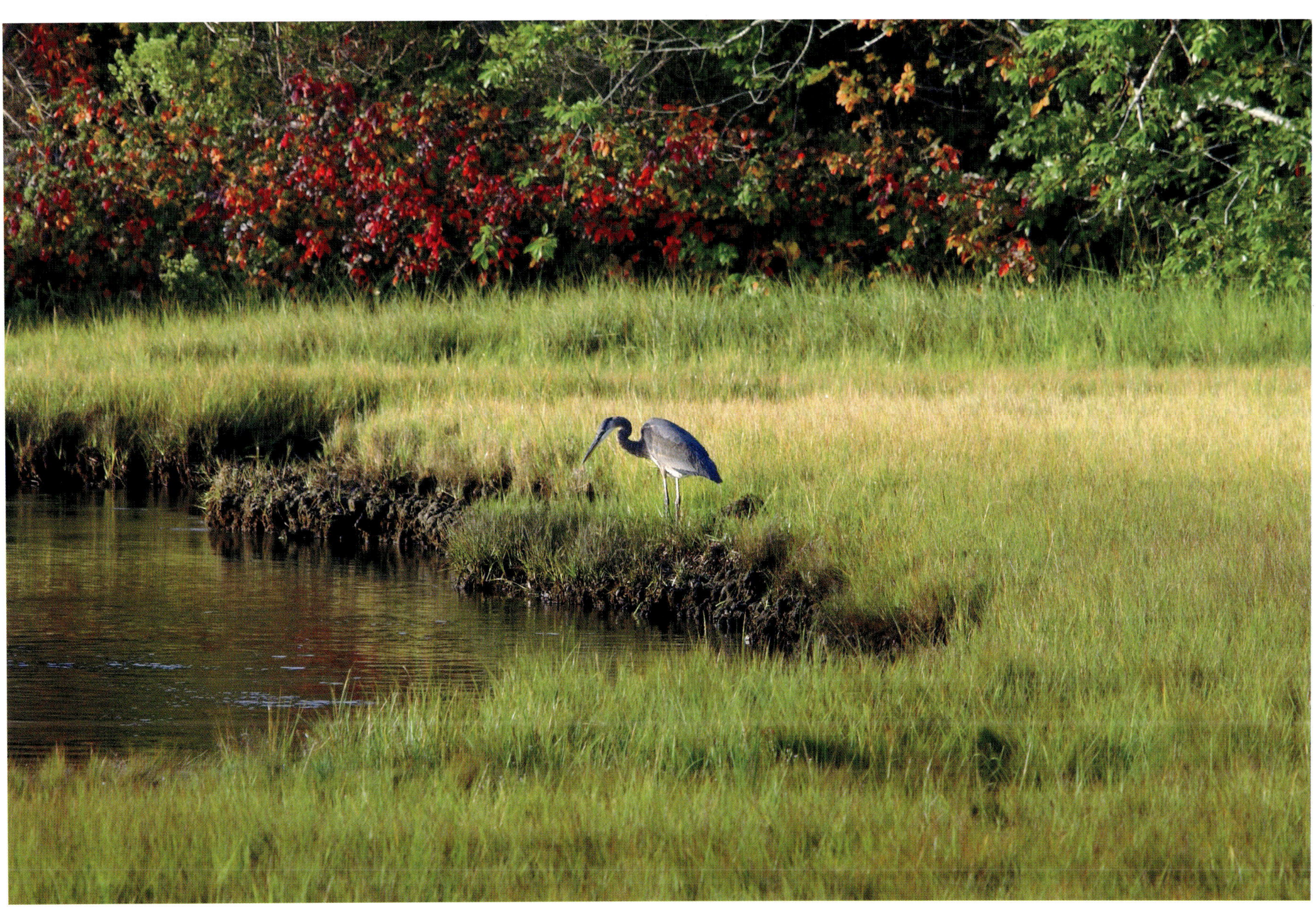

 Bass River, West Dennis

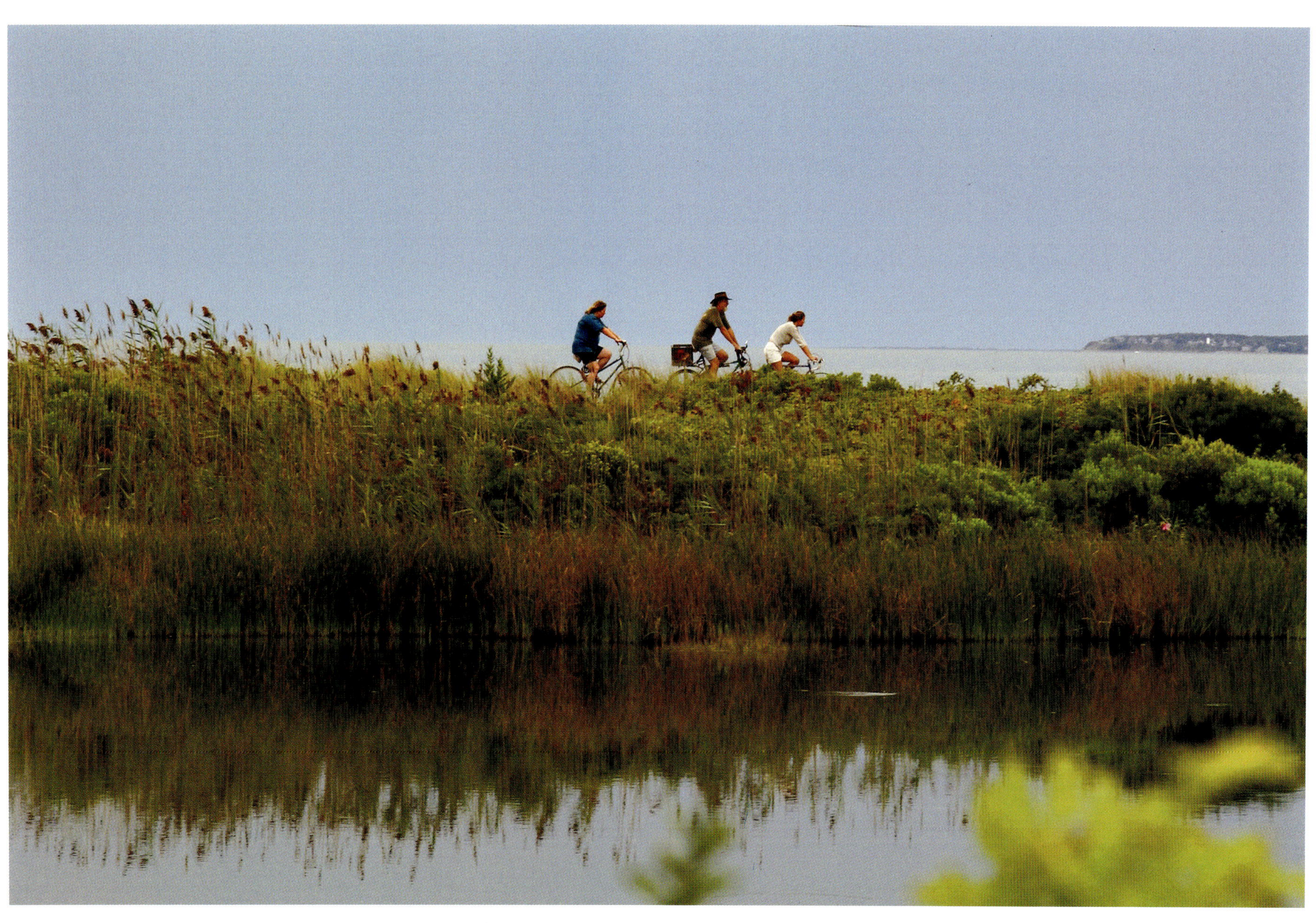

Shining Sea Bike Path, Falmouth to Woods Hole

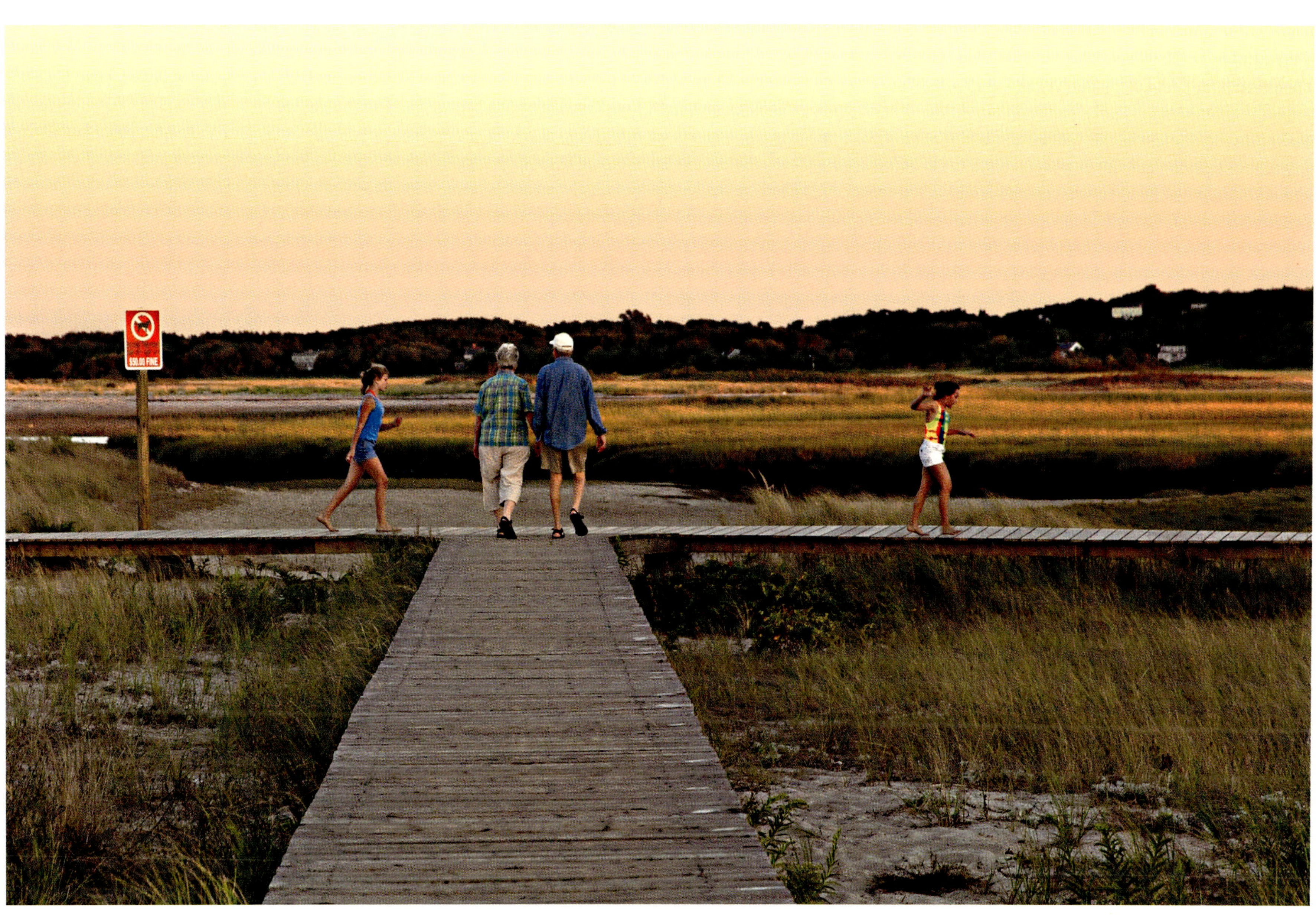

 Boardwalk, Sandwich

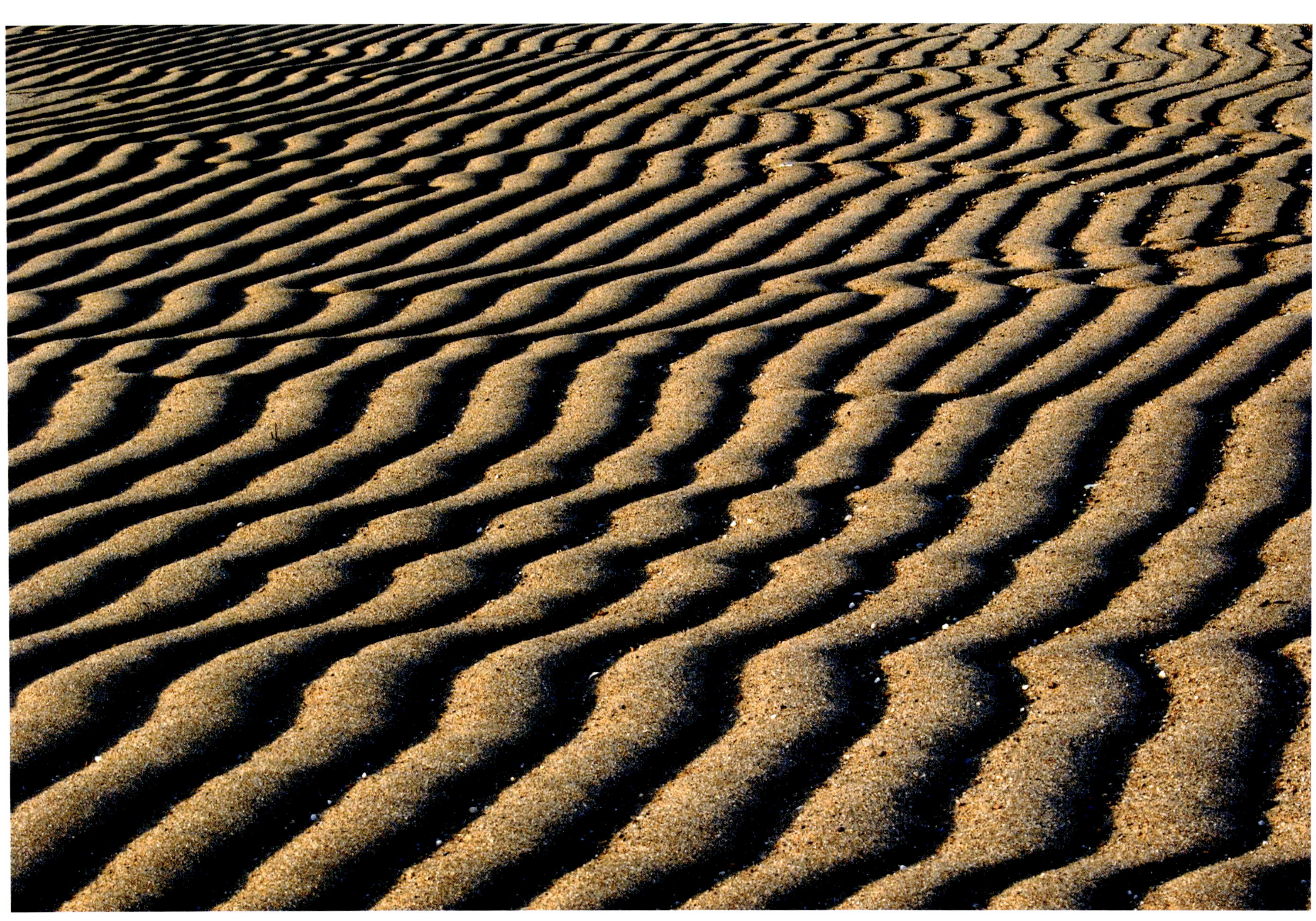

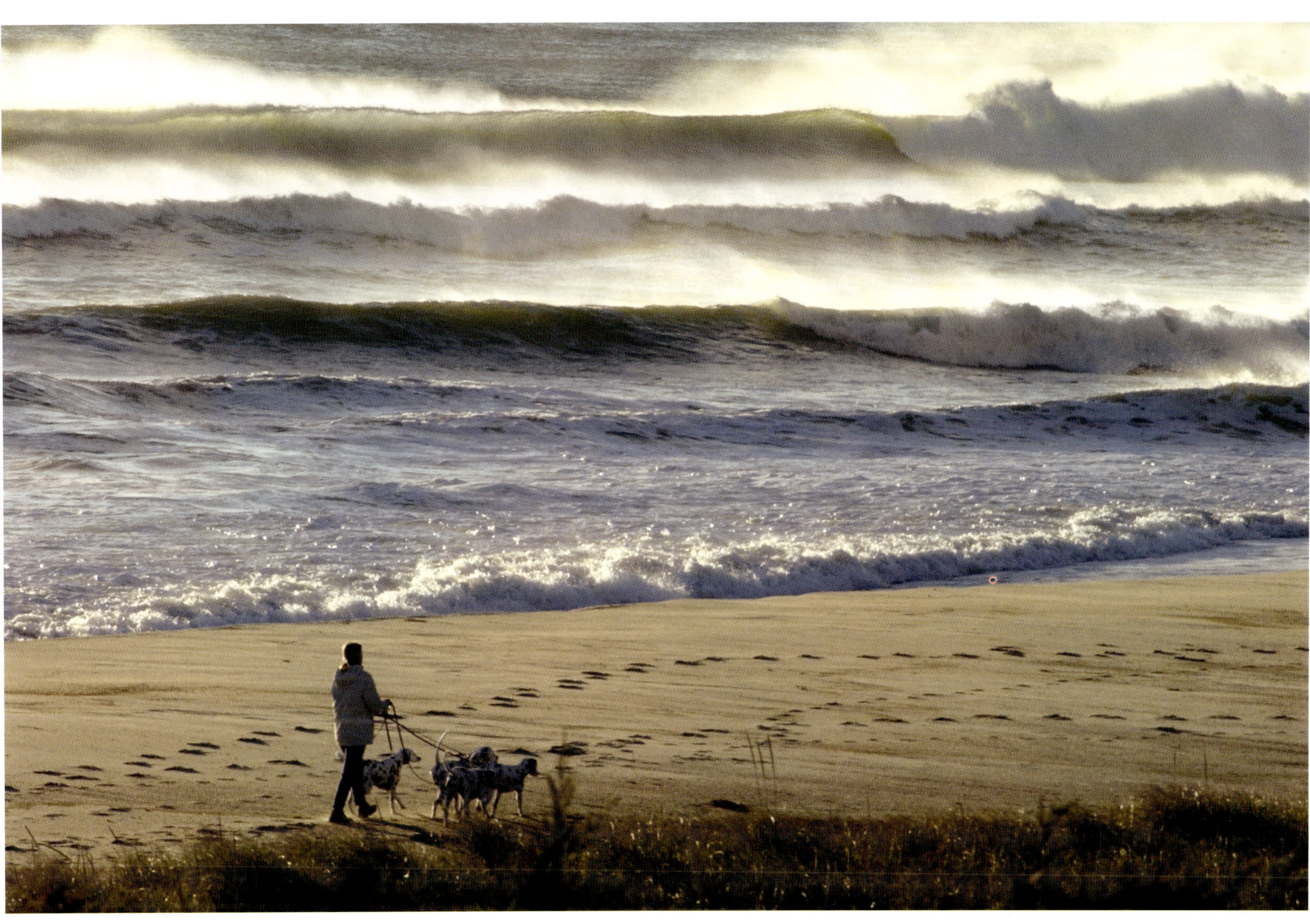

107 **Walking the Dogs, Coast Guard Beach, Eastham**

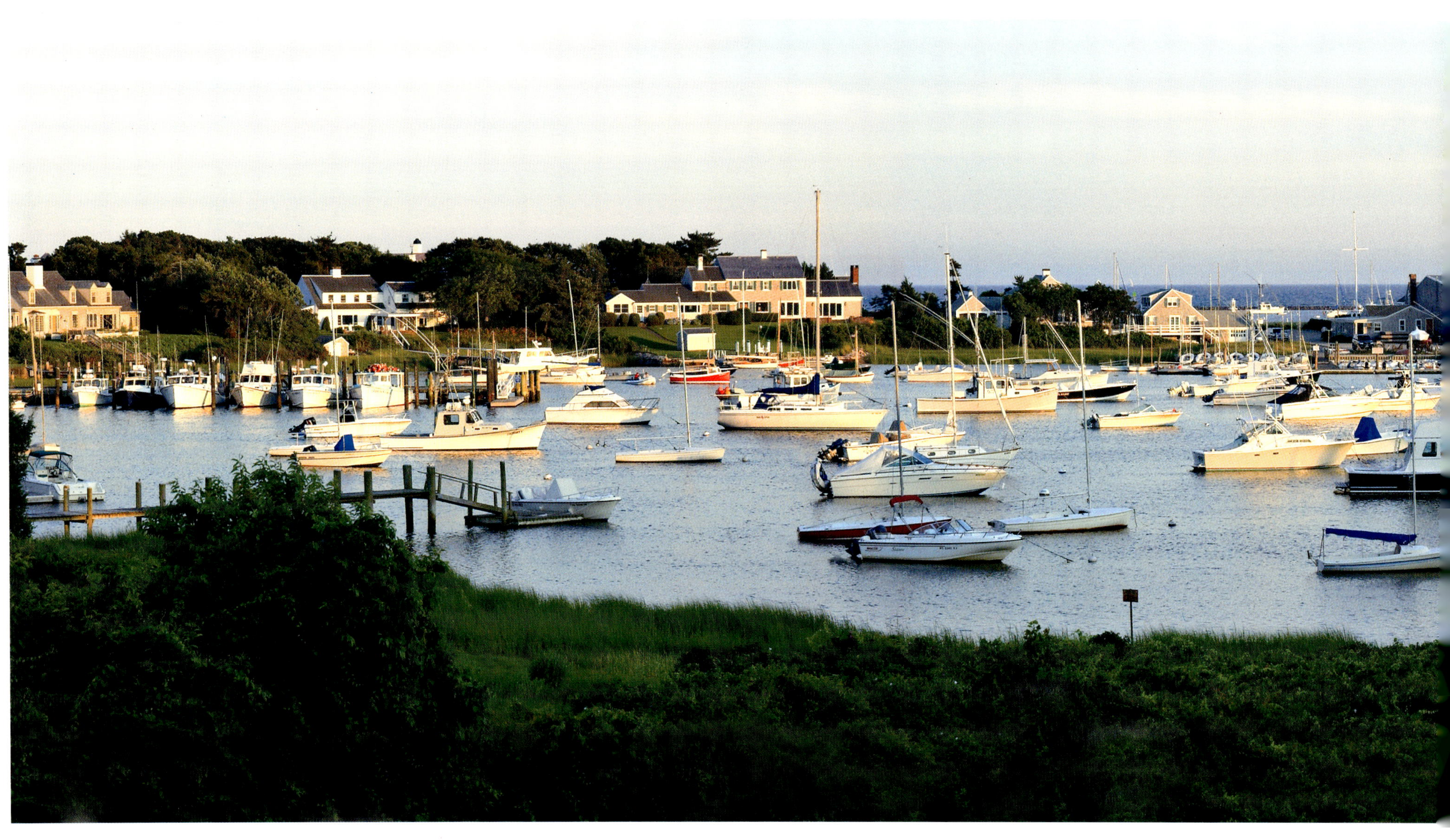

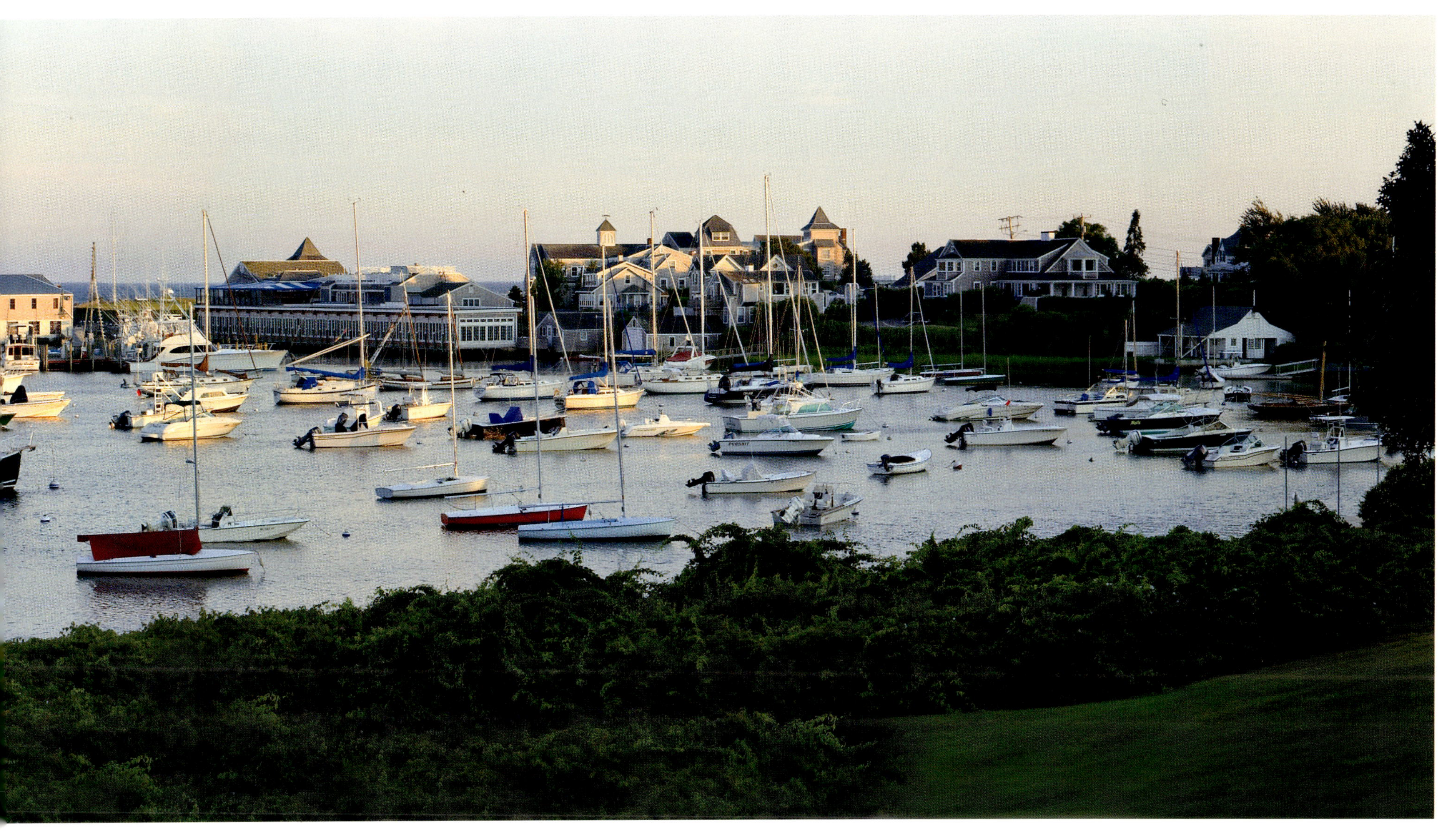

Wychmere Harbor, Harwich Port

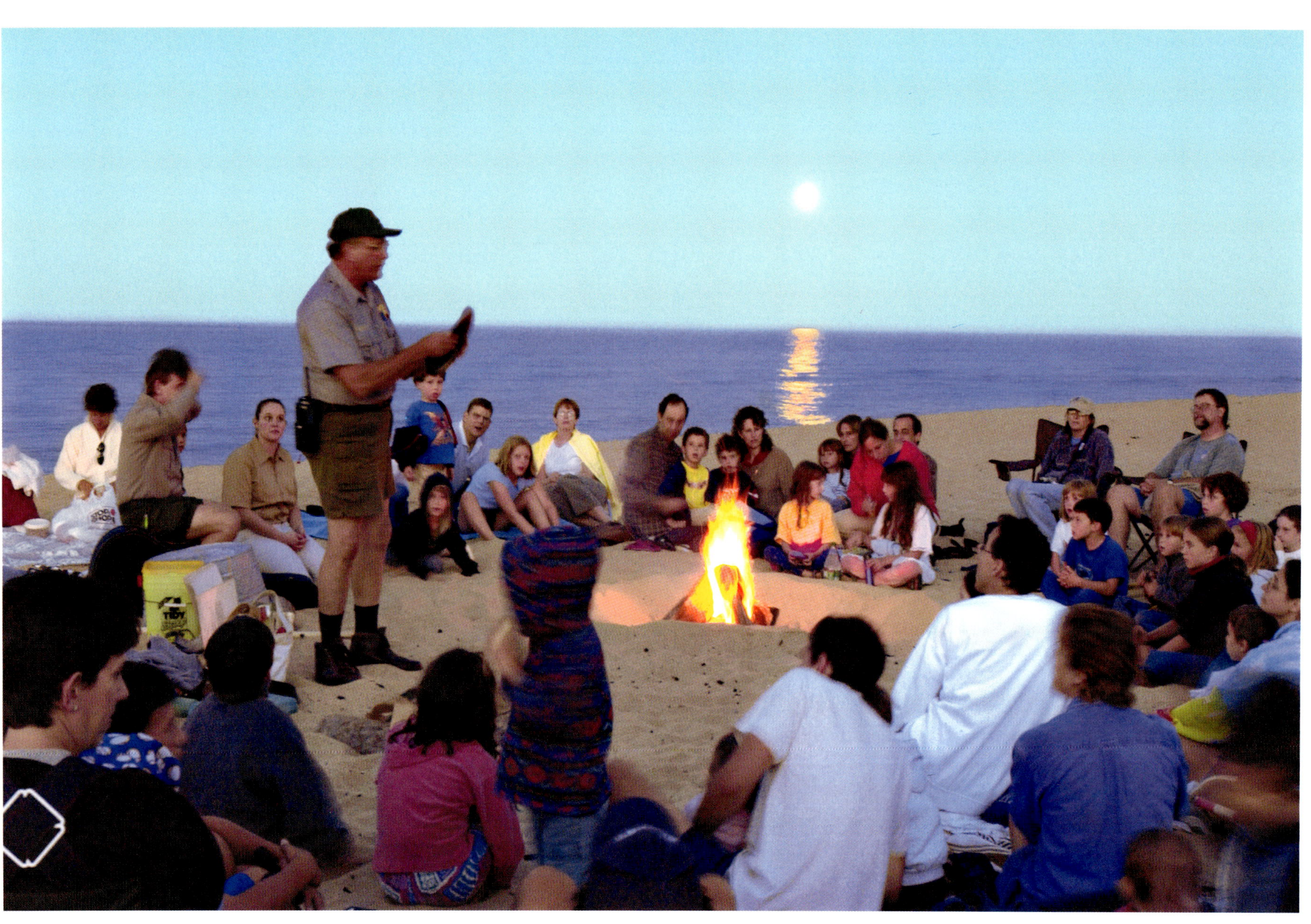

Gathering Around the Campfire with a National Seashore Ranger, Pamet Bay Beach, Truro

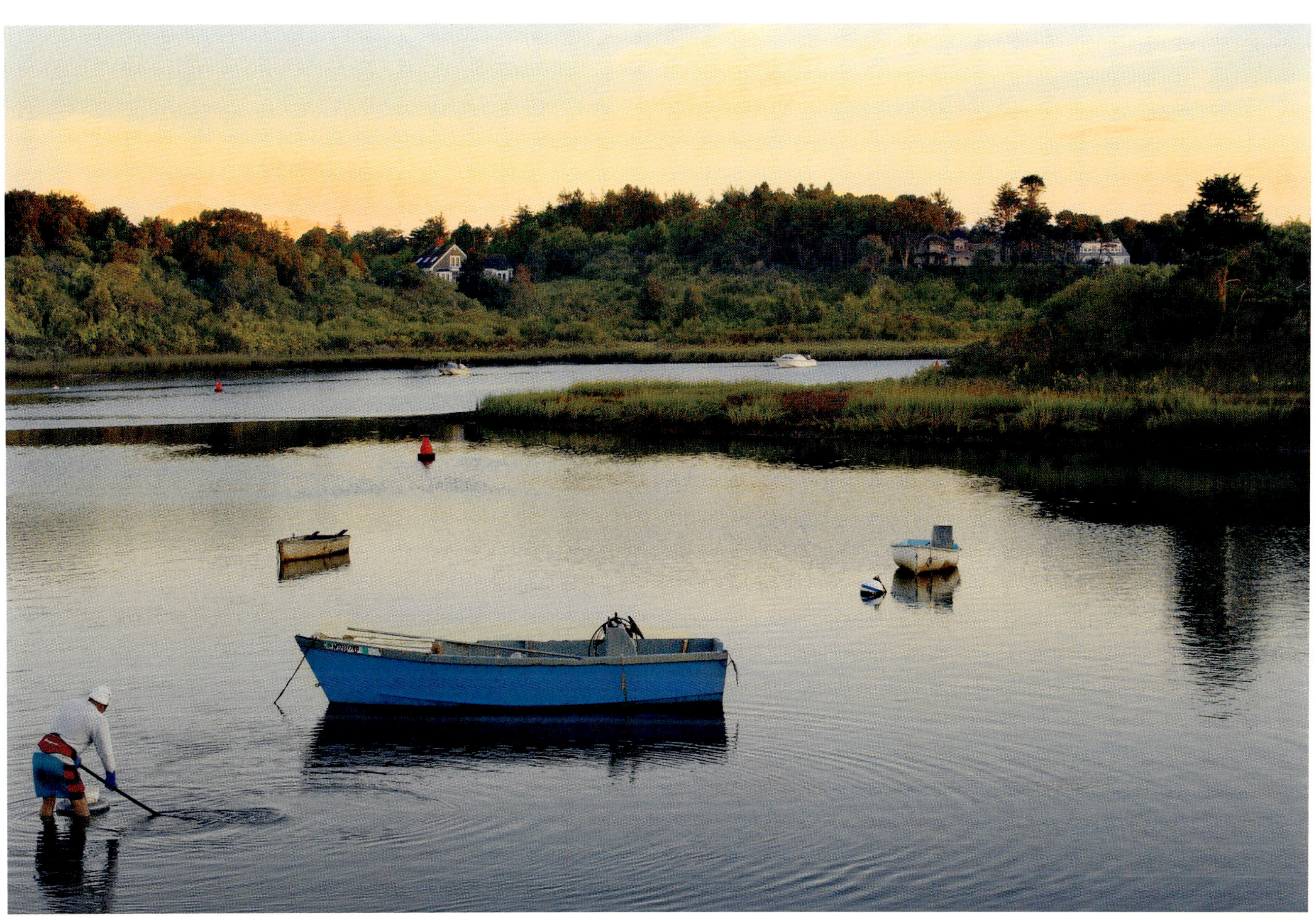

 Oyster Pond Beach, Chatham

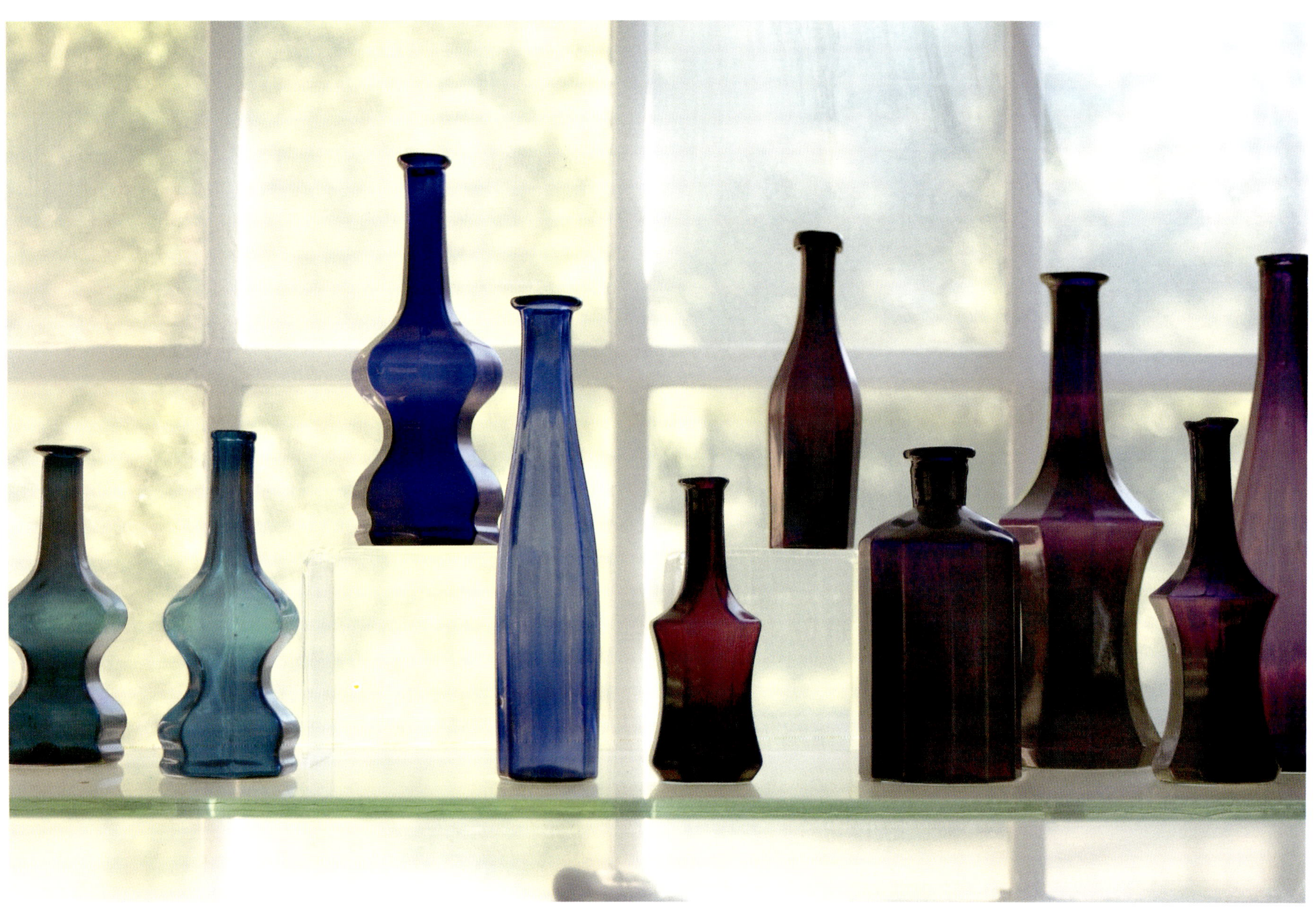

Sandwich Glass Museum, Sandwich

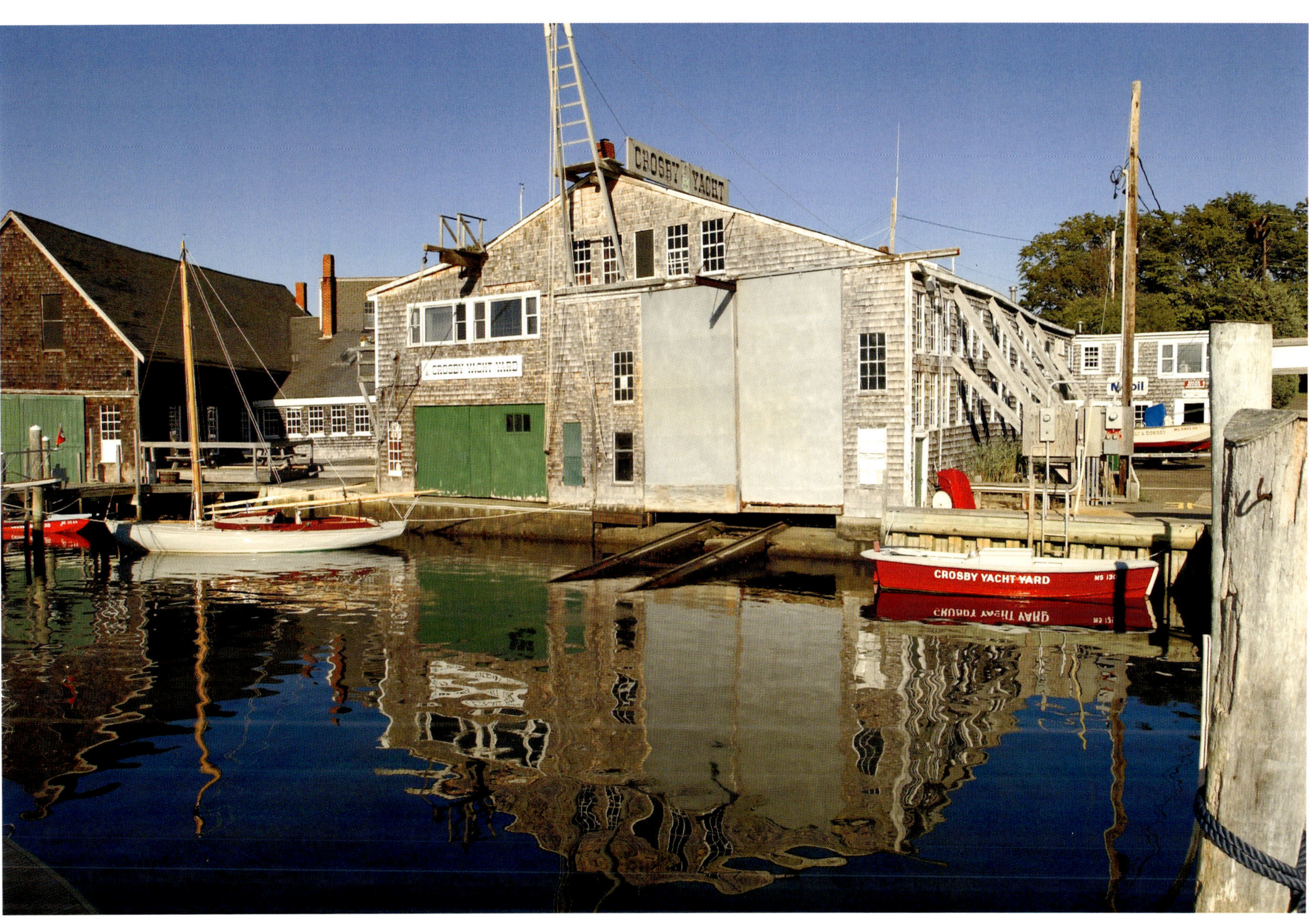

 Crosby Yacht Yard, Osterville

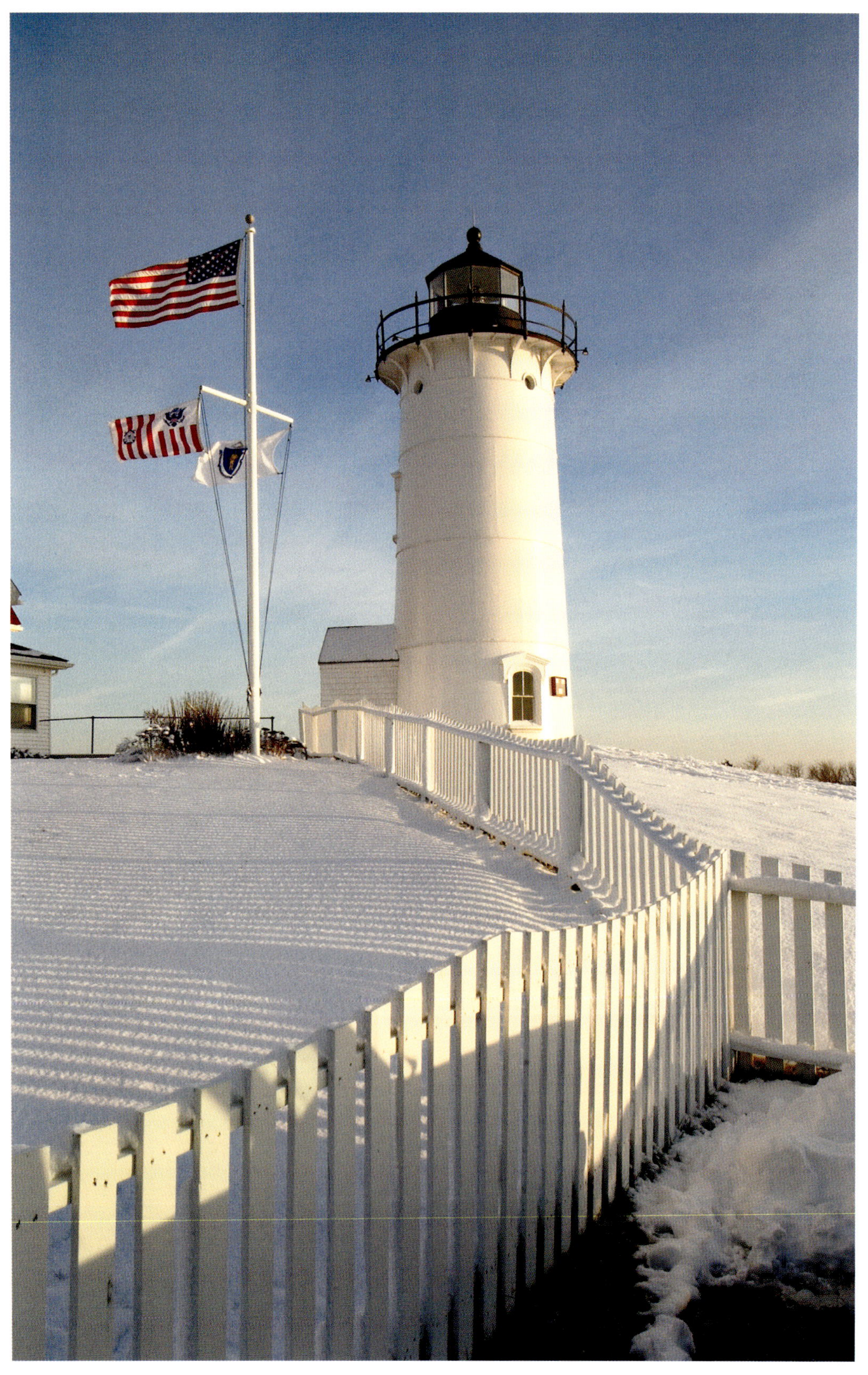

Nobska Lighthouse, Woods Hole

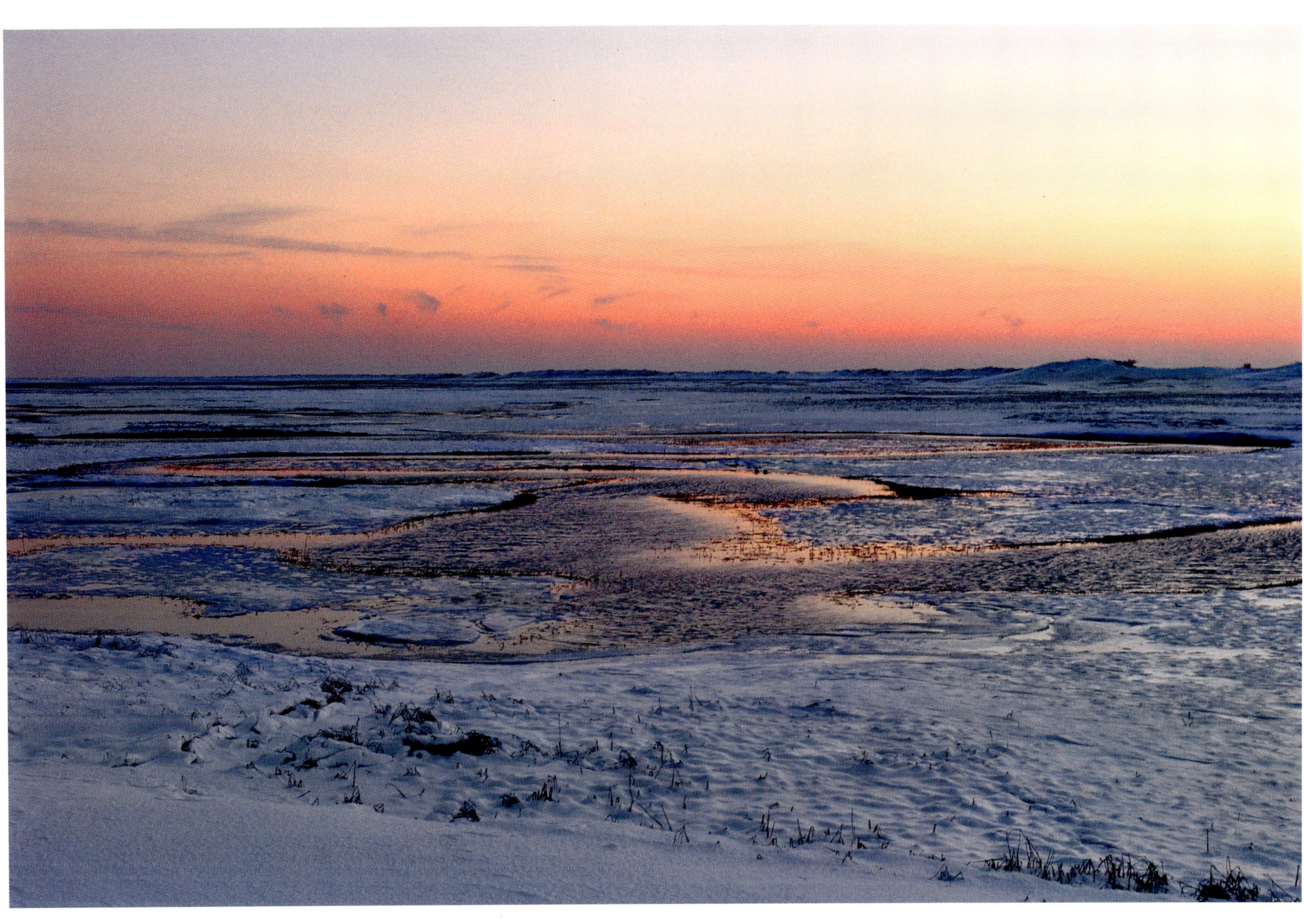

115 **Winterscape, the Moors, Provincetown**

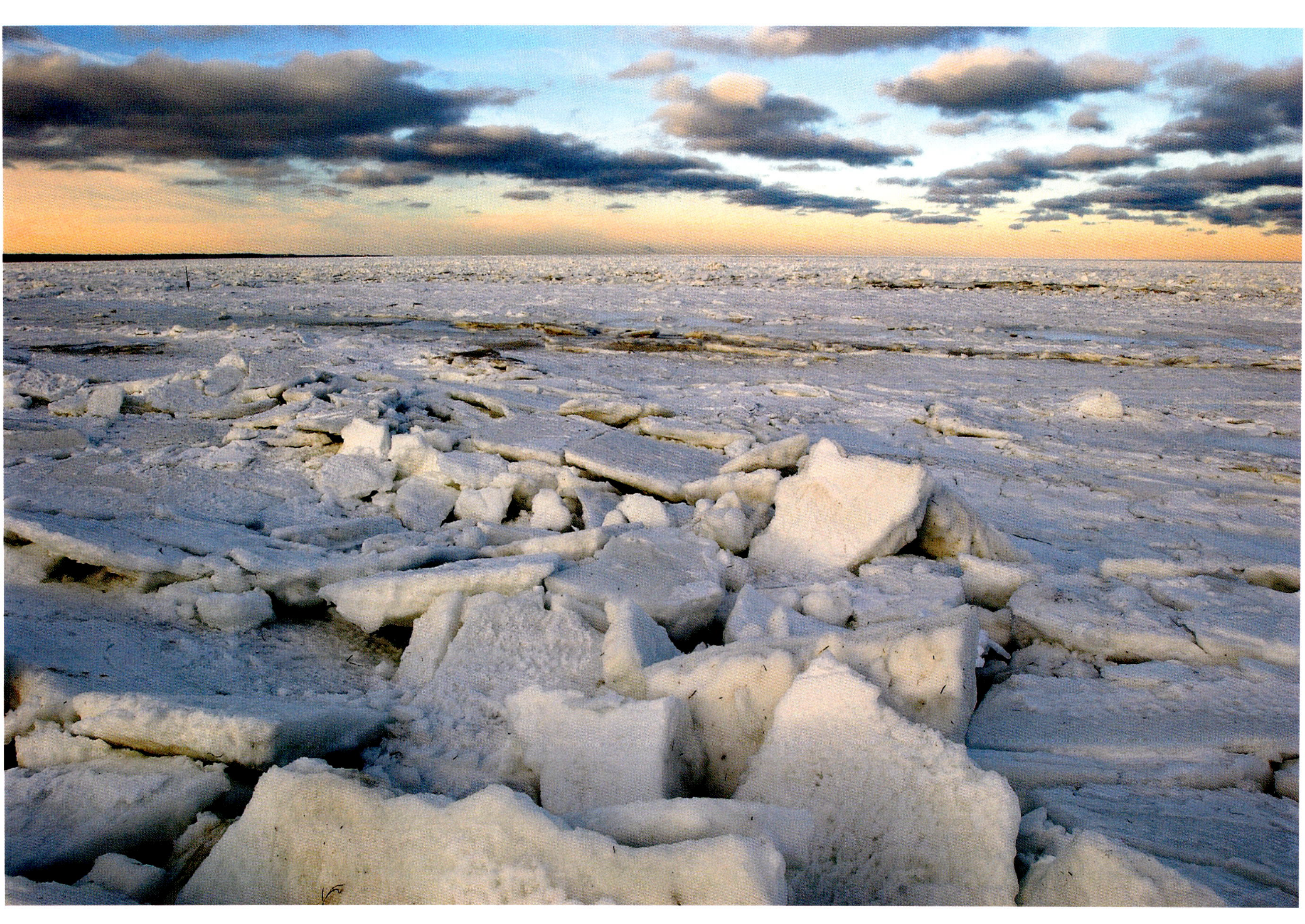

Rock Harbor, Orleans

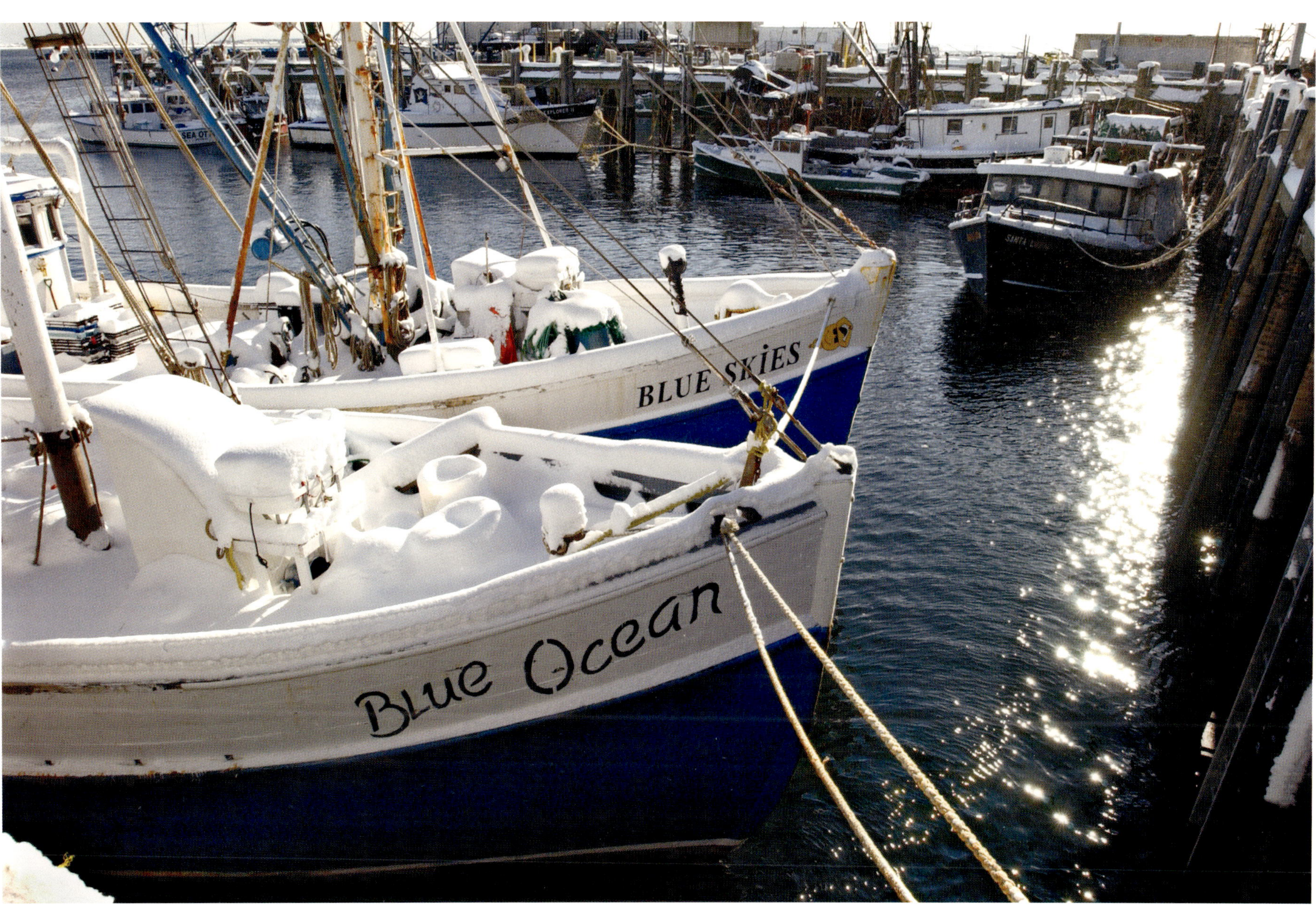

117 MacMillan Wharf, Provincetown

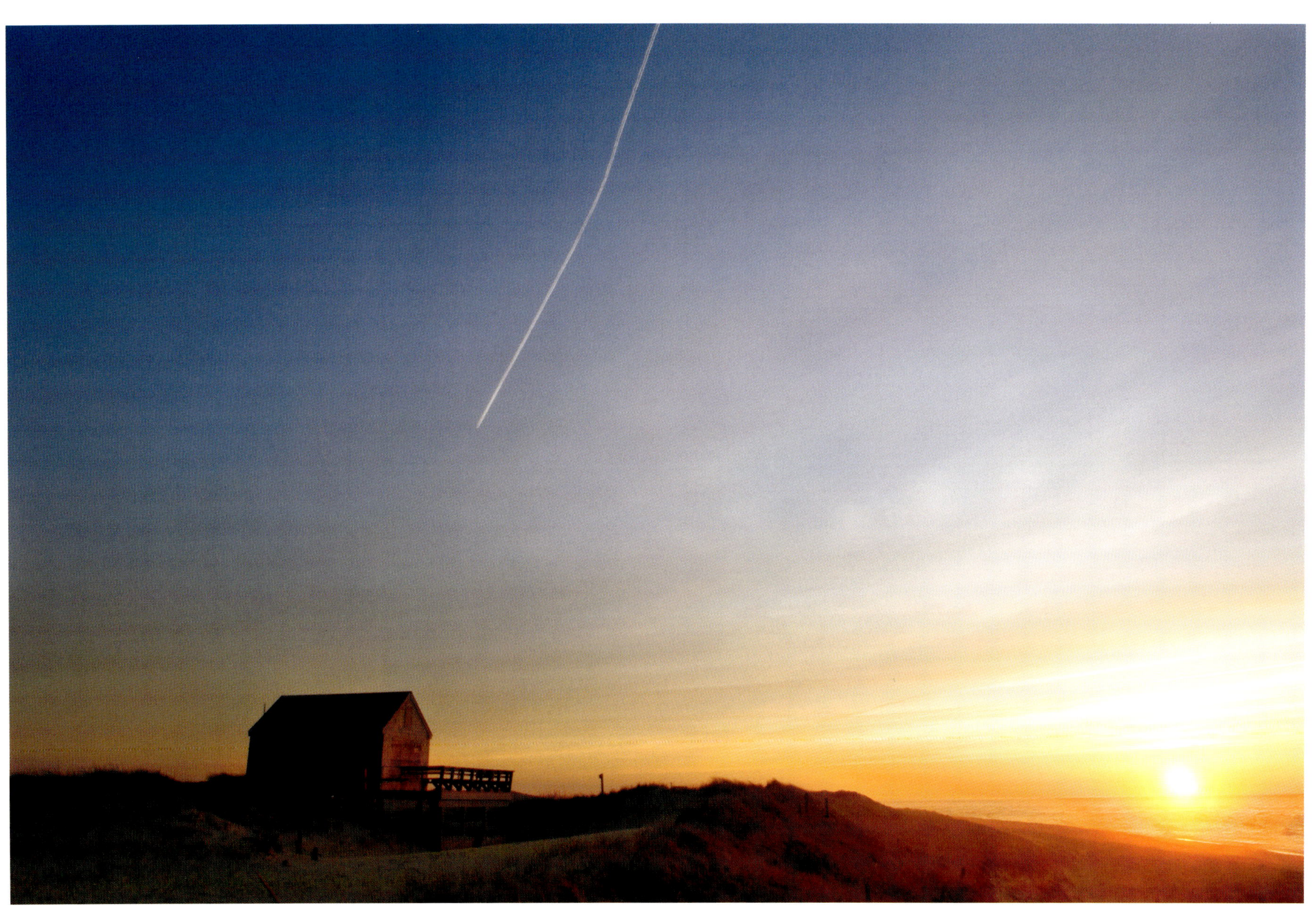

Dune Shack, Provincetown

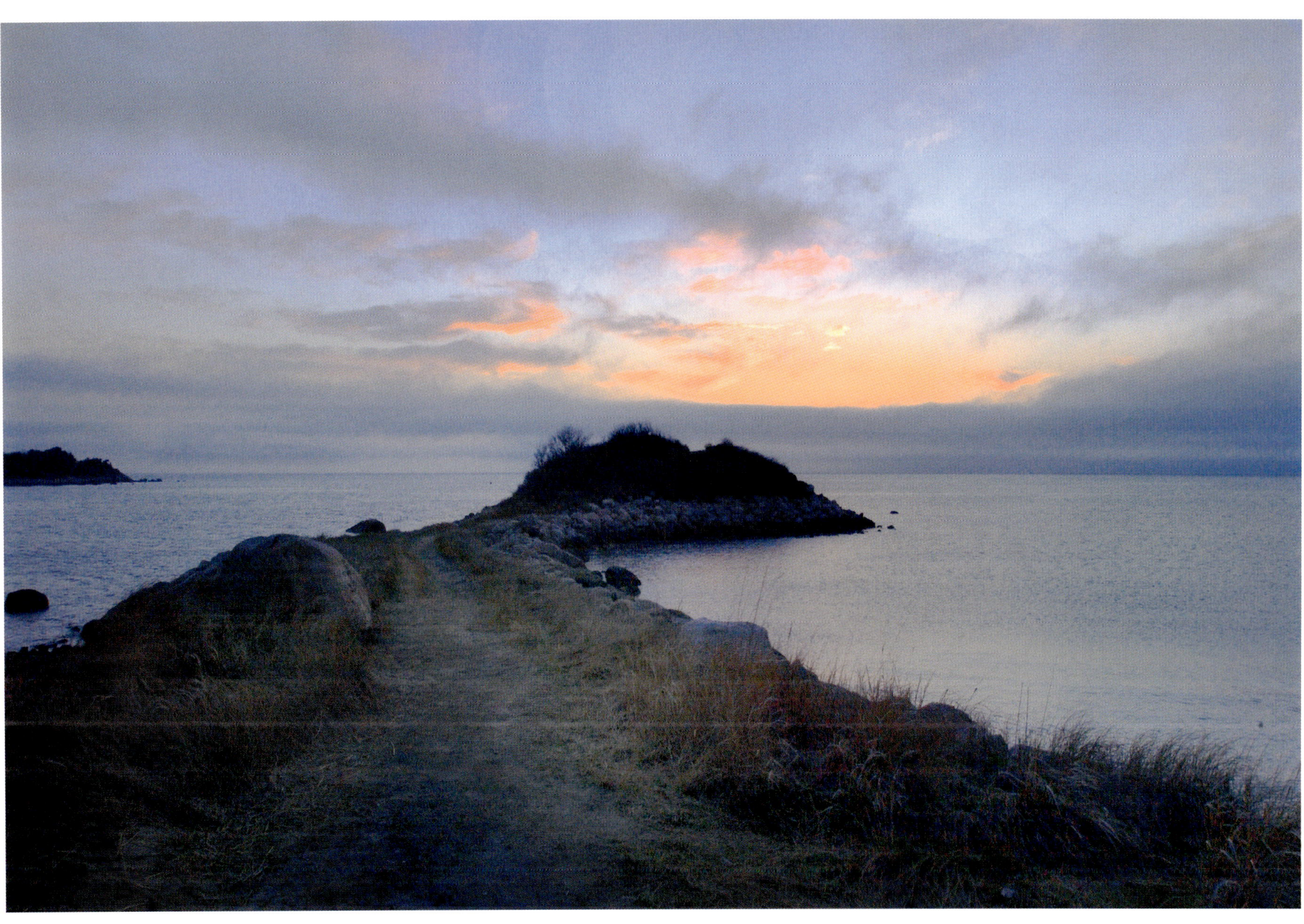

 The Knob, Quissett Harbor, Falmouth

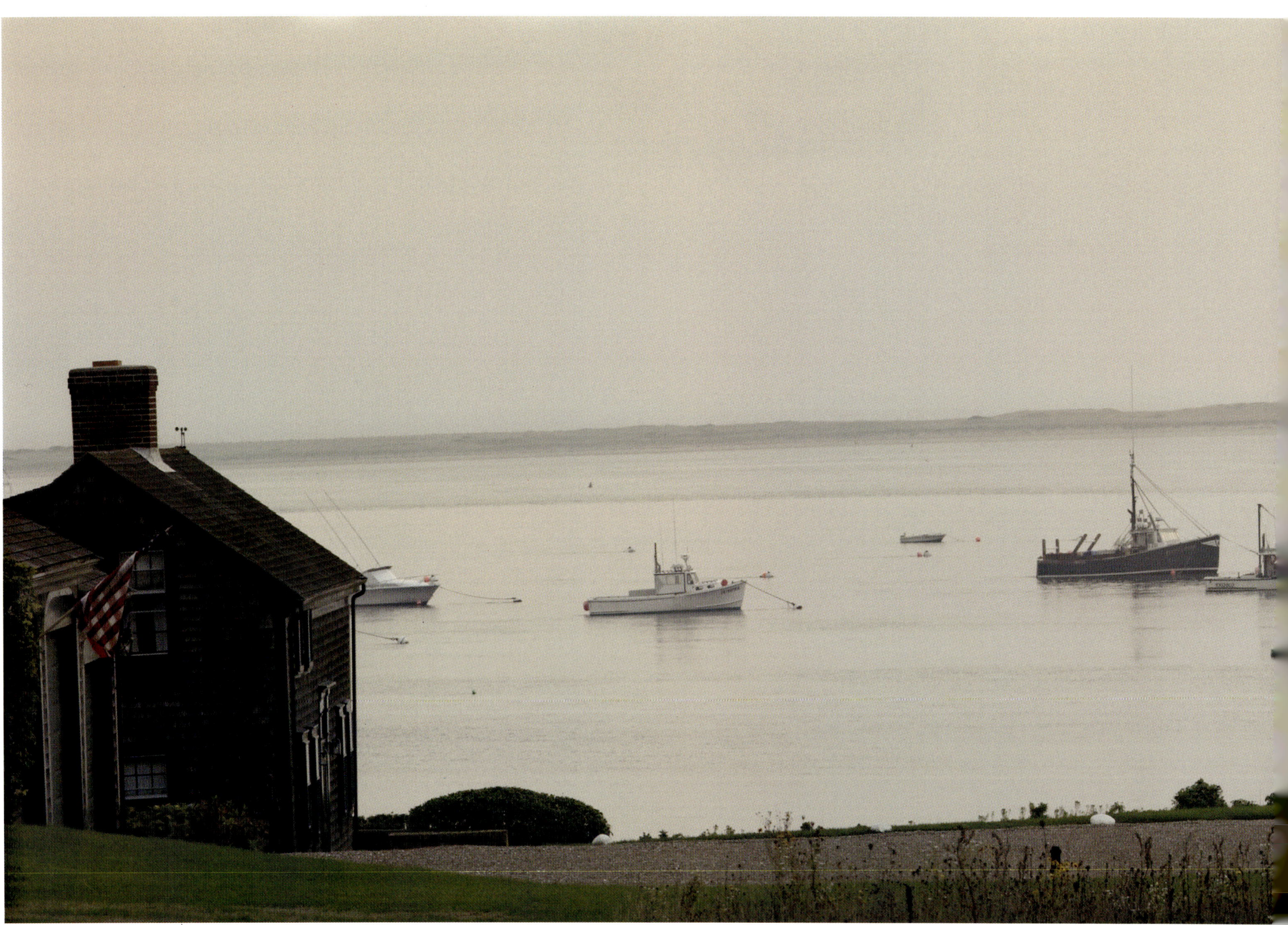

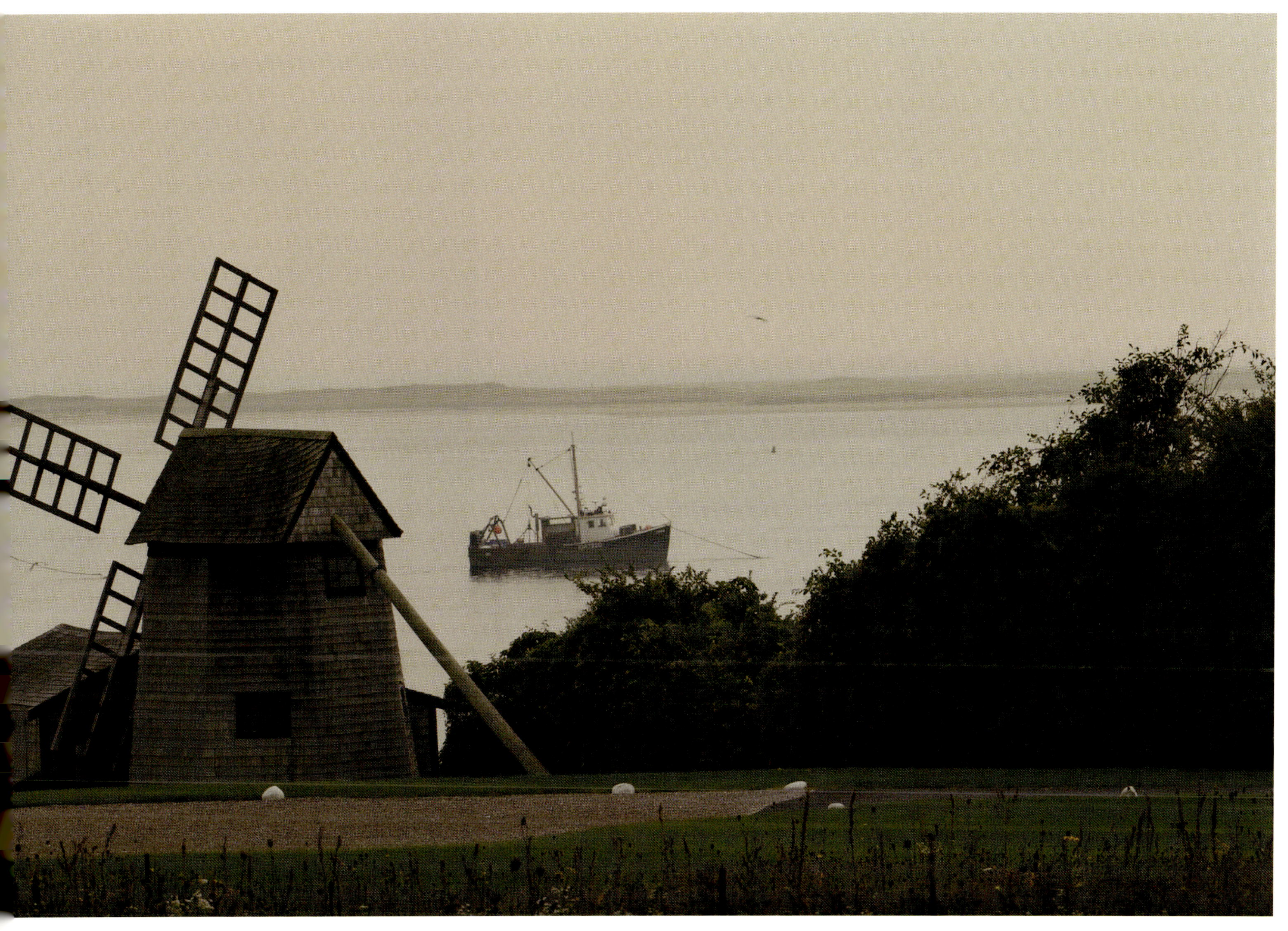

Chatham Harbor

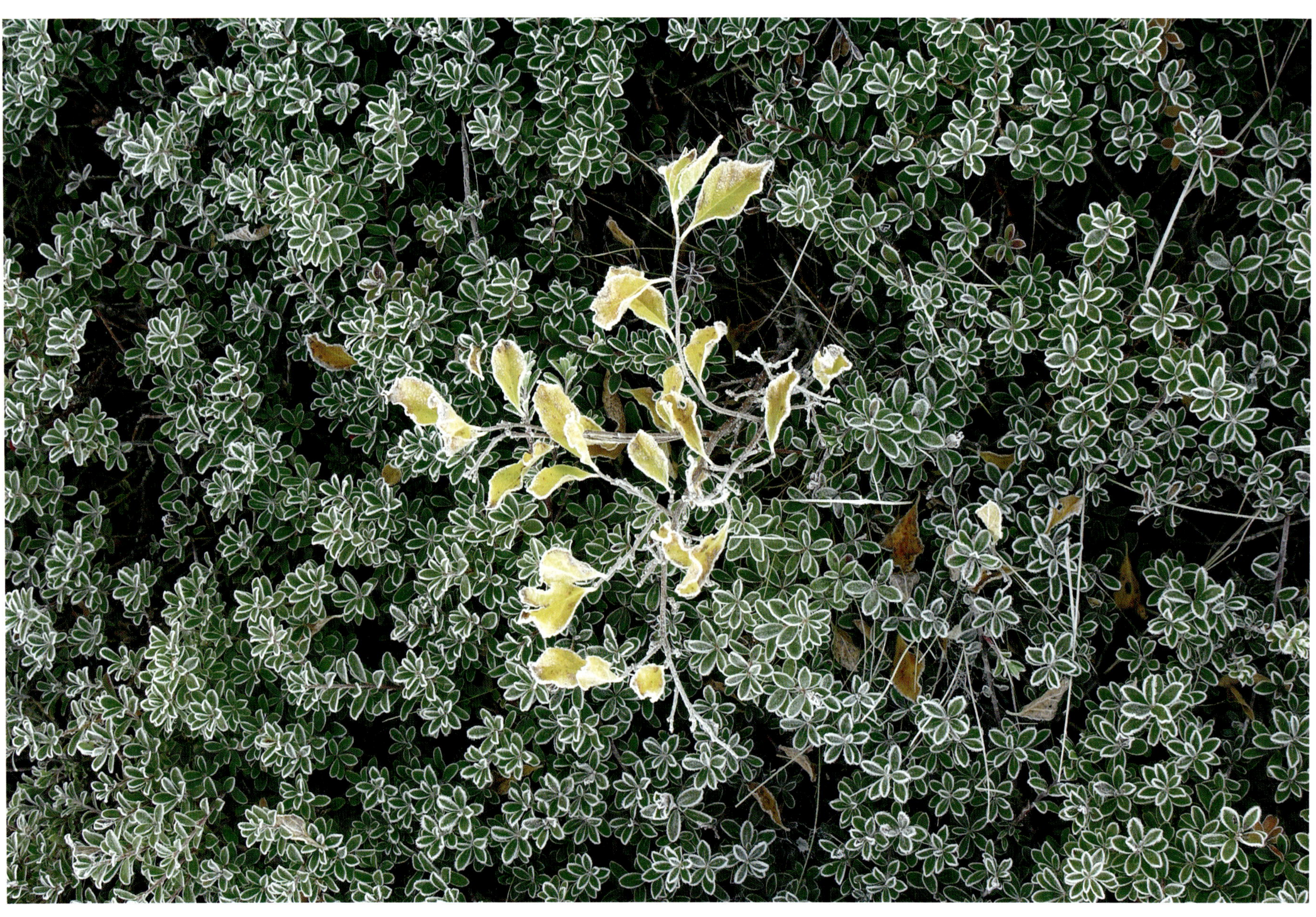

Early Autumn Frost, Wellfleet

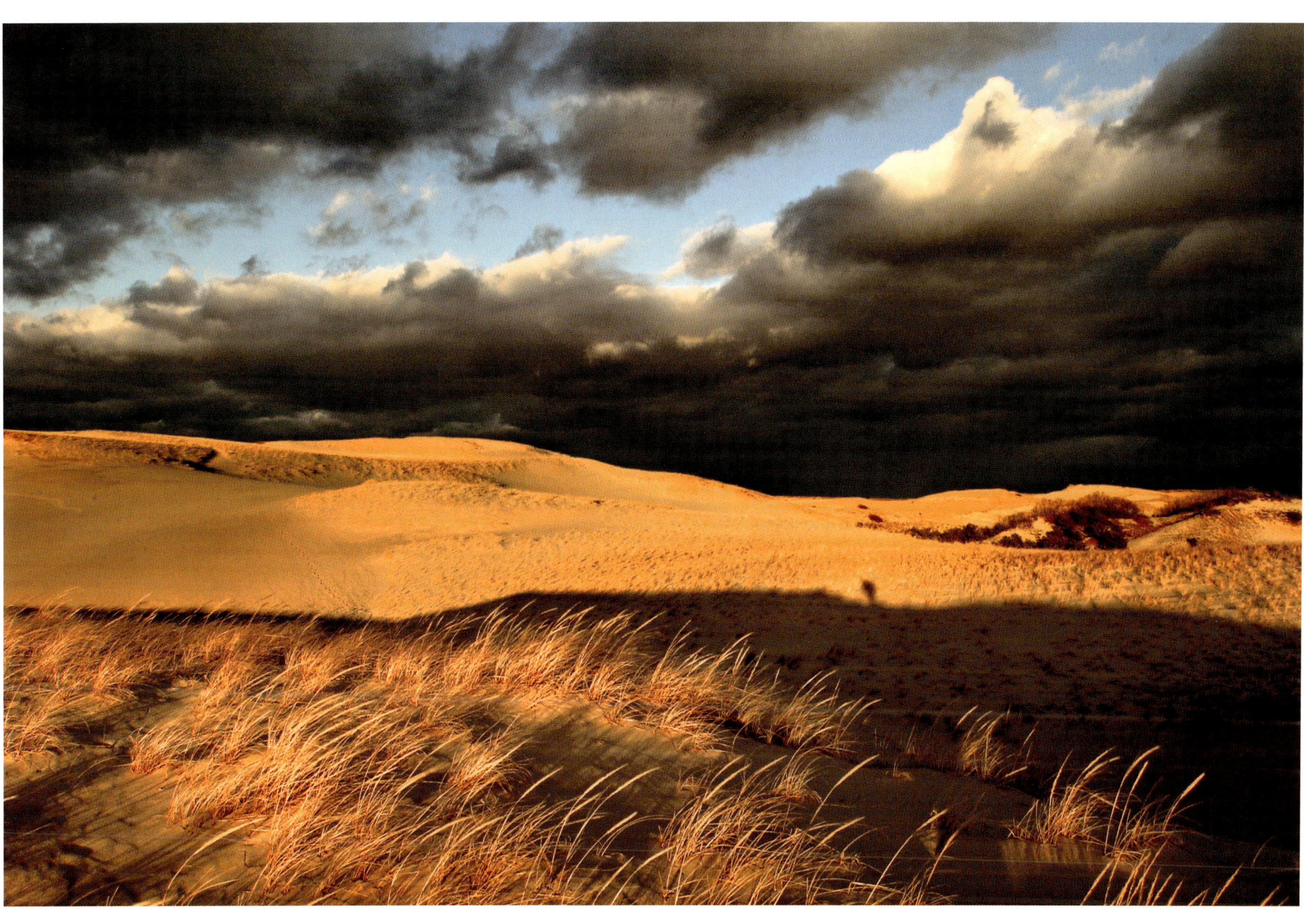

 Storm Clearing, Provincetown

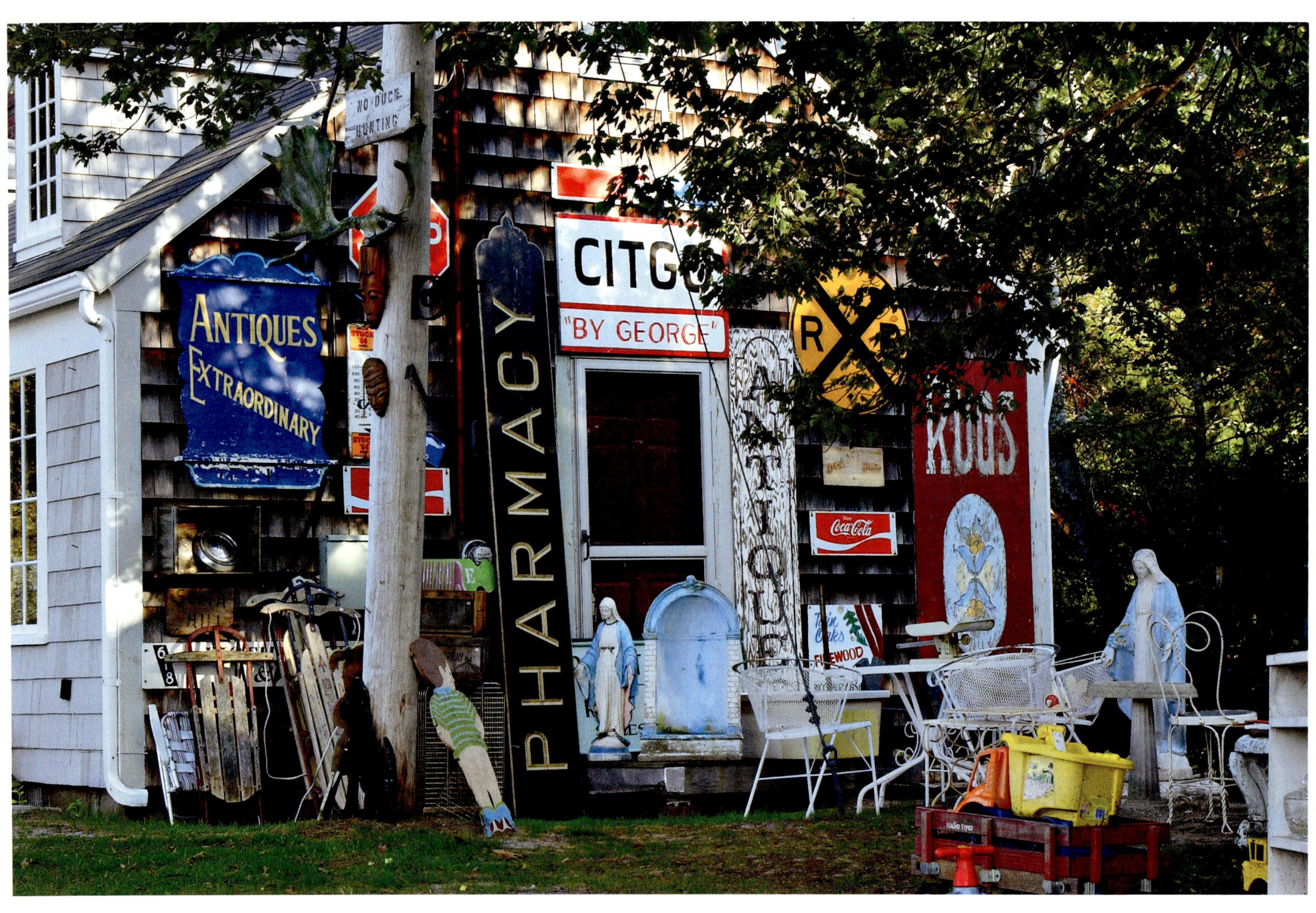

Antique Store, Route 28, Dennis

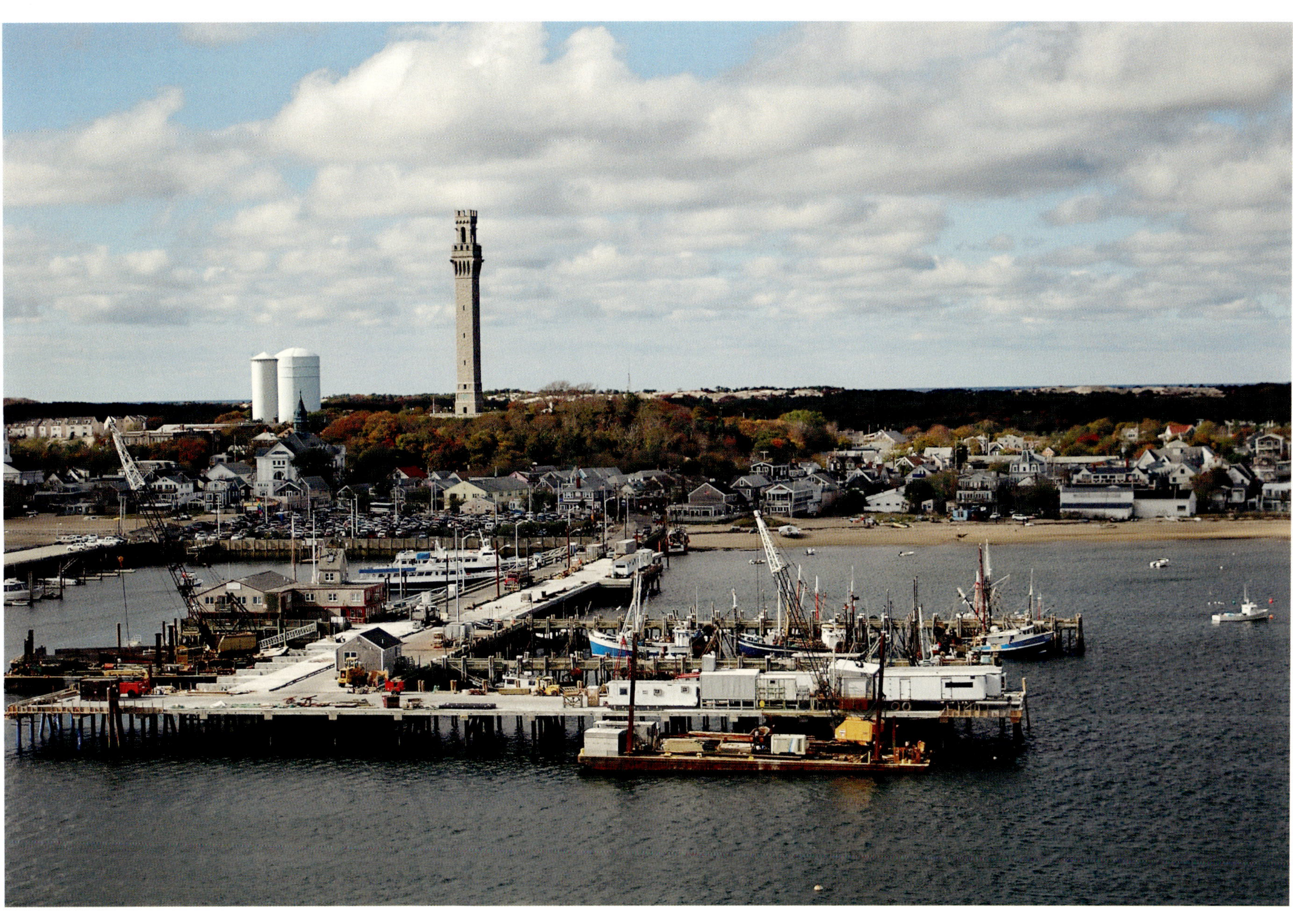

 MacMillan Wharf, Provincetown

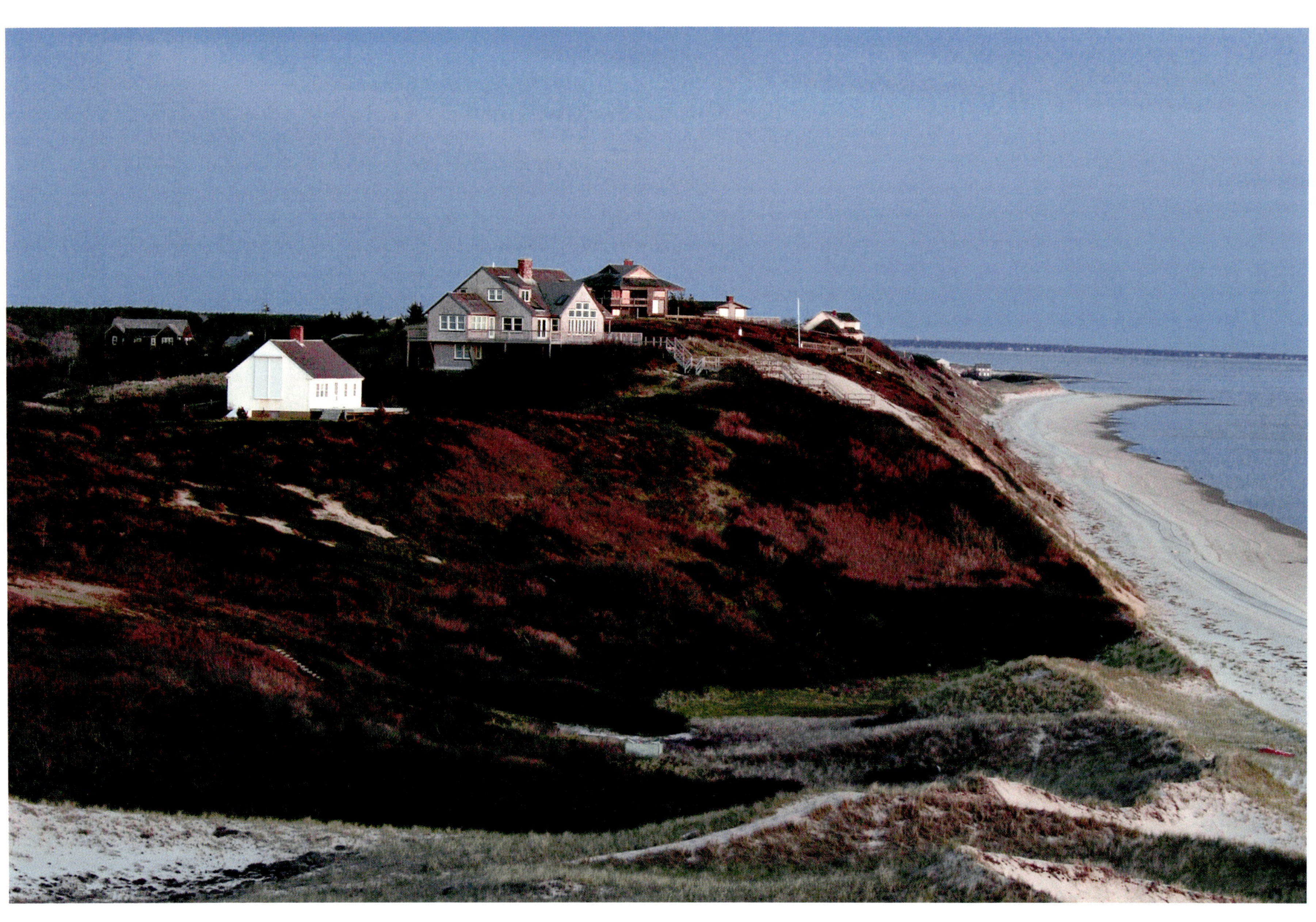

Artist Edward Hopper's Studio, Truro

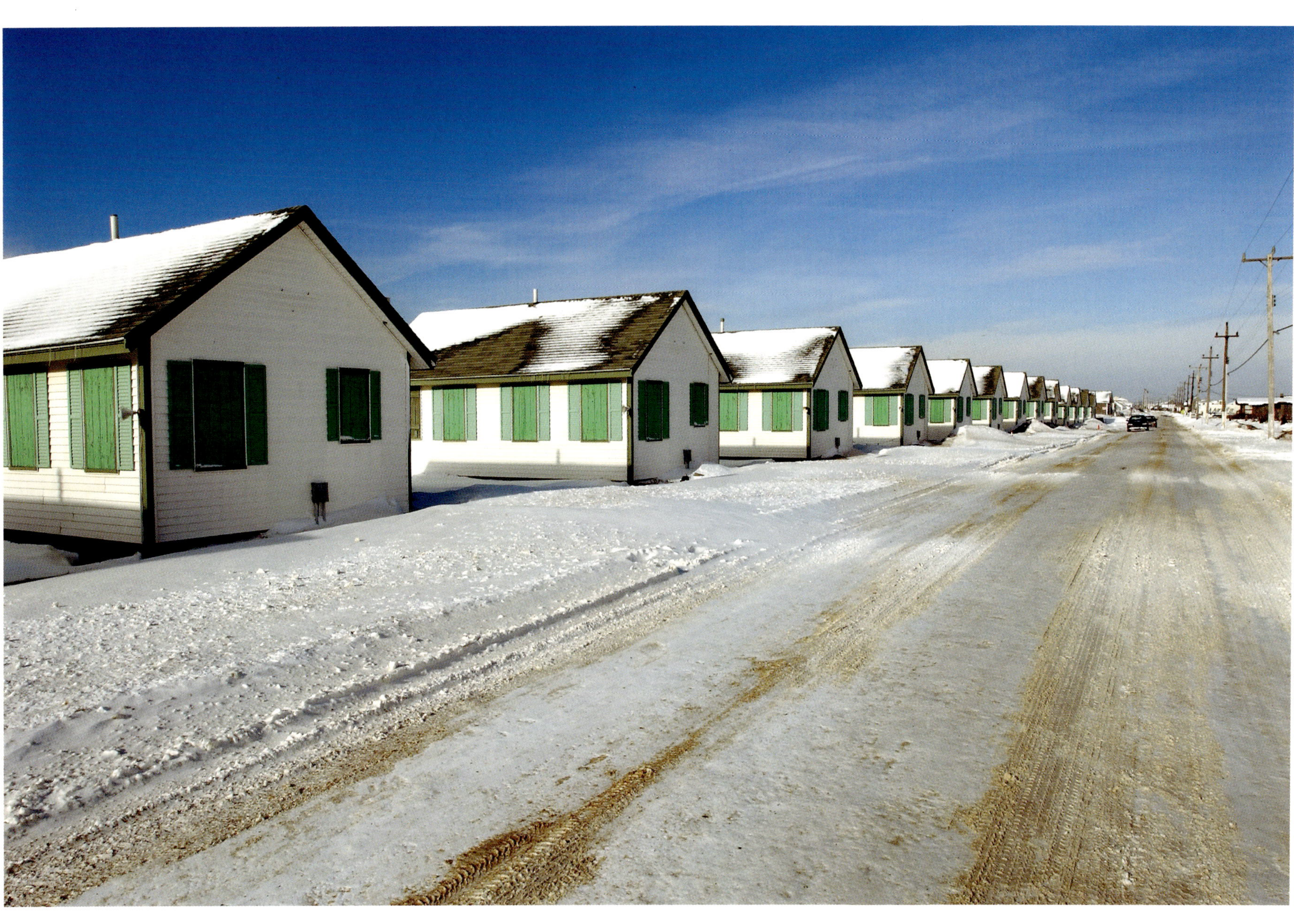

 Bayside Cottages, Truro

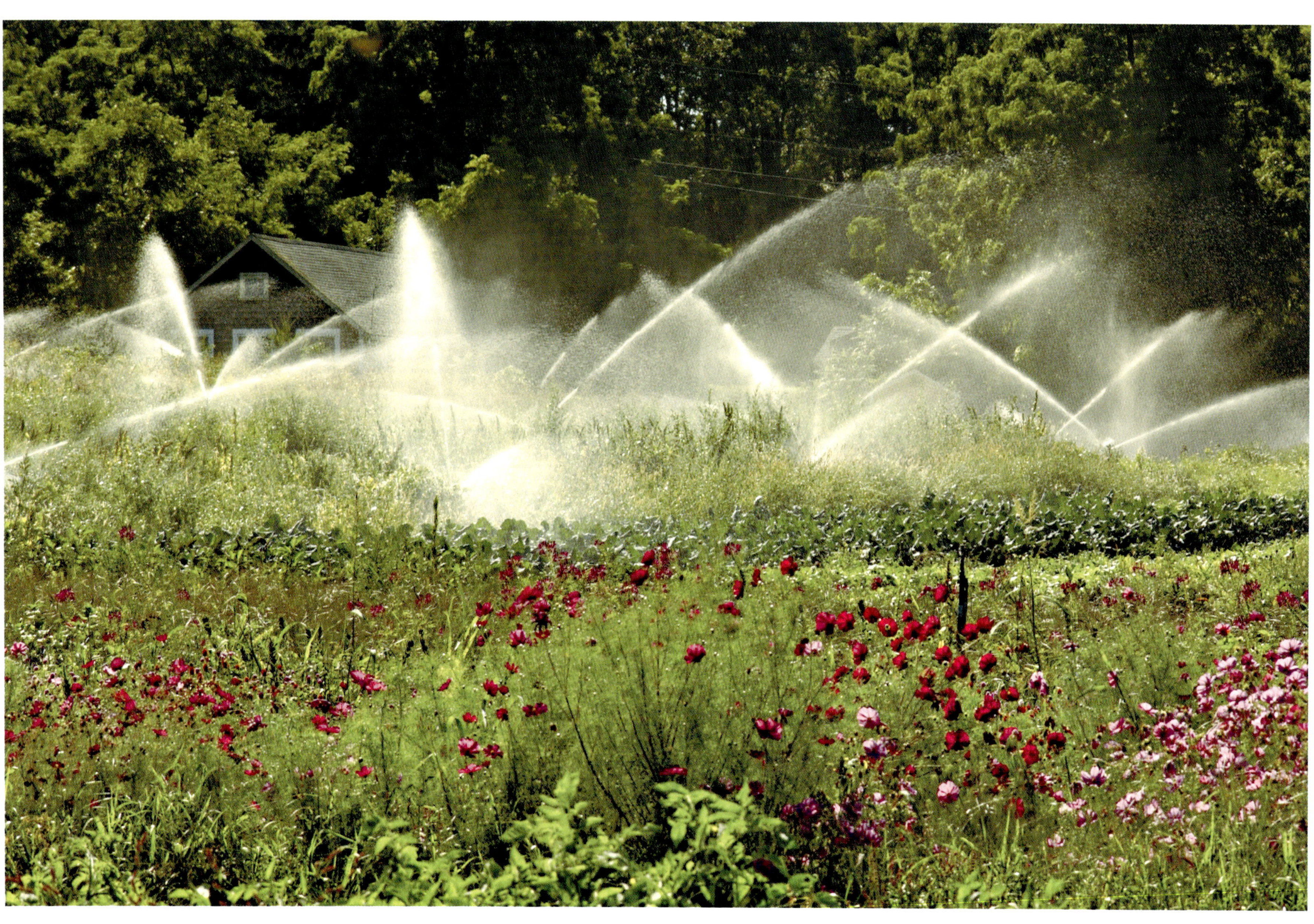

Crow Farm, Sandwich

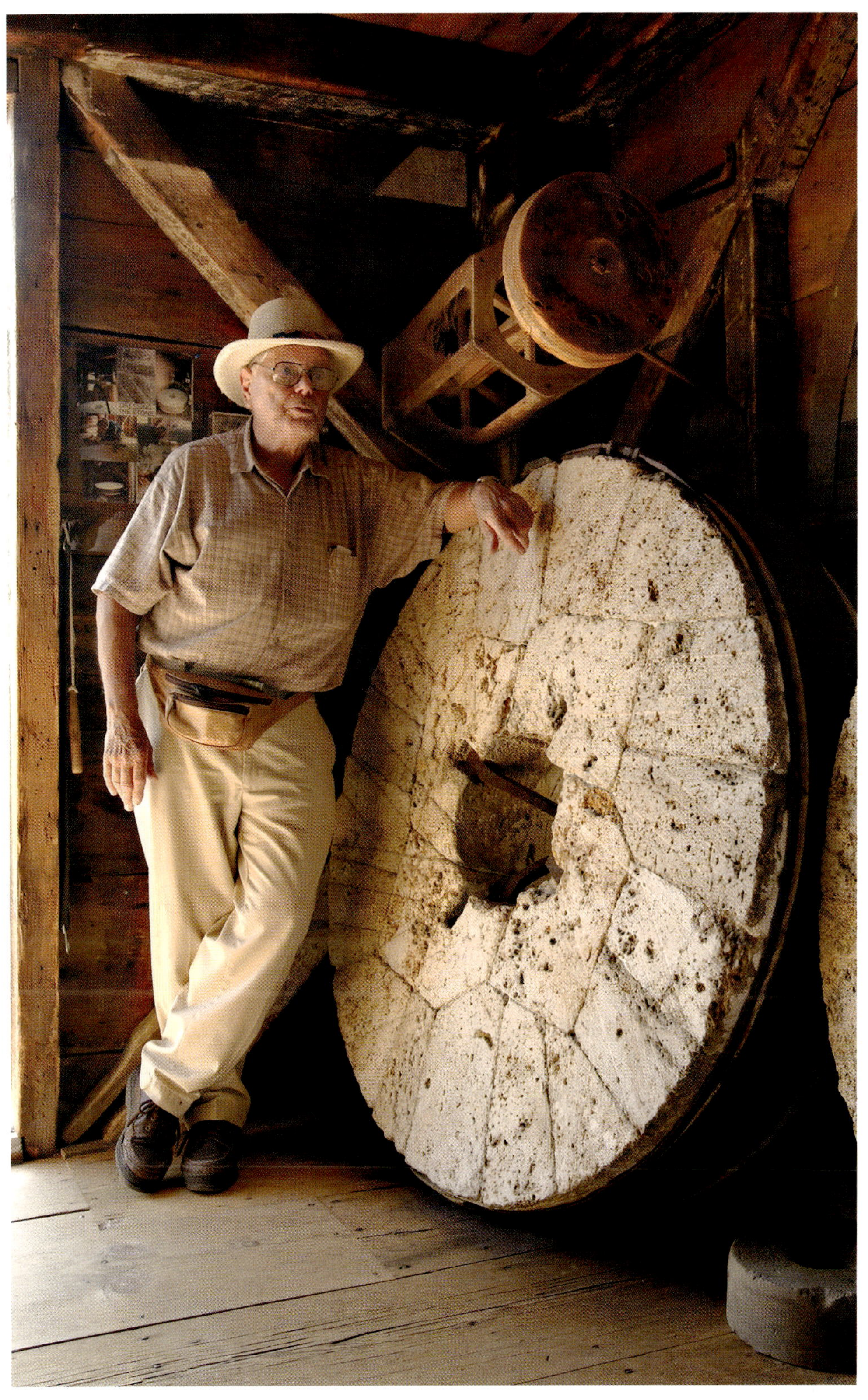

 Dexter Grist Mill, Sandwich

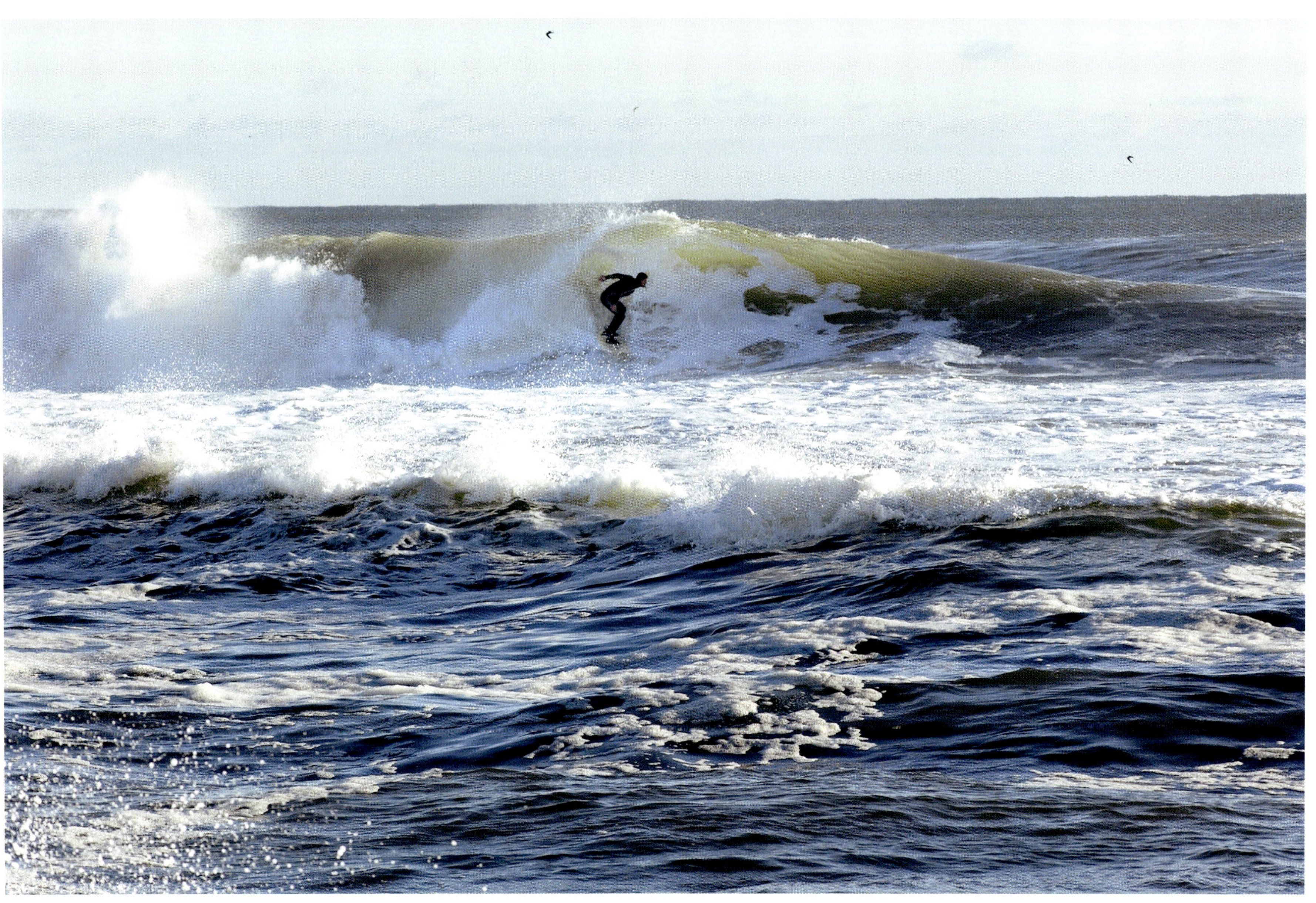

Surfing at Coast Guard Beach, Eastham

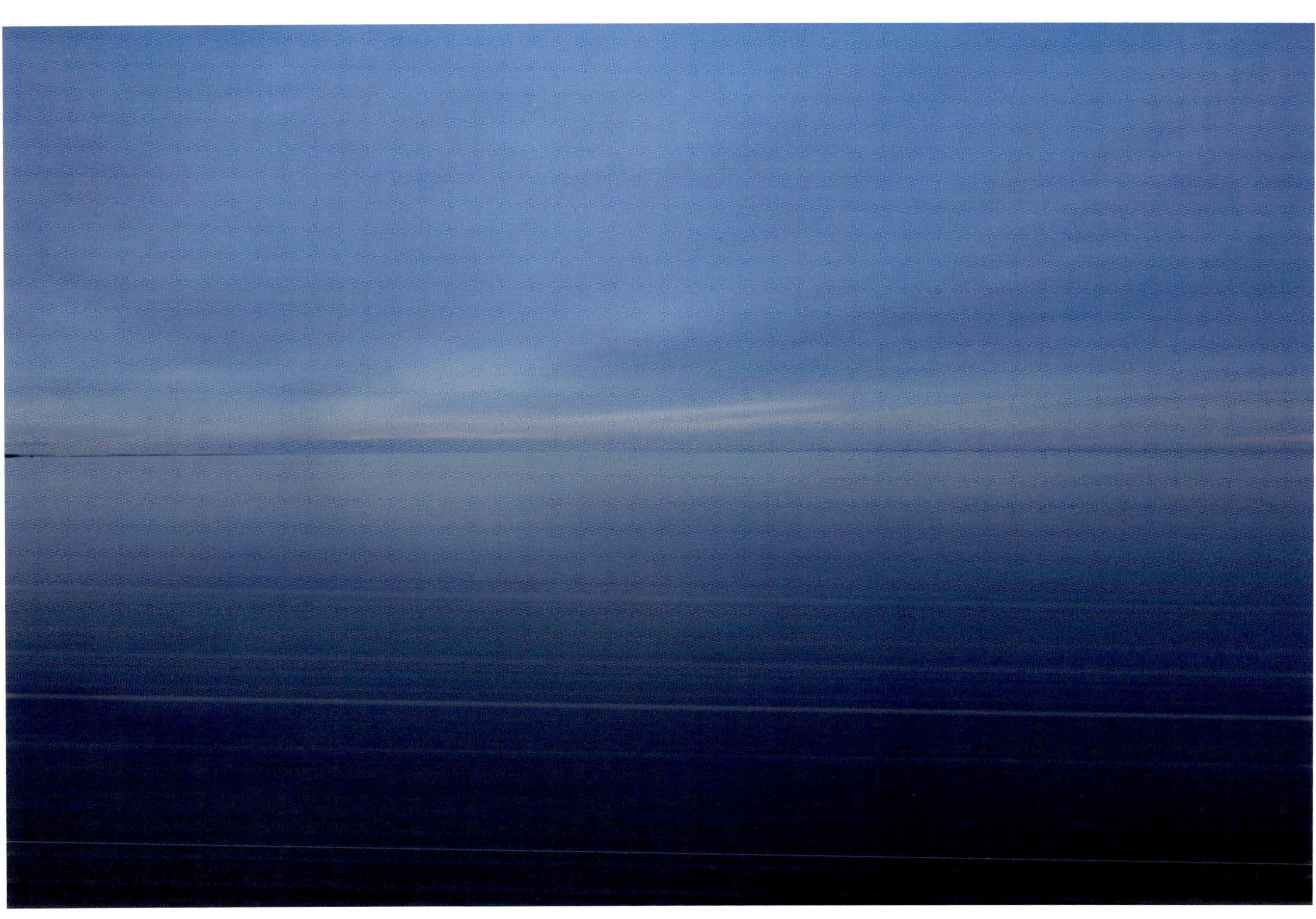

131 **Cape Cod Bay, View from Ocean Edge Resort and Golf Club, Brewster**

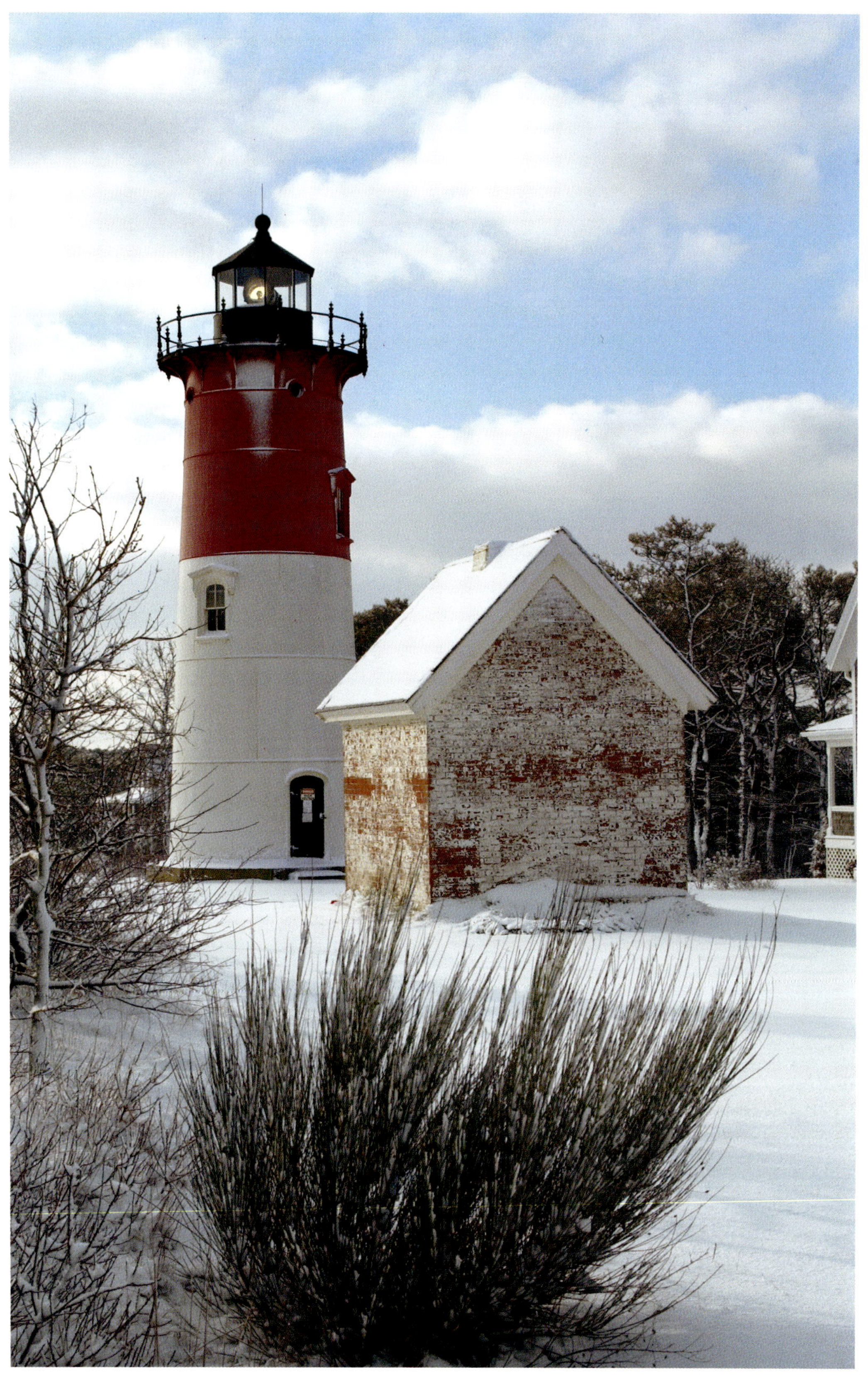

Nauset Light, Nauset Light Beach, Eastham

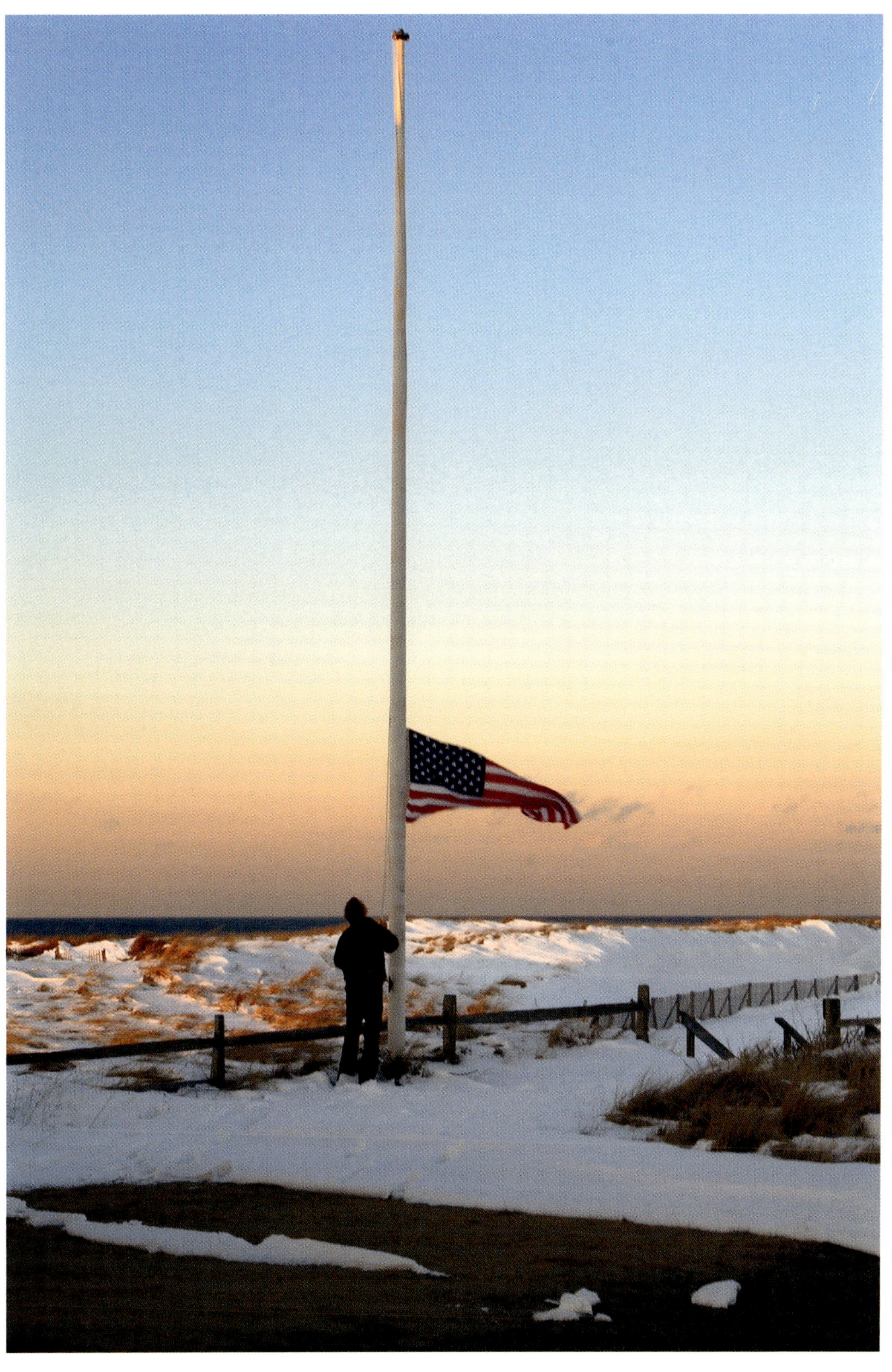

133 **Lowering flag, Race Point Ranger Station, Provincetown**

PHOTOGRAPHIC CAPTIONS

Cover: **Days' Cottages, Cape Cod Bay, North Truro**
This photograph epitomizes what people "feel" about Cape Cod—the freedom of taking flight on the water, a rosy sunrise on Cape Cod Bay, Days' Cottages snuggled alongside Route 6A in North Truro and a SUV ready to take on the mighty dunes and back roads of Cape Cod National Seashore. Taken all together, this image is a montage of the ultimate Cape Cod experience and conveys a feeling of ultimate freedom and serenity…the boat and SUV stand in readiness for the promise of a new day.

2-3 **Coast Guard Beach, Truro**
Truro's Coast Guard Beach—also known as Pamet Beach—sits on the ocean side at the end of Cost Guard Road and should not be confused with Eastham's Coast Guard Beach. This magnificent dramatic vista, perfectly captured by the photographer at sunset, conveys the drama and power of the Atlantic juxtaposed against gentle pink of the setting sun.

8 **Days' Cottages, Cape Cod Bay, North Truro**
See caption for Cover above

11 **Race Point Light, Provincetown**
The first lighthouse at Race Point was built in 1816 and was torn down in 1876 and its height doubled to 42 feet. Today, it is painted white and runs on solar power. The keeper's house, also built in 1876, still stands and a fog horn still operates from Race Point. Access to Race Point Light is only by 4-wheel drive vehicles traveling across the dunes of the Cape Cod National Seashore or on foot.

12 **Great Atlantic Cedar Swamp, Eastham**
Begins at Marconi Wireless Site and runs 1.25 miles through a glacier-formed swamp shaded by white cedar and pine. The inner portion of this trail provides a half-mile of level duckboard boardwalk through the heart of the breathtaking Atlantic Cedar Swamp.

15 **Cranberry Harvest, Abstract**
The cranberry is a native American wetland fruit which grows on trailing vines like a strawberry. Harvested from mid-September through early November, bogs are flooded with up to a foot of water and using a water reel to free the berries from vines. Berries are corralled and removed from bogs by pumps or conveyors; more than 85% of cranberries are wet harvested.

16 **Water Lilies, Kettle Pond, Truro**
The freshwater kettle depressions of Cape Cod National Seashore, also known as kettle ponds, provide important habitat for a great variety of wetland and aquatic plants, amphibians, and aquatic invertebrates. Some of these biological communities, including the shoreline flora of coastal kettle ponds and amphibians of vernal pools, are particularly dependent on seasonal fluctuations in the groundwater table for maintaining habitat characteristics. Increasing human demand for potable water supplies is placing pressure on aquifers throughout Cape Cod, and this pressure is increasing on the Outer Cape, including the land within the Seashore.

17 **Gulls in Flight, Paine's Creek, Brewster**
Inlets and coves cut into the wide beach on this shoreline. Paine's Creek is the home to some interesting wildlife including rare birds and horseshoe crabs.

18-19 **Dunes, Province Lands, Provincetown**
The spectacular ethereal dune landscape of Provincetown has a complex history, primarily resulting from deposition of sand washed from the eroded glacial scarp and built into giant undulating dunes by wind action and stabilized by beach grass.

20 **WWI Statute, Provincetown**
On the corner of Ryder and Commercial Streets is the World War I Memorial. On the top is a life-size bronze statue of a doughboy. On plaques on the sides of the monument are the names of all Provincetown World War I veterans.

21 **Patriot, Mercy Otis Warren (1728-1814) Barnstable Superior Courthouse, Barnstable**
More than two centuries ago, Abigail Adams implored her husband John Adams during the formation of the new American government, to "remember the Ladies." The "first lady of the Revolution" had satirized British occupation of Boston and assisted Sam Adams organize the 'Committees of Correspondence.' On July 5, 2001, a bronze statue of the native playwright and polemicist was unveiled before a giant American flag in front of the Superior Courthouse in Barnstable Village, accompanied by young Hailey Harris' wailing bagpipes and a drum roll by Ann Duffie Fleck, a high official of the Daughters of the American Revolution, in full Revolutionary regalia. The statue was created by David Lewis.

22 **Moon Rising Over Pilgrim Monument, Provincetown**
The 252-foot granite Monument, modeled after the larger Torre del Mangia bell tower in Siena, Italy, is the tallest all-granite structure in America. It commemorates the Pilgrim's first landing in the New World at Provincetown. The entire structure was built of granite blocks from Stonington, Maine. President Theodore Roosevelt attended the laying of the cornerstone in 1907 and President William Howard Taft dedicated the structure on August 5, 1910. It remains one of the most impressive public monuments in the United States.

23 **Highland Light, North Truro**
Also known as Cape Cod Light, at 620,000 candlepower, it is New England's most powerful. Ships from 30 miles at sea can see its welcoming beacon. In 1797, George Washington ordered construction of this wooden lighthouse to watch over shoals which became known as 'the ship graveyard.' This was Cape Cod's first lighthouse. The Light was rebuilt in 1857 with the same 66-foot tower which is still in place today, although in a slightly different spot from where it first stood. A major project during 1996 and part of 1997 moved the brick lighthouse some 600 feet back from the eroding sand cliffs which are slowly being worn away by the turbulent winter surf. The wooden light keeper's house was also relocated and rejoined to the lighthouse. Cape Cod Light now sits between the seventh and eighth fairways of the Highland Links, one of America's ten oldest golf courses. Cape Cod Light is usually the first American lighthouse to be seen by ships crossing the Atlantic and headed for Boston.

24-25 **Bass River, Dennis**
Bass River, a large tidal estuary, is located in central Cape Cod and runs south from Route 6 to the waters of Nantucket Sound at the Cape's south side. It is the boundary between West Dennis to the east and South Yarmouth to the west.

26 **Laughing Gull**
Larus atricilla. A small coastal 15"-17" gull with a dark mantle blending into black wing tips with a white edge on rear of wing. Its voice sounds like human laughter. Its flying range includes the coasts from Nova Scotia to Venezuela. Winters in the southern of US and its habitat includes salt marshes and lakes; in winter, coasts and the ocean.

27 **Laughing Gull in Flight**
Larus atricilla. See caption for page 26 above.

28 **Hatches Harbor, Provincetown**
Remote and unspoiled, the Harbor makes a scenic anchorage for swimming and sunbathing, often right alongside the seals who congregate nearby.

29 **Piping Plover, Provincetown**
Charadrius melodus. The Piping Plover is a small attractive bird habituating lakeshores, river sand bars, and ocean coasts. It nests on sandy or gravelly beaches and feeds at the water's edge. Unlike most shorebirds, which journey to remote arctic and subarctic areas to breed and then may winter as far afield as South America, the Piping Plover breeds and winters primarily in the temperate regions of North America, where much of the habitat that meets its very specific needs is being put to human uses. The pale gray upper parts distinguish the Piping Plover from all other small plovers except the Snowy Plover. The Snowy Plover has a different face pattern in alternate plumage and dark legs and a longer, thinner bill in basic and juvenile plumages.

30 **Race Point Light, Provincetown**
See caption for page 11.

31 **Stony Brook Herring Run, Brewster**
This is where thousands of alewives swim upstream to spawn in freshwater ponds every spring. With the return of these determined herring—which swim and jump up the run against currents to the ponds of their birth to spawn—returns the mystery and awe that this vernal ritual evokes.

32 **Windmill, Orleans**
The Jonathan Young Windmill was returned to Orleans ownership in 1983, after having first been built in the town about 1720. It was moved to Hyannisport in 1897, then given by the Groves family to the Orleans Historical Society in 1983, which donated it to the town of Orleans. The final move brought it back to Town Cove Park, where it now stands.

33 **Old Wireless Road, Marconi Station, Wellfleet**
One can reach Old Wireless Road at a northern "exit" off Atlantic White Cedar Trail in South Wellfleet at a triangle of roads. Despite being part of the Cape Cod National Seashore, this Trail is quiet, particularly at year's end. With its elevated boardwalk, feet remain dry all year. The Trail starts at

the parking lot on the Old Wireless Road near the Marconi Station Site, and do not miss the breath-taking ocean view along the 1.25-mile route.

34-35 Salt Marsh View from National Seashore Visitors Center, Eastham

One-mile trail along Salt Pond and Nauset Marsh and through field and recovering forest offers spectacular vistas. Like all salt marshes, Nauset Marsh provides a fragile link between the land and sea: incoming tides flood the marsh, sweeping in organisms, depositing them on the marsh edges. These, coupled with the marsh's abundant plant life, provide food for the many marine creatures that use the shallow, protected salt marsh as a nursery. The Nauset Marsh Trail is an easy loop walk that skirts the edge of Salt Pond, winds up a hill for a sweeping view of Nauset Marsh, and ends in woodlands. Interpretive markers along the way identify pitch pine, black cherry, eastern red cedar, beach plum, salt-spray rose, and numerous other trailside flora.

36 Corn Hill Beach, Truro

The long, narrow sand beach borders the low running, crab grass covered sand dunes just north of Pamet Harbor. The shallow, sloping ocean floor and typically calm, warmer waters provide the ideal environment for families. Wade along warm ocean inlets which flow behind the beach for a more secluded change of pace. Corn Hill, the historic location where the Pilgrims found a cache of Indian corn, which fed them through their first winter, is also nearby. This is the only bay-side Truro town beach which is open to the public for a daily parking fee.

37 View from East End, Provincetown

Provincetown's "East End" is the place for art galleries and waterfront eating establishments. It also offers incredible vistas of the Pilgrim Monument and the curling fist containing almost all of Provincetown, all the way to Race Point.

38 First Congregational Church, Falmouth

The congregation's Reformed Protestant heritage was brought to these shores by Mayflower Pilgrims and the Puritans of old Massachusetts Bay Colony. The congregation dates to 1687 when newly chartered Falmouth set aside land for a Congregational minister. Members are worshipping in their fifth meetinghouse, whose frame and Paul Revere Bell were moved off the Village Green to its present location in 1857. The Rev. William Bates became minister in 1858, but died the following year just after the birth of his daughter, Katharine Lee. She lived in the parsonage at 16 Main Street, until the family moved to Wellesley Hills. Miss Bates' famous poem, "America the Beautiful," was first published in "The Congregationalist." The Old First Church, including its two additions, still stands as an eloquent witness to the spirit of Congregationalism. Its slender and graceful spire points faithfully Heavenward, a delight to the eye and an inspiration to the soul.

39 First Congregational Church of Yarmouth

Sitting on top of Zion Hill overlooking Cape Cod Bay sits the present Church built in 1870 at a cost of $18,500. The original church, on a different location, was outgrown and replaced by a Church at this location in 1716 at a cost of 400 pounds. A stove was installed in 1727 and parishioners were expected to provide the firewood. If they wanted to sit down, they were also expected to build their own pews! The tall spire became a landmark for the maritime industry and has had to be rebuilt several times after being toppled by hurricanes!

40-41 Sunrise, Chatham

At the confluence of Nantucket Sound and the Atlantic Ocean, Chatham is at once surrounded and defined by the sea. Explorer Samuel de Champlain anchored in Stage Harbor in 1606, before there were any permanent English settlements on Cape Cod, naming the harbor Point Fortune. First named Monomoyick after an indigenous Native American tribe, Chatham was subsequently—and rather poetically—christened "first stop of the east wind." Whether this is true or not is a matter for conjecture by meteorological experts, but, from a marketing and imagery standpoint, the phrase works.

42 Wellfleet Harbor Actors Theater Box Office (WHAT), Wellfleet

Presents some of the most provocative contemporary work on the Cape—perfect fare for the very cerebral types who are drawn here. Founded in 1985 by Jeff Zinn and Gip Hoppe, WHAT features a repertoire of six plays per summer and usually includes some original works, but always includes avant garde selections. Considered one of the top ten regional theaters.

43 Rock Harbor, Orleans

Located on Cape Cod Bay, two miles from the town center at the end of Rock Harbor Road, this is among the most beautiful of all New England harbors. It also happens to be home to Cape Cod's largest (and salty old Orleans fishermen say, the best) charter fishing fleet.

44 Sandy Neck Light, Barnstable

Sandy Neck Light was first established in 1826 when it was built on Sandy Neck spit, a barrier beach that separates Barnstable Harbor from Cape Cod Bay. It served as a beacon for the growing harbor at Barnstable as well as for mariners in Cape Cod Bay. The original Sandy Neck Light was built with the lantern mounted on the roof of the keeper's house, as was the case with many earlier lights. The lighthouse was rebuilt in 1857 with a new separate tower and keeper's house. These both still stand today on the dunes of Sandy Neck. The tower was abandoned as a lighthouse in 1931, when the lantern was removed from the top. The property was later sold by the federal government and remains privately owned today. While no longer home to a light, the lighthouse is beautiful and worthy of a look (it is best viewed from the Harbor).

45 Sunset from the East End, Provincetown

See caption for page 37.

46 Sesuit Harbor Boat Yard, East Dennis

Sesuit Harbor in East Dennis (a marker denotes the former Shipyard's site), manufactured some of the 19th century's finest packet boats, clippers and schooners. The Shipyard, known throughout the nation, built at least eight magnificent clipper ships, all of which were recognized in the Golden Age of Sail. Of these, only one, the Ellen Sears, did not have a Dennis Captain.

47 Cormorant, Craigville Beach, Barnstable

Phalacrocorax auritus (Double-Crested Cormorant). Found all around North America and inhabit marine and inland waters. Cormorant are easily seen on rocks from Maine to Florida. These somber-looking birds have long bodies, necks and beaks with a hooked upper mandible, completely webbed feet, short legs and wedge-shaped tails. Plumage is predominantly black with a greenish or bronze sheen in both sexes. The wings are short and do not permit long flights out to sea and they can be 19-40 inches long, however, they are generally 33 inches in length.

48 Stage Harbor Light, Chatham

Built in 1880 on Harding's Beach, it has also been known as Harding's Beach Light. In 1880, a cast iron tower was constructed next to a typical light keeper's house. The light served as a beacon for Chatham's 'Old,' or Stage, Harbor. In 1933, the tower was replaced by an iron skeleton tower a short distance away. A few years later, the old tower and keeper's house were sold by the government and both remain private property, although the old lantern has been removed from the top of the tower. Admont Clark, in "Lighthouses of Cape Cod - Martha's Vineyard - Nantucket; Their History and Lore," tells several stories about this isolated lighthouse. There was a light keeper suicide in 1919, and, apparently, a hidden cache of booze during prohibition years, according to Clark.

49 Early Morning Ferry from Cape Cod to Martha's Vineyard

Year round ferry service is offered by the Steamship Authority, a quasi-governmental agency, from both Hyannis to Nantucket and Woods Hole to Martha's Vineyard. Steamships run from both ports, but the Fast Ferry, which runs from Hyannis only, is the high-speed catamaran which services Nantucket year-round with one hour passage from Hyannis only. Service from both ports is offered on a regular schedule all day long.

50 Long Point Light Dwarfs Pilgrim Monument, Provincetown

Long Point Light, established in 1827 as a sentinel for Provincetown Harbor, is located on a sandy spit of sand dune sweeping around the outer edge of Provincetown where land dissolves into sea. That first Light was described as a stationary light atop of the original keeper's house; it was 28 feet high and was visible for 13 miles. Long Point is a sandy protection for one of the finest harbors on the Massachusetts coast, with the lighthouse acting as the harbor's official greeter. Looking at the picturesque dunes today, it is hard to imagine that a thriving village was once located on Long Point during the 19th century. All that remains today is the lighthouse, and its oil and keeper's houses; all the other buildings are long gone.

51 Sagamore Bridge at Sunset, Sagamore

During the Great Depression, the National Industrial Recovery Act of 1933 provided $4.6 million to build the present three bridges, employing some 700 workers for two years. These modern bridges were completed in 1935. The Bourne and Sagamore Bridges, each with a span of 616 feet, became among the longest continuous truss bridges in North America. The Cape Cod Railroad Bridge, further west, at 544 feet, remains the third longest vertical lift drawbridge on the continent. You can admire the workmanship of the bridges from the 7-mile paved service road that lines both sides of the canal.

52 "Anything Goes" Cast, Cape Playhouse, Dennis

A landmark, this oldest continuously operating professional summer theater was founded in 1927. The former Nobscusset (Unitarian) Meetinghouse was moved then transformed—after several incarnations as livery stable, smithy, barn, slaughterhouse, and garage—on a 3.5 acre lot into a theater which opened on July 4, 1927 with Basil Rathbone performing in The Guardsman.

53 Snow on the Dunes at Sunrise, Provincetown

See caption for pages 18-19.

54 Sunset, Truro

Sunset from Edward Hopper's studio has not only ethereal beauty, but also special significance. Hopper, a renowned and celebrated icon of Cape Cod realism, was and remains one of the foremost painters who captured Cape Cod in all of her lonely and most revealing moods. Imagine the inspiration Hopper must have realized and wonder he enjoyed spending time throughout the rolling seasons in this magnificent house which presides over the barren cliffs between Ryder and Fisher Beaches in South Truro.

55 Wings Neck Light, Bourne

Wings Neck Light was built in 1849 because of heavy marine traffic traveling in Buzzards Bay to ports in Wareham and Sandwich. When the Cape Cod Canal opened in 1914, Wings Neck Light assumed its real importance for a number of years. The first lighthouse at Wings Neck was a Cape Cod-style light keeper's house with a lantern placed on the roof. In 1889, damage from an earlier fire and general disrepair forced the construction of a new lighthouse. The present keeper's house, with its attached hexagonal wooden tower, was built to replace the old Cape Cod-style house. For many years, Wings Neck was deemed one of the most important lighthouses on the Atlantic Coast because of the heavy shipping traveling the Cape Cod Canal. By 1943, the lighthouse was becoming obsolete and a 'skeleton' tower was constructed to replace the original. The property was sold by the government in 1947 and Wings Neck Light and its surrounding area are now privately owned with no public access.

56 Aerial View, Oyster Beds, Wellfleet

"It was a bold man that first ate an oyster." Yet the concept of eating raw seafood has existed among primitives forever. One wonders how our ancestors discerned the briny, delicious delight that lies inside tightly closed oyster shells. Seafood lovers gratefully pay homage to that brave soul who "first ate an oyster" every time they down a couple of dozen on the half shell. Wellfleet fishermen produce and harvest oysters famous throughout the world. The taste is unique because of the water flow, and an abundance of nutrients, minerals, and fresh water intrusion. Oysters are at their plumpest and sweetest in months with an "r" in them. They spawn in the months without an "r", May through August, and reach their flavorful height by late October. Wellfleet Oysters are prized by chefs the world over for their delicacy and sweetness. Millionaire railroad tycoon 'Diamond Jim' Brady would often just have to have these for a mid-morning snack and no other oysters would do. The town incorporated into the Town of Wellfleet in 1763 and is claimed to be the namesake of the Wellfleet (or Wallfleet), England, another town renowned for its oysters (oysters still are an important commodity to this Cape town). The town has been famous for Wellfleet Oysters ever since these tickled Champlain's Gallic taste buds in 1606 (Champlain christened Wellfleet Port aux Huitres—literally "port of the oysters"). Wellfleeters and gourmands happily agree that these choice shellfish are the most fragrant and sweetest of all oysters.

57 Clam and Oyster Aquaculture Beds, Wellfleet

Aquaculture is the agriculture of the oceans. Culture fisheries involve growing a selected organism, or in some cases several selected organisms, in a controlled environment, where the sole purpose of the organisms is to be harvested and then sold commercially.

58 Oyster Beds, Wellfleet

See captions for pages 56 and 57 above.

59 Clam and Oyster Beds, Wellfleet

See captions for pages 56 and 57 above.

60 Jersey Princess II, Scalloping off Race Point, Provincetown

Cape Cod, from its beginnings when new settlers were still clearing the land, had its economy firmly rooted in the fishing—and whaling—industries. Just down the road from the Chatham Light is the Chatham Fish Pier, where there's always a small crowd gathered on the visitors deck (best viewing is between 12 noon and 2pm, when the Cape's largest fishing fleet is returning). Not only does the pier offer a great view of Chatham's harbor and outer beach with the Atlantic beyond, but when the fishing boats unload their catch, both children and adults get a fascinating glimpse of the Cape's best-known industry. It is a working pier with an observation deck to provide great views of fishermen and the town's active fishing fleet in action. The Pier is also the center for commercial and sports fishermen. Orleans is also home to one of the Cape's biggest charter fishing fleets. During the 18th century, Provincetown established itself as a major fishing and whaling port (third largest after Nantucket and New Bedford, Massachusetts) and 75 wharves could be counted along its shores. Although no longer a major fishing port, a fleet of 40 fishing boats still departs each morning. Provincetown has long been home to a Portuguese community—many of whom are avid fishermen—with deep roots which emanated from the Azores, the Canary Islands and Cape Verdes. Many residents' forbears were drawn here by employment in the whaling trade during the 19th century.

Scallops are found in oceans across the world, comprising a group of several hundred species. The scallops you usually eat at a seafood restaurant are the large northern kinds. These are fished commercially for the large single muscle, which is excellent for eating. Scallops move by snapping their shells together and 'spitting' water out. They propel themselves rapidly in a zigzag direction. Most kinds have a series of brightly colored eyes along the edge of the mantle. These are sensitive to minor changes in light intensity, as might be caused by a passing fish. What appears to be the top and bottom valves of the scallop are actually left and right valves. Scallops are fished for both inshore and offshore although offshore fishing is far more significant. Scallop fishermen fish for scallops all year long. The drag has a metal frame with teeth with a mesh bag that is attached which is dragged along the bottom of the ocean and raked into the mesh bag. The crew take the meat out of the scallops. Some of the scallops' enemies are cod, plaice, and wolf fish; starfish and marine snails destroy adult scallops.

61 Black Fish Creek, Wellfleet

Black Fish Creek flows in a southwesterly direction from east of the Cape Cod Rail Trail, with its headwaters within the boundaries of the Cape Cod National Seashore. It is a large area of salt marsh, with a seaward channel from 15 to 25 feet wide, and is frequently the site of dolphin and other mammal strandings.

62 Cape Cod Canal Control Center, Bourne

At the visitor center, one can see the same array of sensors that the marine traffic controllers watch as they control the passage of vessels through the Canal. The readouts include five radar screens, a dozen closed-circuit video cameras and wind and tide sensors. The controller is ensconced at the other end of the Canal, in the Buzzards Bay administration building, where access if often limited for security reasons. A constant parading flotilla of commercial ships and pleasure craft makes up an ever-changing tableau along this 17-mile man-made waterway.

63 Cape Cod Canal, Railroad Bridge, Bourne

The vertical lift Railroad Bridge spans the Cape Cod Canal, and is located about 50 miles south of Boston. The Canal extends from Cape Cod Bay on the east for a distance of 7.7 miles to Buzzards Bay on the west. The primary purpose of the Canal is to provide a safe navigation channel for vessels seeking the shorter and safer route through the isthmus of Cape Cod. The Canal saves 143 miles of open sea travel out around the tip of Cape Cod. The Railroad Bridge is located close to the western end of the Canal and consists of a 544-foot moveable through-truss span, flanked by a single 128-foot through-truss fixed tower span at each end. The steel structure is 806 feet long, center-to-center of abutment bearings, and carries a single track on an open timber tie deck across the Cape Cod Canal. The bridge is kept in the raised position, with a vertical clearance of approximately 136 feet above mean high water, to allow passage of marine traffic.

64-65 Ballston Beach on a Clear, Crisp Autumn Day, Truro

Ballston Beach is another of Cape Cod's wonders with immense grass-etched dunes shimmering in the sunlight and silky sand. It is nestled along the dunes at the end of North Pamet Road on the Cape's Atlantic side. It is a favorite among surfers, featuring waves of epic proportions and there is a dangerous undertow. Like Longnook Beach, parking at Ballston Beach is limited, with parking restricted only to vehicles displaying a long-term Truro beach parking permit (parking here is free after 4pm). Ballston Beach exemplifies coastal beach processes. While the dune has been breached by the ocean several times in recent years, coastal transport of sand (longshore transport) has reestablished the barrier beach here. Truro's traditionally 'nude' beach is on the ocean side of the Cape, between Ballston and Long Nook Beaches.

66 Sunset, Wellfleet Harbor

During the 17th century, Wellfleet, then known as Billingsgate, was part of Eastham. The town's name may have been a reference to the more than 30 whaling ships—or whale fleet—which once sailed from the harbor. Three of Wellfleet's most distinctive assets are its spacious marina, deepwater ponds and its rich shellfish beds and fishing grounds. Wellfleet is one of the Cape's most tastefully developed resort towns. Its beautiful town, centered on its picturesque harbor, once known as Grampus Bay after the pilot whales which stranded themselves here, contains beautiful historic homes, several fine restaurants and more than two dozen art galleries. Wellfleet's sobriquet 'the art gallery town' is amply supported. This beautifully harbored village has remained remarkably unsullied, essentially non-commercial and incredibly picturesque. Ladies in search of au courant (and surprisingly affordably priced) couture should check out Main Street.

67 John Mulcahy Artist, Wellfleet

Mulcahy has been an artist on Cape Cod for more than four decades. Born in Hingham, he has always been inspired by Cape Cod. "I can not express with words the joy, happiness and fulfillment I have in my mind and heart when painting," claims Mulcahy. His sentiments are likely shared by many Cape artists.

Cape Cod. Those two words evoke myriad images. To the architect, it is a style of house. To the child, it means seemingly endless strands of beach and equally endless curls of ocean surf. But, to the artist, it conjures the ethereal light which envelops its 559.6 miles of beach, endless crescents of powdery sand and fog-swarthed harbors. This is no ordinary destination. American art icon Edward Hopper found the Cape's light ideal for his brand of austere realism. He summered, hermit-like, in South Truro for nigh on 40 years (1930 to 1967) in near total contentment. In 2000, AmericanStyle magazine readers chose Cape Cod as #1 Arts Destination in the United States, an appropriate appellation. One respondent claimed "Art is a way of life on the Cape." Spend a day exploring the Cape's wondrous and arty byways, and you'll soon agree.

Art lovers visit Cape shores to enjoy its ubiquitous galleries, museums and historic landmarks. And meeting its hundreds of artisans, visiting their studios and galleries and watching them work is inspirational, imbuing their works of art with even more meaning.

Artists have been coming to the Cape since 1899, when artist Charles W. Hawthorne founded the Cape Cod School of Art in Provincetown, introducing the near-derelict fishing town to Greenwich Village intelligentsia. He was so besotted by its "jumble of color in the intense sunlight accentuated by the brilliant blue of the harbor" that he ended up teaching here for 30 years. Other artists drawn to the Cape include such luminaries as Edward Hopper, Jackson Pollock, Robert Motherwell and Mark Rothko. Another bright star on our cultural scene is actress Julie Harris of Chatham. Harris has received numerous national theater honors, including several Tony Awards. In 2002, she received a special Tony Award for lifetime achievement in theater. She has also received an Emmy Award and an Oscar nomination. Harris, 77, is well-known locally for her support of the arts community of Cape Cod, where she has made her home for more than 20 years. Visitors soon sense the special connection this peninsula shares with the arts and the art world. Cape artists and artisans pay homage to the land they love, the air they breathe, the water they sail. Art can be found on the beach, in sunrises and sunsets, on the dunes, at low tide, in sculpture gardens and art galleries and open studios, in theatres and auction houses. Cape Cod—it embraces artists and, then, will simply not let them go. Cape Cod—#1 Arts Destination in the United States—one visit will explain why.

68 Duck Creek and Uncle Tim's Bridge, Wellfleet

This winter shot of a much-photographed and beautiful vista crosses marshland and tidal Duck Creek, leading to a small wooded island.

69 Green Briar Jam Kitchen, Sandwich

"Tis a wonderful thing to sweeten a world which is in a jam and needs preserving," wrote conservationist Thornton Burgess to Ida Putnam. The young Burgess wandered the woods surrounding Putnam's jam kitchen. Children will love this center with changing natural history exhibits, a full summer program of nature classes, self-guided walks through 52 acres of Sandwich Conservation land and weekday tours of the Jam Kitchen, which makes natural jams, jellies, and pickles from Putnam's original recipes. The Center is nestled deep in the woods adjacent to a pond—the scene looking rather like an illustration from one of the Burgess storybooks.

70 Windsurfing, West Dennis

Cape Cod has some of the best windsurfing beaches on the East Coast, including Hyannis' Kalmus Park Beach and West Dennis Beach. There is a huge following for this sport on Cape Cod, which has become kind of a windsurfing Mecca and is home to the King of the Cape windsurfing competition every summer. Wave surfing is superb on the Outer Cape's oceanside beaches, too.

71 Windmill Park, Eastham

Located on the green in Eastham Center, the windmill was built in Plymouth about 1680 and moved to Truro in the 1770s, then to Eastham in 1793, first to where the National Seashore Salt Pond Visitor Center is now located, and then to its present site in 1808. Lovingly restored and maintained, it is the oldest and last working gristmill on Cape Cod and is owned and maintained by the Town of Eastham.

72 Tall Ship Kalmar Nyckel at Sail, Provincetown

This 141-foot tall ship is an accurate re-creation of a Dutch-armed trading vessel built in the early 1600s. This replica sports a figurehead of a bright red fierce-looking, twin-tailed lion named Leo.

73 Little Pamet River, Truro

Also called 'Payomet" in days past, this river cuts across the forearm of the Cape from ocean to bay. It has a valley filled with 18th Century homes, rich human history and a dramatic geologic story. Two roads lead down either side of the valley and dead end at Ballston Beach. Traveling north on Route 6, 2.2 miles from the Wellfleet/Truro line, the highway begins a moderate descent into the Pamet Valley, an ancient melt water channel sculpted from the land thousands of years ago by melting glaciers. From the highway, you can quickly glimpse up and down the valley. Running through the valley is the Pamet River, a meandering creek that begins near the ocean and empties into Cape Cod Bay at Pamet Harbor. The river turns from freshwater to brackish and then salt by the time it reaches the bay. In the early 19th Century, the river was wide and navigable. Houses could be floated on it to new locations. A trip to the end of South Pamet Road ends at Ballston Beach. Along the way are numerous 18th and 19th Century houses, one of which was a stage coach stop at the corner of Collins Road (formerly a portion of the Old King's Highway).

74 Ocean Edge Golf Club, Brewster

Located in Brewster, the Club is located within Ocean Edge Resort's 400 acres and features 6,665-yard championship course with five ponds, a driving range where one can arrange for golf lessons with PGA pros. The Resort's stylish restaurant, Linx, offers casual and al fresco dining overlooking the golf course.

75 Cranberry Bog, Brewster

See caption for page 15.

76 Fort Hill, Eastham

Fort Hill was the highest point adjacent to the meetinghouse erected by Pilgrim residents of Nauset (later called Eastham) shortly after they settled here in 1644. Scholars still speculate on the naming of Fort Hill, but similar names were given to high points at other settlements along the eastern seaboard during that period. A hill of this sort would serve as a natural point of defense from which defenders could shoot at attackers from their aerie. The most probable threat to the Pilgrim residents during that period was from fellow European settlers such as the Dutch in New Amsterdam (New York). Some farmland here was likely the former property of Governor Thomas Prence (Prince), governor of Eastham for some years. The Reverend Samuel Treat, who was 'assigned' to Eastham in 1672, also owned about twenty acres of land at Fort Hill. The boundaries were marked by a stone inscribed with a "T," and the northwest marker still exists.

77 Artist Anne MacAdam at Her Easel, North Truro

As a long-time resident of Provincetown, McAdam is inspired by its magnificent light, its surrounding waters and panoramic landscapes to be found all over Cape Cod. She enjoys working outside on large canvases and has a prolific and handsome repertoire of Cape landscapes. McAdam is represented by the Berta Walker Gallery.

Also see caption for page 67.

78 Sunrise Nauset Beach, Eastham

Nauset Beach's ten-mile sweep of sandy ocean beach features long, low dunes and sometimes-wild ocean surf and has always been a favorite of body and board surfers. Off-road vehicles (with permits) may select the choicest spots, because the parking lot, while massive, fills early on beautiful summer days. This is not the same as Nauset Light Beach, which is part of the National Seashore in Eastham.

79 Cape Cod Canal from Scusset Harbor, Sagamore

Scusset Beach State Reservation comprises nearly 500 acres adjacent to the Cape Cod Canal and offers nearly 100 RV and five actual tent-sites. It is a pleasant locale for a swim, jog, walk, hike or cycle ride and is located along the mainland side of the Canal in Sagamore near the Sagamore Bridge. There is a also pier which is popular for fishing.

80-81 Great Harbor from Penzance Point, Woods Hole

Woods Hole is the infamous water passage between Buzzards Bay and Vineyard Sound which is located between the southwest tip of Cape Cod, at Falmouth, and two of the Elizabeth Islands, Nonamesset and Uncatena. The name comes from the passage (or hole) between Penzance Point and Nonamesset Island. Bartholomew Gosnold reportedly charted this area in 1602. Early settlers farmed, raised sheep, or fished; and from 1863 to 1897, the Pacific Guano Company had a booming fertilizer business on Long Neck (later renamed Penzance Point). That area became a haven for the rich, coined "Bankers Row" in historic accounts. During the heyday of whaling, candles were made from spermaceti in the historic Candle House on Water Street in this timeless and interesting village.

82 Below Zero, A Frozen Morning at Marconi Station, Wellfleet

In March 1901 Marconi and Vyvyan initially identified Cape Cod as a suitable place to receive a wireless signal from Poldhu, England, in Cornwall. Vyvyan, who oversaw construction, said: "The work proceeded rapidly and by the end of June, I had completed the circle of masts and the buildings... It was clear to me, however, that the mast system was distinctly unsafe. In August, under the influence of nothing more than a stiff breeze, the heads of the masts on the windward side bent over to a dangerous degree, and I reported this to the London Office, asking permission to lower the royal masts for safety. Meanwhile a similar ring of masts was being erected at Poldhu, England, but before the system was completed the masts collapsed during a gale on 17 September 1901, and the masts at Cape Cod suffered a like fate a few weeks later." *Source: Wireless Over Thirty Years by R. N. Vyvyan published 1933.*Cape Cod Station narrowly missed being a part of a historic 'first' after tests between Poldhu and Ireland prompted Marconi to take the decision to aim for the nearest landfall Newfoundland. The famous signal, the letter 'S,' which was sent to Newfoundland from Poldhu, England, was received on 12 December 1901, while Vyvyan and his staff were working to clear the wreckage at Cape Cod.

In February 1902, work commenced at Cape Cod to construct four 210-foot high timbered towers, which were solidly anchored with concrete footings. On 18 January 1903, a message was sent from Cape Cod to Glace Bay for re-transmission to Poldhu from Theodore Roosevelt, President of the United States, to King Edward VII. Conditions were so good that night that Poldhu picked up the message directly, making this the first wireless message from the United States to England. Cape Cod continued to work as a station, until it was closed in 1917 by the Navy for safety reasons.

83 **Chatham Light, Chatham**

In 1808, the first of three sets of twin lighthouses was built at Chatham Beach. The two wooden light towers distinguished the site from the single light at Highland to the north in Truro. In 1841, the original wooden lighthouses were replaced by a set of brick towers which presided over the bluff until 1881, when erosion toppled them over the edge and when a new pair of brick-lined iron design lighthouses was built at Chatham.

84 **Gail Dreaming on the Dunes, Harry Kemp Dune Shack, Provincetown**

Provincetown Dune Shacks are where creative souls commune with their muse in two week increments. Six of these shacks were preserved by the Cape Cod National Seashore for their use, and must be applied for seasonally. The first such shack was built in 1794 as a refuge for shipwrecked sailors. Four of the shacks are available to artists and writers who receive residencies through a lottery system. Some notable tenants include Jack Kerouac, e.e. Cummings, Eugene O'Neill, Norman Mailer and Jackson Pollock. For information on membership, contact P.O. Box 1705, Provincetown, MA, 02657.

85 **Book Shelves, Harry Kemps' "Poet of the Dunes" Dune Shack, Provincetown**

Harry Kemp had undistinguished beginnings, born to parents of modest means in Youngstown, Ohio in 1883. In 1908, Kemp became a close friend of Upton Sinclair, riding the crest of fame as author of The Jungle. Both Upton Sinclair and William Allen White were convinced that in Harry Kemp, America had found its new Walt Whitman, a poet who spoke to all of us. Between 1907 and 1908, White arranged for 30 of Kemp's poems to be published in The American Magazine and succeeded in finding the impecunious poet a patron, millionaire Charles Crane, who offered to subsidize Kemp for a whole year. To Kemp's enduring credit, two items are worthy of mention: he was the first to establish theatre on the lower East Side and call it 'The East Village;' and a 19-year-old boy, who came down from the Bronx by subway, credited Kemp with giving him his first exposure to theatre. His name was Clifford Odets. In the summer of 1928, Kemp moved out to the dunes of Peaked Hill where he would spend summers for 30 years, becoming its most dedicated and lyrical resident, determined to leave his footprints in the sands of time. Home was a tiny sandblasted shack on the ocean's edge, less than a mile from the Coast Guard Station where Eugene O'Neill lived from 1919 until 1924. O'Neill's home was lavishly refurbished by Mabel Dodge, its previous owner who spared no costs in providing all the comforts of home. Kemp's shack was built by Frank Henderson for the Coast Guard Station to serve as its hen house. It was a model of survival minimalism, about ten feet by ten feet on six cement blocks, two railroad ties and timbers across the blocks, a triangular saddle roof, two windows facing east and west, and out the front door, in Kemp's words, "an ocean that doesn't stop 'til it strikes the coast of Europe." Rent? An alien term which never entered Kemp's glossary; in town and on the dunes he was a delinquent non-payer for all seasons. Kemp died August 8, 1960 at the age of 77. The day after friends scattered Kemp's ashes on the dunes out at Peaked Hill, a powerful hurricane battered the entire northeast and reconfigured the sands on the back shore.

86-87 **Morning, Wellfleet**

See caption for page 66.

88 **Coast Guard Station, Eastham**

This Coast Guard station was built in 1915 and replaced in 1936 because of rapidly eroding dunes. This building is now home for employees of the National Seashore's summer staff. A nearby service building contains old life saving equipment.

89 **Highland Light, North Truro**

See caption for page 23.

90-91 **Osterville**

Osterville, nee Oysterville, was purchased from Native Americans for two cooper kettles and some fencing—a cheap price for what has evolved into Cape Cod's most prestigious address. Many of the Fortune 500 Company CEOs and some du Ponts, Cabots and Mellons summer at Wianno or Oyster Harbors—Osterville addresses even more affluent than Osterville itself. Along its white clapboarded Main Street, one observes Jaguars, Mercedes, Volvos, BMWs, Alfa Romeos, Saabs, stretch limos and a parade of obviously affluent residents with their black labs in tow.

92 **Sunrise Paine's Creek, Brewster**

This genteel town, occupying eight miles along Cape Cod Bay—named for Mayflower passenger Elder William Brewster—was part of Harwich, named North Parish, until 1803 when the towns separated. Considering that Brewster has no harbors, it was the domicile to sea captains galore—and their legends endure. Early town settlement was centered around the area of what is presently Route 124 and the Brewster Store. During the early 19th century, Brewster was the terminus for Boston-Brewster packet cargo service. Throughout the 19th century, Brewster sea captains were paragons of adventure, commerce —and profit. Their stately mansions, built with the profits of their global trading forays, are testaments to the affluence of the age of sail. Today, 22-square mile Brewster, comprising three villages—Brewster, East and West Brewster—has remained primarily free of the commercial encroachments of other Cape towns and it remains 'apart.'

93 **Sunrise Days' Cottage, North Truro**

See caption for Cover.

94 **Spring, A Clutch of Black Locust Trees, Wellfleet**

Wellfleet is a town which evolved from an agrarian village to a town devoted to maritime trades and basks today in the sunshine of the tourism industry. Its idyllic location—between the sandy beaches of the Atlantic Ocean and the harbors and inlets along Cape Cod Bay make it perhaps one of the Cape's most scenic and bucolic places to visit. The past has hardly been forgotten in this small and serene town. It is a most comfortable amalgam of old and new—its authentic general store stands today where the old train station once discharged its Cape-bound passengers. Restaurants, art galleries and au courant boutiques line the streets and byways of this treasure trove. Many freshwater ponds grace this diminutive town—and their narrow sandy shores and peaceful waters bubble with delight during the summer and offer restful vistas in the colder months. And there is plenty of activity along the waterfront. Sail and fishing boats ply its wonderful harbor on their way out to Cape Cod Bay and beyond. The Cape Cod Rail Trail starts—or, as some say, ends—here and the Audubon Society has many interesting and exciting trails to explore. No matter the season, this small town—named after Wallfleet, England—is always in season, And do not forget Wellfleet Oysters are the ultimate oyster and are highly prized and recognized by chefs worldwide. The town has been famous for Wellfleet Oysters ever since these tickled Champlain's Gallic taste buds in 1606 (Champlain christened Wellfleet *Port aux Huitres*—literally "port of the oysters"). Wellfleeters and gourmands happily agree that these choice shellfish are the most fragrant and sweetest of all oysters.

95 **Winter Forest, Truro**

Truro has less residents now than it did in 1840 (when Pamet Harbor was a whaling and shipbuilding port), which is possibly one of the best reasons to go there. The 'town' comprises several stores and public edifices plus scores of off-beat and pricey residences built into hidden dunes (a sign facetiously indicates that this modest clutch of buildings is 'downtown Truro.') This bucolic village qualifies as the Cape's 'sleepiest' community. Writers, artists, politicos and mental health types are wont to vacation and live here and American art icon Edward Hopper—who found the Cape's light ideal for his brand of austere realism— summered, hermit-like, in South Truro for nigh on 40 years (1930 to 1967) in near total contentment. And while many visitors are drawn by this relative isolation, they can be comforted by the fact that lively Provincetown is but a short drive away. This monied town celebrates in true Yankee style with its late-September 'dump dance' at the town's recycling center.

96 **Days' Cottages, North Truro**

Days' Flower Cottages run along Shore Road, Route 6A, North Truro, in a neat row—orderly and identical. Each of the 23 units is a simple clapboard cottage painted white and trimmed in sea foam green. Each is 18 feet from its neighboring cottage, has ten windows, two bedrooms, living room, bath and open-air porch with Cape Cod Bay view. All measure 28 feet x17 feet and are only distinguishable from one another by signs above the doorways, each of which bears the name of a different flower: Aster, Rose, Lilac, Tulip, Peony, Violet, Crocus and so on through 23 flower names. These 23 original cottages have seen seven decades, two major wars, three hurricanes and 68 winters.

97 **View from Paine's Creek, Brewster**

This peaceful and scenic inlet has been photographed many times for promotional pieces and postcards featuring Cape Cod and, now for this book. Going from west to east, Paine's Creek is the first town beach on the bay. As its name implies, it is fed by a creek and is the perfect calm water beach for children. Early arrivers get the best spots on this diminutive beach, which is a favorite of toddlers' parents and sunset seekers. On clear days, the Pilgrim Monument and distinctive curve of the Cape along Cape Cod Bay are clearly visible.

98 Stage Harbor Light, Chatham

See caption for page 48.

99 Quissett Harbor, Woods Hole, Falmouth

Quissett Harbor is the perfect place for peaceful walks any time of the year-merely follow the path that leads to the "Knob." This little chunk of land overlooking Buzzards Bay is the perfect viewing place for the most spectacular sunsets. A small parking lot provides limited parking at this small, secluded harbor.

100 Sunrise, Chatham

See caption for page 40-41.

101 Sand Pipers, Chatham

Charadrius melodus. Sand-pipers trot close to each wave, waiting for the sea to cast up their breakfast. Sand pipers run with great speed and then stand remarkably still and erect, sometimes blending in with their backgrounds due to the remarkable coloring, which can be akin to beach camouflage.

102 Corn Hill, Pamet River, Truro

See captions for pages 36 and 73.

103 Bass River, West Dennis

See caption for pages 24-25.

104 Shining Sea Bike Path, Falmouth to Woods Hole

Shining Sea Bike Path's four-mile route from Falmouth to Woods Hole takes cyclists past arresting shoreline vistas, serene woodlands along an old rail bed route, passing sandy beaches, ocean harbors, marshes, ponds and woodlands. The Path is flat and paved. An additional six miles of bike path are currently slated for the cycling path and have been budgeted and funded and is in the planning stages.

105 Boardwalk, Sandwich

The Sandwich Boardwalk fords Mill Creek across Sandwich Harbor to a lovely public beach. In 1991, Hurricane Bob and subsequent storms destroyed the original boardwalk here. Right after its destruction, an appeal went out for people to purchase 1,700 individual planks which would be engraved for $25 and $50 to complete the new 1,350 foot walkway. The new boardwalk was completed in 1992. Half the fun of visiting this boardwalk is reading the contributors' messages carved into the planks. Some pay tribute to loved ones lost. Others like "Friends from Connecticut," "Mom's Beach 1992" and "Squibby from M.V." remind us of past visitors. "Old Man River" and "Hey Diddle Diddle" grace two of the planks. A third cautions "Slippery when Wet." Perhaps, though, our favorite is "Meet Here," a cryptic invitation to visit often.

106 Ripples in the Sand

Cape Cod is a geological time capsule. From the Brewster Flats at low tide to the ever-changing face of Provincetown's Race Point and the Atlantic-facing seashore—Cape Cod is a treasure trove of geological history. Sea shells and rocks given up by the ocean each contain eons of history. Wind and sea have played more than a nominal role in shaping this peninsula, too. Marine erosion gave birth to the Outer Cape's tall cliffs. The 'Chatham Break,' resulting from 1991's Hurricane Bob, forever changed the shore and harbor of this pristine Cape village. Ocean currents carried sand to create the Province Lands in Provincetown. The Cape is a dynamic place—shifting sands, wind and the ocean work their sometimes nefarious magic to continually change the face of Cape Cod. Almost five thousand years ago, the rugged eastern and-southern shores extended two miles further into the ocean than they do today. Gradually, wind and waves smoothed the ocean-facing coast. Scientists tell us that Cape Cod loses three feet of Atlantic coast annually (nearly five acres). Much of this eroded sand and rock (about two acres' worth)—is deposited further north on the outer Cape in stages—sandbar, sand spit and land—to form an ever-lengthening beach. Nauset Beach and Nauset Spit (Eastham) and North Beach (Chatham) are all sand spits. In Wellfleet, Billingsgate Island, once domicile to dozens of families, is today merely a sandbar. Water and wind are ever removing land from one Cape location and depositing new land in another, however, the Cape sustains a net land loss of two acres every year. Conservation efforts, such as planting beach grass on bare dunes, have helped make these sandy mountains resistant to winter storms. But these grasses have but a fragile hold in the sand, and only by prohibiting foot and other traffic can these dunes—and the dry land they call home—survive.

107 Walking the Dogs, Coast Guard Beach, Eastham

Coast Guard Beach has consistently won kudos for Cape Cod and has won the appellation as one of the "ten best beaches in the United States" by many magazines and the Travel Channel. It is on the Atlantic Ocean and is the spot for surfers and sunbathers. The Coast Guard station here was built in 1915 and replaced in 1936 because of the rapidly eroding dunes. This house is now a home for employees of the National Seashore's summer staff. A nearby service building contains old life saving equipment. There are beautiful hiking and trails throughout the Coast Guard Beach area and the beach is backed by low grass and heath land. At high tide, the ordinarily wide high low-tide swath of beach shrinks considerably.

108-109 Wychmere Harbor, Harwich Port

Wychmere Harbor was once a salt pond with no access to Nantucket Sound. It was first named Annosarakumitt by Cape Native Americans. It was later christened Oyster Pond and then Salt Water Pond by early settlers—neither was particularly creative. In the 20th century, summer residents re-christened it Wychmere and the name stuck. It is perhaps Harwich Port's most beautiful harbor and has a perfectly formed knoll which is ideal for picnic lunches overlooking its beautiful waters. Wychmere Harbor boasts the largest active fleet of J-22 and Flying Scot sloops under the umbrella of the Southern Massachusetts Yacht Racing Association and is the winter home base for the Cape Cod Frosty Dinghy.

110 Gathering Around the Camp Fire with a National Seashore Ranger, Pamet Bay Beach, Truro

The Cape Cod National Seashore has two visitor centers with staff to assist visitors with orientation and trip planning, eleven self-guiding trails which are open year round and all kinds of activities. These include early morning birding walks, surfcasting lessons, hikes, walks, canoe lessons and trips and many other activities.

111 Oyster Pond Beach, Chatham

Only a block from Chatham's Main Street, this sheltered salt-water pond is popular with parents of young children—and they are there in abundance. It is a great spot for sunrises and sunsets and is loaded with Cape charm.

112 Sandwich Glass Museum, Sandwich

In the 1820s, Boston glass merchant Deming Jarves established a glass factory, Boston & Sandwich Glass Company, having recognized that the town's location and natural resources were near perfect for such an undertaking. His master glassblowers and colorists produced exquisite glasswork. By the 1850s, the town boasted two glass factories—manufacturing the entire spectrum of glassware, from the functional-to the strictly decorative—making Sandwich one of the foremost glass capitals of the world. Jarves' factory closed in 1888, but Sandwich glass is still highly prized by collectors and even museums. The Museum contains one of the largest collections of Sandwich glass in the US. The dazzling display of glass is displayed to optimal effect along banks of sunny windows through which sun illuminates the glass, lighting up the Museum in a kaleidoscope of colors, which is illustrated in this photograph.

113 Crosby Yacht Yard, Osterville

Established in 1850 in Osterville, Crosby Yacht Yard is the original designer and builder of the world famous Crosby Catboat, Wianno Senior, Crosby Striper, Canyon, Hawk, and its complete line of TUGS. During World War II, the U.S. Army Corps of Engineers took control of the Crosby Yacht property to conduct landing boat training for the Normandy invasion. A restaurant here, overlooking the Crosby Basin, serves breakfast, lunch and dinner from May through September.

114 Nobska Lighthouse, Woods Hole

Woods Hole, jumping off point for the Steamship Authority's Martha's Vineyard ferry, is also home of beautiful Nobska Light. Built in 1828, the original lighthouse was replaced in 1879. This lighthouse is unusual because, when seen from the perpendicular, its beacon appears white, but when viewed from other angles, it appears reddish. This helps orient sailors to their position relative to the lighthouse.

Nobska Light stands on a rise of land towering over the water and is a beacon for Woods Hole Harbor, guiding mariners traveling between the Cape Cod mainland and Martha's Vineyard. The 1876 keeper's house, which has grown and expanded over the years, now serves as housing for the commanding officer of the U.S. Coast Guard Group Woods Hole.

115 Winterscape, the Moors, Provincetown

This flat expanse of terrain is alive with heath and other flora and fauna. It is particularly atmospheric at sunrise and sunset, when Provincetown's ethereal light makes photographing the moors such a joy. This wonderful photograph brings the winter moors to life with its vibrant and pinks, corals and reds fading to purple and azure. One can almost feel the warmth of the setting sun, in spite of the winter landscape.

116 Rock Harbor, Orleans

See caption for page 43.

117 MacMillan Wharf, Provincetown

The first pier on the site was built 1873 and named Railroad Wharf or Town Pier. By the mid-1950s, Town Pier was 75 years old and showing signs of aging. Westcott Construction Company of West Attleboro, MA, won the contract to build MacMillan Wharf replacing the sagging, deteriorating Town Pier with a spic-and-span structure, built to fully embrace the sea traffic at Provincetown. At that time, the cost to build the Wharf was $600,000. The MacMillan Wharf, also called MacMillan Pier, reconstruction project of 2002 cost $18 million. It is from this maritime transportation hub that whale watch excursions, ferries to Boston and yacht and fishing charters arrive and depart.

118 **Dune Shack, Provincetown**
See caption for page 84.

119 **The Knob, Quissett Harbor, Falmouth**
This bucolic retreat at Quissett Harbor, with its diminutive parking lot, provides one of the Cape's wonderful 'escape routes.' Here, visitors can walk through and along its 13 acres of waterfront trails taking in this picturesque harbor, Buzzards Bay and seaward vistas. Thus named because of its rounded shape, this promontory provides a wonderful spot for sketching, painting, reading, relaxing and taking in its incomparable and magnificent sunsets. Gentlemen take note: The Knob is a wonderfully romantic spot to propose to your prospective bride.

120-121 **Chatham Harbor**
This serene and peaceful view of Chatham Harbor belies the disaster which struck in January 1987. On that fateful day, a powerful nor'easter broke through the lower end of Nauset Beach, allowing the Atlantic Ocean to surge into Chatham Harbor. This breach of the barrier beach is responsible for strong and dangerous currents and considerable wave action, all of which can make both boating and swimming somewhat dangerous. Notwithstanding the 'Chatham Break,' as it has been christened, it has brought many visitors into town to observe the phenomenon. Chatham Harbor had been shielded from surges of the open Atlantic Ocean by the lower end of Nauset Beach, a barrier beach.

122 **Early Autumn Frost, Wellfleet**

123 **Storm Clearing, Provincetown**
This magnificent vista over the dunes exhibits perfectly the drama of time and place which Cape Cod exemplifies. A short while before this photograph was taken, this scene was a tempest, with wild winds and threatening purple-black clouds. The soft setting sun creates a wonderful tableau juxtaposed against these ominous, but retreating, clouds captured so perfectly by the photographer in time and space.

124 **Antique Store, Route 28, Dennis**
There are several auction houses on Cape Cod which regularly present auctions where trained eyes—or early birds—often mean a great piece at an even better price. Outdoor flea markets in Wellfleet and Mashpee are an entire day's entertainment mixed with the thrill of a bargain hunt. However, the Cape Cod antique trail takes visitors Cape-wide, for every town has at least one, and several are nearly defined by antiques shops. The Old King's Highway (Route 6A), is a treasure trove of shops and antique centers. Spring and fall, watch the roadsides for tag and estate sales. Here, naïve sellers often sell real treasures for a few dollars. From Chinese cloisonné to Chippendale chairs, from art glass to Erte prints, from primitive furniture to oriental carpets, the Cape Cod antique scene has it all.

125 **MacMillan Wharf, Provincetown**
See caption for page 117.

126 **Artist Edward Hopper's Studio, Truro**
1882-1967, American painter and engraver, born in Nyack, NY and studied in New York City with Robert Henri. In 1920 the first one-man show of his paintings was held; in 1933 a retrospective exhibition of his works took place at the Museum of Modern Art in New York. He excelled in creating realistic pictures of clear-cut, sunlit streets and houses, often without figures. His paintings exhibit a frequent atmosphere of loneliness—an almost menacing starkness—and a clear sense of time of day or night. In 1913, he moved to the Greenwich Village quarters he would occupy for the rest of his life, and soon thereafter began a longtime tradition of summering on Cape Cod. His work is distinguished by his enigmatic yet precise representation of the solitude inherent in urban landscapes and interiors, human relationships, the open road, and the expansive sea. From 1930 to 1966, Hopper's family stayed in a house and studio that they had built in South Truro on Cape Cod. This house still stands, somewhat changed, today and is pictured here.

127 **Bayside Cottages, Truro**
Along Route 6A in Truro there are literally hundreds of bayside cottages. These cottages, known to provide some of the best locales for viewing Cape Cod sunsets, are often rented years in advance and sometimes, generations of families rent the same cottages year after year and extended families meet, during the same weeks in the summer—kind of a Cape Cod family reunion tradition. Sitting facing Cape Cod Bay, these wonderful diminutive cottages are well located for long, lazy days on Cape Cod Bay and are but a short drive from the color and excitement of Provincetown.

128 **Crow Farm, Sandwich**
The Cape's oldest town began as a trading post in 1627, was settled in 1637 and incorporated two years later, in 1639, by a splinter group of Puritans. Plymouth Colony's records claim "tenn men from Saugust (presently known as Lynn, Massachusetts) were granted "liberty to view a place to sitt down & have sufficient lands for three score famylies." The land was cleared and homes built by Edmund Freeman and his compatriots. Small wonder they liked this area so much, for it had plentiful fresh water, fish and salt marsh hay for livestock. The settlers named the town after the town of Sandwich in East Kent, rather than the Earl of Sandwich (who was born 118 years after the town's incorporation). The English town of Sandwich was renowned for its salt marsh. Sandwich today—with 22,000 residents—comprises 42 square miles and the villages of Sandwich, East Sandwich, South Sandwich, Scorton Neck, Wakeby and Forestdale.

129 **Dexter Grist Mill, Sandwich**
This circa 1640 grist mill is located off Water Street, south of Main Street and is the real McCoy, built by Thomas Dexter, and was one of several turbine-powered workhorses used during the glass factories' Halcyon days. It went out of use in 1880s, when coal-powered western mills provided cheaper flour and sat idle until the 1920s, when it was resurrected in a new incarnation as a tea room to cater to a tourists driving to the Cape by a comparatively new invention, the automobile. Its cypress wood waterwheel and wooden gears are powered by pond overflow. Today, the mill's output is cornmeal which is happily sold in cloth bags.

130 **Surfing at Coast Guard Beach, Eastham**
Board surfers perennially inhabit this 'temple of surfing' on the Outer Cape. The surf is treacherous with a strong undertow and only surfers who are strong swimmers should attempt to surf its waters. Backed by low grass and heath, the width of the beach shrinks considerably at high tide. From Nauset Light Beach in Orleans and this beauty begins an unbroken 30-mile stretch of barrier beach extending all the way to Provincetown—Thoreau's "Cape Cod Beach." Coast Guard Beach has been acclaimed 'one of the America's ten best beaches' by The Travel Channel, Condé Nast Traveler and many other publications. There is no parking here, so park at the Salt Pond Visitor Center or you can park and shuttle from a lot at Doane Road.

131 **Cape Cod Bay, View from Ocean Edge Resort & Golf Club, Brewster**
This southern arm of Massachusetts Bay on Atlantic coast is enclosed by Cape Cod peninsula and is 25 miles, or 40 km wide. This Resort's property, located directly on Cape Cod Bay, offers watersports and play in its calm waters. Known for its impossibly stunning sunsets and amazing salt flats at low tide.

132 **Nauset Light, Nauset Light Beach*, Eastham**
Before Nauset Light was moved from Chatham (where it stood next to Chatham Light) in 1923 and erected, three lights—'Three Sisters'—stood watch, guiding sailors home. Nauset Beach Light Station was established in 1839 with construction of three small brick towers. The light station was known as 'Three Sisters of Nauset.' By 1892, the encroaching Atlantic Ocean nearly claimed the towers and the Lighthouse Board commissioned construction of three wooden towers. In 1911, two of the wooden towers were discarded before they, too, fell over the bluff. The center tower became part of the keeper's house. This tower was known as 'The Beacon.' By 1923, the Lighthouse Service, finding it expensive to maintain a set of twin lights at Chatham, replaced 'The Beacon' with one of Chatham's superior cast iron, brick lined towers (constructed in Chatham in 1877). Chatham's former 'north tower' was moved to Eastham in 1923 and became Nauset Light. In 1940, the tower was painted a distinctive red and white to match its light characteristic. Threatened by shoreline erosion throughout the 1980s and 1990s, the historic 114-foot tower was, again, in very real danger of being lost. The lighthouse was moved to a new location the west of its former site in 1996. In 1998, the 1875 lighthouse keeper's home was also moved and reunited with the light tower. The second set of triple lights (built in 1892) has been reunited, restored, and preserved by the Cape Cod National Seashore. *(not to be confused with Nauset Beach, in Orleans.)

133 **Lowering flag, Race Point Ranger Station, Provincetown**
Named for the fierce rip tides that come around the point of the Cape, Race Point beach is the wilder ocean sister of Herring Cove. Since it is on the Atlantic side, the water is colder with more wave action. The beach is managed by the National Seashore.

ACKNOWLEDGEMENTS

I would like to express my gratitude and appreciation to the following for their contribution to this project:

Cape Codder Resort and Spa (Deb Catania), 1225 Iyannough Road, Hyannis, MA 02601

Captain's House Inn (Jan and Dave McMaster), 369-377 Old Harbor Road, Chatham, MA 02633

Chatham Bars Inn (Linda Kelleher), Shore Road, Chatham, MA 02633

Dan'l Webster Inn (Deb Catania), 149 Main Street, Sandwich, MA 02653

Hy-Line Cruises (Betsy Koch), Ocean Street Dock, Hyannis, MA 02601

Ocean Edge Resort, (Susan Cotton), 2907 Main Street (Route 6A), Brewster, MA 02631

Orleans Inn, (Ed Maas), 3 Old County Road, Orleans, MA 02653

Shore Way Acres (Dorrie Ketterer) 59 Shore Street, Falmouth, Box G MA 02540

The Cape Point, (Paul Schwartz and Sue Raynor), 476 Route 28, West Yarmouth, MA 02673

The Belfry Inne & Bistro, (Chris Wilson), 6-8 Jarves Street, Post Office Box 2211, Sandwich MA 02563

The Lighthouse Inn (Nelson Cook), 1 Lighthouse Inn Road, Post Office Box 128, West Dennis, MA 02670

Wingscorton Farm Bed & Breakfast (Dick Loring and Sheila Weyers), 11 Wing Boulevard, Olde King's Highway, E. Sandwich, MA 02537

Bill DeSousa, Michael Patrick Destinations & Communications, 396 Main Street, Suite 3, Hyannis, Cape Cod, MA

Glenn Faria, Michael Patrick Destinations & Communications, 396 Main Street, Suite 3, Hyannis, Cape Cod, MA

ORDERING INFORMATION
BOOKS & CALENDARS

- Provincetown and the National Seashore: A Photographic Essay by Charles Fields, 144 pages, hard cover, 11" x 12", $49.95
- Cape Cod and the National Seashore: A Photographic Essay by Charles Fields, 144 pages, hard cover, 11" x 12", $49.95
- Provincetown and the National Seashore Calendar, 12" x 12", $11.95
- Cape Cod and the National Seashore Calendar, 12" x 12", $11.95

PHOTOGRAPHS

Archival Photographic Prints from the above publications are available. Printed on the professional Epson Stylus 2200P using archival inks and paper. All photographs are produced in limited editions of 50 or 100 each signed and numbered with archival matting and frames. Matted and framed prints 11" x 14"- $235, 16" x 20" - $295, 18" x 24" - $320 For additional information on panorama prints and shipping...

CALL 866-487-5901

Fields Publishing, LLC • PO Box 698, Provincetown, MA 02657 • www.charlesfields.net • email cgfields@earthlink.net